My Diamond Days
with Osho

ma prem shunyo

FULL
CIRCLE

FULL
CIRCLE

OTHER OSHO TITLES *published by* FULL CIRCLE

India, My Love
(Hardcover • Gift Edition)
Tantra : *The Supreme Understanding*
The Goose is Out

OSHO LOVE SERIES

Love and Hate
Love and Relationship
Love and Freedom
Love Yourself
Love and Being

OSHO MEDITATION SERIES

Surrender to Existence
Say Yes!
Love is a Free Bird
Life is a Gift
Stranger to the Earth
Be a Lamp unto Yourself
Alone We Fly
Live Dangerously
I Teach Fearlessness
Become One with Yourself
A Dewdrop in the Ocean
Meditation — An Ecstasy

My Diamond Days
with Osho

ma prem shunyo

FULL
CIRCLE

MY DIAMOND DAYS WITH OSHO
Copyright © Osho International Foundation
All right reserved.
First Paperback Edition, 1999
First Paperback Reprint, 2000
Second Paperback Reprint, February, 2004
ISBN 81-7621-036-6

Published by

FULL CIRCLE *PUBLISHING*
J-40, Jorbagh Lane, New Delhi-110003
Tel: 24620063, 55654197 • Fax: 24645795
E-mail: fullcircle@vsnl.com • website: www.atfullcircle.com

Print & typesetting: SCANSET

J-40, Jorbagh Lane, New Delhi-110003
Tel: 24620063, 55654197 Fax: 24645795

Printed at Nice Printing Press, Delhi-110051

PRINTED IN INDIA

99/04/03/02/21/SCANSET/SAP/NPP/NE

Contents

Foreword

It is fitting that I should write a foreword for Shunyo's book, for it is I, as she puts it, who started her off on her adventure and waved goodbye as she boarded the plane to India seventeen years ago. She was to become an intimate disciple of the Indian guru Bhagwan Shree Rajneesh, who became known as Osho (Zen Master) shortly before he died in January 1990.

This is a story of what it's actually like, in our lifetimes, for a Westerner to tread the path of the *bhakti,* the way of devotion...to seek, recognize, and follow one's true Teacher — the gateway to one's own enlightenment. He may not be your master or mine, but in Shunyo's limpid telling, the truth becomes abundantly clear in the old saying: All pathways with heart lead to the summit of the same mountain — and the nearer they are to the top, the more they resemble each other.

In Shunyo's case, her path was the notorious "sex guru" of the popular press, thumber of his nose at the establishment values, amasser of Rolls Royces and tens of thousands of uninhibitedly joyful red-robed *sannyasins.* The guru who was unceremoniously deported, vilified by the media, his Oregon Ashram crushed, was then — in ill health, with a few close disciples — hounded by the U.S. government from nation to nation for a year until returning to India where he died shortly afterwards of unclear causes.

For fifteen years Shunyo devoted herself to following Osho's pathway to enlightenment, as well as to washing his clothes and caring for his basic needs. She was always the "quiet one," the "Mary Magdalene" of the long-surviving intimates.

A dark Celtic beauty from the wilds of Cornwall, Sandy Pengelly danced, looked for love and meaning, and strived to make a living in the flower-child years of London. In 1975, she abandoned everything and went to Poona, India, to see if Osho matched up to his writings. He did. He renamed her Chetana. And much later, shortly before he died, he renamed her again: "Shunyo" — which she rather proudly explains means "Zero."

This is the diary of the roller-coaster ride of her inner and outer adventures, which proved to be both life and sanity threatening yet profoundly rewarding.

After six years in Poona, Shunyo accompanied Osho when he visited America. She was washing his clothes for him in Oregon during the explosive years of ascent to international attention and infamy. She shared with him being shackled in chains and imprisoned in North Carolina (with no charge against her) and finally being deported — with no explanation. The ailing, fragile Osho, with a few intimates, was hounded from nation to nation, seeking refuge under constant threats and harassment. This vulnerable and astonishingly special family of people experienced years of hatred and rejection, on an international scale, before braving the return home to India — which Osho had last left under a political cloud. At Bombay airport they were nearly crushed by the tumultuous welcoming crowd.

Shunyo was with him over the following years, as he withered quickly — in body, but not in light — of a fatal, wasting disease, which was unanimously diagnosed by various independent sources as resulting from thallium poisoning, administered while in the jails of America. It was in these final months that Osho, as he was now called, released Shunyo into the understanding that she had really been following her own path all along, and it was now, like her prose and her heart, clearer than ever.

I'm sure you'll recognize this book as truly written from the heart. It has three powerful things going for it. First: it describes the inner path of a 20th century *bhakti* with such innocence and literacy that it speaks to everyone who has ever tried going inwards regardless of their path.

Second: for those who haven't, and wonder what all this "enlightenment" bit is about anyway, it's a record of what it's actually like to be a high mountaineer of the often cynically referred to "consciousness movement" of the last thirty years, a fly on the wall at one of the most interesting events of our time, and witness to the perennial mustering of the dark forces of ignorance against the candles of predictive clarity.

Third: because Shunyo's path happens to have been the man who cast as long a shadow as any cult leader recently in the popular imagination, her tale is a sobering and valuable contribution to our time. And anyway, on looking back, who in history is more interesting than those who lived ideas which cast the longest shadows, and caught the greatest flack in their own lifetimes?

DR. LAWRENCE BLAIR, AUTHOR:
RHYTHMS OF VISION
AND *RING OF FIRE*.
FILM MAKER AND LECTURER.

Prologue

A woodcutter used to go into the woods every day. Sometimes he had to remain hungry because it was raining, sometimes it was too hot, sometimes it was too cold.

A mystic lived in the woods. He watched the woodcutter growing old, sick, hungry, working hard the whole day. He said, "Listen, why don't you go a little further?"

The woodcutter said, "What am I going to get a little further? More wood? Unnecessarily carrying that wood for miles?"

The mystic said, "No. If you go a little further, you will find a copper mine. You can take the copper into the city, and that will be enough for seven days. You need not come every day to cut the wood."

The man thought: "Why not give it a try?"

He went in and found the mine. And he was so happy. He came back and fell at the feet of the mystic.

The mystic said, "Don't rejoice too much right now. You have to go a little deeper into the woods."

"But," he said, "what is the point? Now I have got seven days' food."

The mystic said, "Still..."

But the man said, "I will lose the copper mine if I go further."

He said, "You go. You certainly will lose the copper mine, but there is a silver mine. And whatsoever you can bring will be enough for three months."

"The mystic has proved right about the copper mine," the woodcutter thought. "Perhaps he is also right about the silver mine." And he went in and found the silver mine.

And he came dancing, and he said, "How can I pay you? My gratitude knows no bounds."

The mystic said, "But there is a gold mine just a few steps deeper."

The woodcutter was hesitant. In fact, he was such a poor man, that having a silver mine...he had never dreamed of it.

But if the mystic is saying it, who knows? — he may still be right. And he found the gold mine. Now it was enough to come once a year.

But the mystic said, "It will be a long time — one year from now you will be coming here. I am getting old — I may not be here, I may be gone. So I have to tell you, don't stop at the gold mine. Just a little more..."

But the man said, "Why? What is the point? You show me one thing, and the moment I get it, you immediately tell me to drop that and go ahead! Now I have found the gold mine!"

The mystic said, "But there is a diamond mine just a few feet deeper in the forest."

The woodcutter went that very day, and he found it. He brought many diamonds, and he said, "This will be enough for my whole life."

The mystic said, "Now perhaps we may not meet again, so my last message is: now that you have enough for your whole life, GO IN! Forget the forest, the copper mine, the silver mine, the gold mine, the diamond mine. Now I give you the ultimate secret, the ultimate treasure that is within you. Your outer needs are fulfilled. Sit the way I am sitting here."

The poor man said, "Yes, I was wondering... you know all these things — why do you go on sitting here? The question has arisen again and again. And I was just going to ask, "Why don't you get all those diamonds lying there? Only you know about them. Why do you go on sitting under this tree?"

The mystic said, "After finding the diamonds, my master told me, 'Now sit under this tree and GO IN.'"

"I'm Here!"

"**A**nything to say?"
A voice inside is screaming "I'm here, I'm here," but I am struck dumb. And then... the eyes.

When the Master looks into the eyes of the disciple, and He looks, and looks... He is seeing the whole story; everything, past, present and future. The disciple is transparent to the Master and He can see the unrealized Buddha. I could only sit there, letting Him in, because it is the only way to find the diamond. Fear is there that He may see things in the unconscious that I would rather keep hidden; but He looks at me with such love that I can only say, yes. Sometimes, such a look can leave no trace in the memory — just an ecstatic feeling, an intense rush of joyful energy that leaves me fit to burst.

This was my first meeting with the mystic, Osho. It was spring, 1976, in India.

Almost a year before, I had stood in the neat white kitchen of my London house, and I felt that my life, or the way I was living it, was finished. It was as certain as a feeling in the bones when rain is coming. And yet there was no apparent reason for it. Friends would ask me, "But, why?" What could I say? Why do the swans fly to Lake Mansarovar in the Himalayas, each summer? How do they know the way? It happened at a time when I had everything I wanted. Life was easy, I was happy; I had good friends, a great boyfriend, I did exactly the work I wanted to; and I thought, "This is it, there is nothing more that I want to do." I could smell the wind of change, but I had no idea what kind of change it could be.

I came across my first Osho book *The Silent Explosion.* It smelt of incense.

I had been riding the crest of a wave for years, I knew the wheel would turn, and I wanted to be prepared. I went to Ibiza with my boyfriend, Lawrence. He was a tall, dark, handsome doctor in mysticism, who saw magic everywhere and was gifted with the ability to communicate it both verbally and through the medium of film and writing. He had just finished his first book *Rhythms of Vision* and was taking a well earned rest. Arriving at Ibiza airport, I saw Lawrence's mother, Lydia, for the first time. She was standing with both her arms raised in the air in greeting to us and I still have the image of that first meeting in my mind, as though it was yesterday. Lydia is a spiritual mother to me and our connection is deep and ancient. She had been with a spiritual group in Indonesia for many years, and also studied with Gurdjieff people. In her beautiful traditional Ibiza house, the three of us sat by the pine cone fire and discussed *The Silent Explosion.* I wanted her advice about whether she thought it "safe," and she said yes I should try the meditation techniques. The only doubt I had about the book was that at the back there was a biographical note that said Osho had been in Tibet seven hundred years before in his last incarnation. This sounded too fantastic to be true, but I can remember how Lawrence raised his eyebrows, when I said, "Anyway, I don't expect to find a perfect spiritual master, because how can he be perfect in my eyes, when I don't even know what to look for."

Anyone who has visited Ibiza will know that it is an island that brings up intense feelings. It is ruled by the Goddess Thanet, who takes care of women, and astrologically it is Scorpio. Depth and intensity, darkness and magic. Anyway, I was just on holiday, and I wasn't looking for weird experiences; I was very happy working in Lydia's garden all day. The connection with the earth felt good and I was not interested in going to the beach, or the usual tourist spots.

It was here that I had my first experience of meditation, of being in the moment. It happened out of necessity.

Lawrence and I went on a picnic with a few friends. I wandered away from the group to find some flowers to take back to Lydia. She had not been feeling well and so had not come with us. I came across a grove of bushy plants as tall as I was, on which were huge pink and white flowers. As I reached up to pick them I saw that they would not break easily, and so I had to tear the branches in a rather clumsy way that broke the bush. I looked at the wreckage I had caused and saw that the branch was oozing white sap, where I had torn it from top to bottom. I felt bad, it looked like it was bleeding. I said to the plant, "Well, if I can tear you open like this, then I can at least lick you better." So, I licked, with my tongue, the weeping sap out of the branch, and walked back to the picnic with my flowers. My tongue and the back of my throat started feeling numb, as though I had had a shot of Novocain at the dentist's.

As I approached my friends, who were seated around on the ground, one woman jumped up and said, "Throw those flowers immediately, and wash your hands — those flowers are deadly poisonous." The white sap was inside me. I saw that if I tell these people what I had done, they are going to freak out. And if they freak out, then I will freak out, and I will get sick. "There's no hospital here anyway," I reasoned to myself, "And so what can be done? Better I accept the "poison" in my body and let it become part of me." So I didn't tell any of my friends what I had done.

It was a long drive back to the house in the car and I was very silent. My friends were telling stories of people who had died from these poisonous flowers. One family, the parents and their two children, had died only a couple of months earlier because they had a barbecue and had used the branches on the fire to cook their food.

It was very hot and crowded in the car and I was sitting on Lawrence's knee. I bent my head and looked out of the window and felt the numbness in my throat, and told myself that I would be alright if I could accept the poison and relax. I made a deal, silently, with the flowers that their poison would lie dormant and would not harm me unless one day I poisoned myself. I don't know what I meant by that, but that is what my mind was saying.

It was early evening when we reached Lydia's house, and I can still remember the colors of the setting sun on the blossoming almond tree. We prepared dinner. We ate dinner. I did not say a word. I was being moved into the here and now, because each moment was possibly my last. I felt a little dizzy and very high. Everything I did had great meaning and intensity. I was aware of everything around me like never before and I was aware of myself — my body, each heartbeat, each movement. I had the feeling to keep moving, so I spring-cleaned the kitchen. Lydia and Lawrence would call in after me to come and sit down and what the hell was I doing cleaning the kitchen all the time.

I felt very calm. I was not thinking much about anything. I went to bed that night and wondered if I would wake up. I can still see the room as I took my last look at it that night — it has become an indelible impression. Anyway, I woke up, and was perfectly healthy. Later, I looked up the flowers in an encyclopedia, and it read:

"Oleander :

...and having a poisonous milky juice. The best known is the common oleander often called rosebay, a native of the Mediterranean region, characterized by its tall shrubby habitat, and is well described by Pliny the Greek, who mentions its roselike flowers and poisonous qualities."

But that is not the point. I had had my first experience of how it feels to live in the moment, to be aware and conscious of each moment. I had one foot on 'The Path.'

On another occasion, I was at a cocktail party with Lawrence and Lydia. The guests were an assortment of rich, titled and rather stiff people. Our friend, whose party it was, delighted in collecting interesting people around him and I guess that's how we were invited, because we were rather on the "eccentric fringe" in comparison to the rest of the guests.

During the party, outside in the narrow street, a dog must have been hit by a car. Its cries and screams filled the open house and balconies, where titled guests were quietly sipping from their glasses, as they stood murmuring in polite conversation. Now, understand, I had never caused a scene anywhere. I am, after all, British, and am actually a "quiet type" of personality. The howls and cries of the dog hit me so deep that I started to howl in unison with the dog. No thoughts crossed my mind that "This is not ladylike, this is not sociably acceptable, or people will think me mad" — it just happened! I actually fell to the floor, howling like a dog. I was completely lost in the pain of the animal.

When I opened my eyes, the last guest was disappearing around the corner of the door. The room was empty except for Lawrence, Lydia, myself and our host. Even Lydia, who was pretty unconventional herself, looked embarrassed and a little worried as she knelt beside me and asked, "Are you alright dear?" I had never felt better in my life. Something had been released and I felt wonderful. Our host was also happy. I think he was rather pleased that his party had been such a great subject of gossip.

I was having quite a holiday! During the next few weeks

I was to see a few disembodied faces that no one else was aware of, and I heard, on one occasion, voices singing. I decided that as soon as I arrived back in London I would go to the Rajneesh Meditation Center and start meditating, because something was definitely unraveling in my life.

I had never been with any religious group, or teacher. I had read a book here and there on Zen, Krishnamurti, but I never felt myself to be a seeker. What is it to be a seeker? For me, it is when you know there is more than you are experiencing. A part of you is alive, and you know it, but you are not totally in touch with it. You know that the life you are leading is not enough — you know there is more. You know there is something to be found, and so you start searching.

Some part of me was stirring, as if turning in its sleep. Maybe I was hearing the distant call of an ancient seer. I have understood Osho to say that although we think we have found Him, it is not like that. "I have been calling you," He said.

I knew I was not seeing everything quite as it really was. I remember when I left my home in Cornwall to come to India, I went to say good-bye to the cliffs and the small cove where I spent a lot of my childhood. I looked up at the cliffs and the rocks and I said to them, "I won't come back to you until I can really see you" — I knew I could not really see them.

The first time I visited the Meditation Center, I arrived late and the meditation had just finished. The center was in the basement of a building in Bell Street, London. Outside was a vegetable market and the streets were crowded. Inside, I entered a long white painted tunnel that was barely five feet high. Either side were cushions. This was the 'sitting room', as it were, where the *sannyasins* met to drink tea and gossip. Walking through this rather narrow white tunnel I encountered the meditators coming towards me. There were men and women and they were all naked and covered in sweat! "This is not meditation," I told myself. I looked around and saw that the walls were covered in photographs of a man who I presumed must be Osho. So many photos, and people sitting at his feet! "Who do they think he is?" I asked myself, "A movie star, or something!" This was clearly not the place for me and I stormed out angrily, and stamped my feet all the way home. I was too fired up to even catch a bus or cab, and it was a long way.

That night I dreamt that I was working very hard. It was more a dream of feelings than visual. I was working in a determined manner in the dream, and at the end of two years I was given a gift. The gift was given to me by a friend who I had known and loved for years, and he had recently taken *sannyas* and changed his name to Rishi. I held out my hands to receive it and my hands were empty. A voice from somewhere said, "Well, I don't think much of that! You have worked two years for that and you don't even understand what you have got. You can't even see it!" And I didn't care. I knew I would work for another two years, and another two years. With that, I felt a wind sweep up behind me and I looked towards the horizon and could see forever into the distance. The dream was so strong it woke me up and I said to myself that it was the Meditation Center that had caused this dream and I must go back. I went back the next day and started doing Osho's 'Dynamic Meditation' technique.

Doing 'Dynamic Meditation' changed my life. Everybody did the meditation naked, and I soon realized that there was nothing sexual in this. I had no feeling that anyone was interested in my body at all; on the contrary, we all wore blindfolds. The first stage is chaotic breathing to a background of taped music, and the second stage is cathartic, to release suppressed emotions. I thought I had no suppressed emotions, and I had nothing to scream about, so I gently danced about during this stage. It was a few days into the meditation that I was surprised one day, when in the cathartic stage, I witnessed myself as a tall Amazon female standing on a hill, and a scream erupted out of me so loud, so primordial, that it filled the whole universe. I was screaming into the darkness and it was an expression of the agony and pain for the whole of humanity's past. But I felt detached and separate, as though I was watching and hearing the scream coming from someone else.

The catharsis is a cleansing process before meditation can happen. I knew I was not capable of simply sitting silently and letting meditation happen, because my mind was too busy. At this point in my life I actually thought I was my mind. There was no separation between the thoughts that moved constantly through my head, and my being. I had no feeling of consciousness. I knew only my thoughts. But after this experience I was beginning to understand that there is much much more to "me" than I think.

I had another experience during the cathartic stage some days later when I felt my body as not "me". My body became that of a hunchback. My face changed, my mouth hung open and my eyes peered curiously sideways. My whole left side seemed to collapse and from my mouth came strange sounds as though I couldn't speak. I crouched in a corner and had a feeling of being misunderstood, but the strongest feeling was of love. A feeling of love surrounded this "creature" that was my body. I felt male, and this deformed male was filled with tremendous love, such a sweetness and gentleness that it was a beautiful and touching experience. I needed no explanation for it, as once again I had felt myself separate, as though watching, and I felt no fear because in a strange way it had felt natural. However, I did not mention it to anyone until years later, for fear of being thought mad.

The third stage is to jump up and down with arms in the air, shouting "Hoo! Hoo!" for ten minutes and then

"STOP" is shouted and you stop exactly as you are. In this third stage meditation happens of its own accord. There is nothing to be done. The final stage is to dance in celebration, and that too happens on its own.

I did this meditation technique every evening for about six months. But I was caught the first few times I did it. Leaving the Meditation Center each night, I was completely blissed out, as though on some kind of drug. Bell Street is in one of the worst parts of London. It is off the Harrow Road and under a flyover. Trucks and heavy traffic are constant. It is near Paddington train station and the red brick buildings around there are old and ugly. I would come out into this grim chaos of traffic and grayness, looking up at everything and saying, "It's all so beautiful." Also, it was the first thing in my life that I was on time for. Every night I would be sitting on the bus on my way through Paddington at exactly six o'clock, and I would say to myself, "What is the matter with me, I must be mad. What's happening to me? I have never been on time for anything in my life, not school, not work, not any date."

Sannyas consisted of three small commitments in those days. One wore a *mala*, — a necklace of 108 wooden beads — with a plastic locket showing a photo of Osho. *Malas* (without the locket) have been worn by the traditional *sannyasin* in India for thousands of years. Orange clothes were worn at all times, and a Sanskrit name was given as a change from the old name and its associations. I was shocked when, in India, I saw my first "traditional *sannyasins*". They were dressed just the same as I was in orange and *mala* and I could understand what a blow it must be for an Indian to see a Westerner (especially a woman) dressed as one of their "holy" men. The traditional *sannyasin* has renounced the world and is usually an old man and rarely a woman, who would never be seen with a girlfriend or boyfriend. We no longer wear these colors or the *mala* now (at the time of writing!). It seems its "work" is done.

To wear orange came naturally, as I didn't even realize that it was one of the "rules". The *mala* became a necessity, as I was constantly feeling that I had lost something. This had begun to happen shortly after I started the meditation. I would gasp and clutch at my breast, as though I had lost a necklace. This became embarrassing, as it would happen anywhere, at any time. Eventually I thought, "Hell, I will have to get one of those necklaces."

The *sannyasins* that I met at the center didn't appeal to me as personalities. For instance, I had never even met a woman who didn't wear make-up, and here were these women with the pale faces, and their soft white skin, and long shapeless hairstyles. And the men looked very feminine to me. They were not the kind of people that I wanted to take home and introduce to any of my friends. However, I was attracted to them in a way that I did not understand and I spent more and more time at the Meditation Center and went out less and less to parties with my friends.

There was a woman I saw each night sitting in the round white tunnel, knitting a multi-colored, ethnic patterned scarf. She was not a *sannyasin*, and from what I heard, her young and very attractive face and penchant for Afghani clothes and Tibetan boots, hid the fact that she was a successful businesswoman and lawyer. She was called Sue Appleton, and her name would soon be changed to Anando. Little did I know then that our lives were to become as colorfully interwoven as her ethnic knitting.

I met another woman called Susan, and her name was to change to Savita. She was an accountant, and her plain and homely looks disguised her well, as she was to become a main player in the destruction and ruin of many lives. Her talent with figures was to give her access to millions of dollars, and make her a criminal. We were doing a group together in a country house in Suffolk. Throughout the group we made no contact, but at the very end, in darkness, the group was told to take off all their clothes and place them in the corner of the room. We were then to take something from the pile of clothes and put it on. When the lights went on, I was wearing her dress, and she was wearing mine. We eyed each other warily, and I felt strange, as though unwillingly and ceremoniously we had become blood brothers. A bond I was not to honor.

It happened to me that doing the meditation not only gave me great joy, but I was also feeling increasingly aware that everything I had known was losing meaning for me. Whereas I was once thrilled to go out to night clubs and dinner parties with friends, I began noticing that all the faces I was dressing up for were empty and dead. Even the richest people looked like they had nothing. My intellectual friends had great discussions while vaguely looking over the shoulder of the person they were talking to. Once, while talking to a friend at one of his art gallery openings, I noticed that although we were talking, he wasn't there! There was nobody home, behind those eyes! He didn't even notice when I stopped speaking in the middle of a sentence and stood staring at him in wonder.

Everything looked false. I wrote pages and pages to Osho, asking, "Why is nothing real?" Luckily, I had the sense not to post most of my letters. These were the beginning days which were quite unsettling, because when I first started looking at my life, and the people around me, it was hard. I really saw some things that were frightening. So, during these first few months as a meditator there was a lot of unveiling going on. A lot of looking at things for the first time. Dynamic Meditation awakens a vital energy that brings freshness and clarity to the seeker's eyes.

I was working as a secretary two days a week for some fashion photographers and an artist friend of theirs, who always wore blue, and lived with his blue-clad wife, and blue-clad child, in a blue house, with blue carpets, blue furniture, and blue paintings on blue walls. When I started to wear only orange clothes he thought *I* was mad! He rang the photographers and they discussed me, saying they were worried I had gone crazy because I was meditating. They said to me that of all the people they knew, I didn't need to meditate. "You are always so happy and relaxed," they said.

Two other friends took me aside, with serious faces and asked me if I was "doing hard drugs." "No, I'm meditating," I replied.

I worked for an actor one day a week, as what he called his personal assistant. Actually what I mostly did was listen to him when he talked. He was an extremely handsome, rich young man and yet he would periodically get drunk and destroy all the furniture and windows of his mews house with his bare and bleeding hands. He told me I was "wasting my life by meditating," and that he would not help me in any way financially, even though he could afford to.

I needed to meet the man who had invented this meditation and had changed my life so much, and I couldn't wait another day before taking *sannyas*. I took *sannyas* in London from Shyam Singha, a rebel disciple; a tiger of a man, with flaming yellow-green eyes. A man with tremendous charisma and wisdom and he helped me a lot, but then our paths were to take different turns. He gave me a name on a piece of paper written in Osho's hand — Ma Dharma Chetana. There was a new moon eclipse in Scorpio, in the eighth house, and I felt this an auspicious beginning.

I wrote my first letter to Osho (addressing Him as Lord of the Full Moon, which is the meaning of Rajneesh) saying that I had heard him talk of 'The Path,' but I was so lost that I couldn't even find my feet to put on the path. His answer was "Come, just come, with or without your feet."

So romantic, and right from the beginning a twinkle, a sense of humor.

I set myself a date on which I was going to leave for India. I had no money, but when that date came I was going to leave, with or without a ticket.

I packed up everything as though I would never return. I took my two cats to an eccentric old lady in the country, who had about two hundred cats. To my two, she gave a private caravan in her garden.

I took my Shih Tzu dog, 'The Beast', to my parents in Cornwall. They were very accepting of my "new fad that wouldn't last," and my mother even accompanied me to the beach early each morning where I did Dynamic Meditation. Taking me with her around our small town while she shopped, she proudly told neighbors and storekeepers that, "Our Sandra is doing meditation now." But after a few days she was worried that to meditate every day was too often, and she prophesied that I would "either go mad, or end up in a nunnery." My mother's great beauty is her innocence. My father's is his sense of humor. I said good-bye to my grandmother, my brother and my sister. I wept when I said good-bye to my parents, and hung out of the train window as it pulled out of the quaint old station on the hill in Liskeard. I thought I was going forever and would never see anyone again.

Lawrence took me to London airport to see me off on my adventure into the interior, as he was about to start his adventure into the exterior world: from Hollywood — to wild primitive tribes in New Guinea. We didn't know when we would meet again, and through tears, I asked him, "Do you think I'll be able to learn Yoga there?" He put his arm around me and said, "Oh, I'm sure you will learn many things there."

CHAPTER TWO

Luminous Darkness

After my first night in an Indian hotel, in Pune, I decided to abandon the search for 'Truth'. The hotel had appeared to be a good one from the outside, and I arrived tired and shaken at my first experience of an Indian airport and train station. The station looked like a refugee camp with whole families asleep on their pathetic bundles of possessions, right in the middle of the platform, where passengers rushed past and over them. Maimed, starving people pulled at me, begged from me, and stared as though they wanted to eat me. Porters and taxi drivers shouted at each other and even had a fist fight, punching each other's faces and half strangling each other over who was to have a customer. And so many hundreds of people — everywhere. Population explosion!

On the wall of my hotel room was the most repulsive, crusty-backed creature I had ever seen. It was a three-inch long cockroach, and it flew at me. It actually flew, and I screamed so loud that people came running. I can still remember the incredulous look on the man's face when he saw that I was making so much fuss over a cockroach.

Turning on the bathroom taps I was surprised when the water went straight through the sink and splashed onto my feet. The plumbing had never been completed and there was no pipe connecting the sink to a drain. I went to the reception desk and tried to explain what had happened, and then took the manager to my bathroom and pointed at the bottomless sink. But he could not see the problem, and anyway didn't have another room free.

The bed was a metal frame that had once been painted blue, with springs that almost penetrated the thin mattress, and on top of this were two well-worn sheets that hadn't been changed in a long time. But the worst thing was what I understood to be a large *swastika* painted in blood on the wall. This, I thought, was some kind of black magic. I didn't know then that the *swastika* originated in India and is a symbol of good fortune. It was Hitler who, reversing the direction of the cross unknowingly changed the *swastika* to symbolize evil. And it was not painted in blood but a herb that, when chewed, becomes red. It has a similar effect to tobacco, and it's very popular and spat everywhere.

It was late at night and I didn't want to go back out into the madness of the street, so I sat fully dressed on the bed all night, not daring to lie down on it — and cried.

Awaking in a crumpled heap on the bed to the sounds of a very loud radio playing Indian film music and people shouting, I decided to take a quick holiday somewhere in the sun and go back to London. I had some books to deliver to the *ashram* for Osho's library, so I took a rickshaw to the *ashram* and from there was leaving for the coast. I had only one foot outside the rickshaw, and as I looked up I saw Rishi. He was the man who, in my dream, had handed me my "gift" for which I had been striving for two years. He took me to his house, put me in the bed and there I stayed for one week. Then I was ready.

I started attending Hindi discourses. Osho talked alternate months in English and Hindi. This was the Hindi month. I didn't have the eyes to see Osho's grace and beauty at first, but I was certainly feeling something.

To sit and listen to a talk in an unknown language for two hours sitting on a marble floor, seems a bit daft. But Chuang Tzu Auditorium, with its extremely high roof supported by pillars and open on all sides to a garden, so lush and exotic, was a very special place. Osho's voice while speaking Hindi is the most beautiful music I have ever heard. I never missed a Hindi discourse; I even preferred them to English.

In monsoon there were very few people (sometimes no more than about one hundred) and the rain would be pelting down on the surrounding jungle. It was the easiest way to slip into meditation and not even know it. Discourse would end with the Hindi *"Aj Itna Hee"* (enough for today) after two hours, and I would think, "Oh, no! I just sat down." Osho always lowers His voice as He reaches the end of a discourse, in a way that one is gently nudged over the edge, into oblivion. Time loses all meaning and two hours can be as two minutes.

I was feeling tremendously alive. It felt as though Osho had given me life. I was alive before, in body; I was enjoying myself, but I could feel a qualitative difference now.

The first few days that I attended the discourses a strange thing would happen. Each morning I would run out of the auditorium and head for a large clump of bushes in a secluded spot of the *ashram* gardens, crawl under the bushes, and howl my eyes out. Sometimes I would sob and blubber until lunch time. This continued for months. I never understood what I was crying about. It didn't feel like sadness, more like an overflow of awe.

The body can certainly have strong reactions to meditation in the beginning. Any sickness we got while we were doing intense meditation camps, or groups, we were advised to wait five days before seeing a doctor. These sicknesses always changed and went without medicine, because they were basically being created by the mind. It became quite obvious that the body and mind are interconnected in a way that, if understood, could enable us to avoid many illnesses.

As each month passed, marked by the change from

Hindi to English discourses, I would marvel that I was still in Pune with Osho. Even though I had come "forever", I had no idea how this was going to happen. Rishi was taking his spiritual path quite seriously at this time. He was celibate and eating only brown rice. So after the first week of taking care of me he asked me to find my own place.

When I became a *Sannyasin* I had found the *Sannyasin* men too soft and effeminate. I thought, "Well, obviously my love-life is finished if I get into this trip." But I didn't care. At twenty-nine I felt I had done enough. However, walking into the local snack bar, "Cafe Delight" one morning to drink a sugarcane juice, I met a tall, slim, blond Englishman called Prabuddha, and 'fell in love'. We were staying in the same hotel, and after a week decided that we might as well live in the same room as it was cheaper. It was not quite as bad as the first hotel I stayed in, but did not lack cockroaches, stinking bathrooms, and screams in the night. It was the hottest time of the year and the electricity was continually being cut off, but I had never been happier in my life.

Each night Osho met about twelve to fifteen disciples on the porch of His house overlooking the garden. This was called *darshan* (literally translated it means seeing). In this intimate atmosphere He would meet new people and help anyone who was having difficulties with meditation, or as happened a lot with Westerners — relationship problems. At my first *darshan* I was sitting by the side of Laxmi, a small Indian woman who was Osho's secretary, when my name was called. I can't remember Him walking in, in fact I can't remember much except the fresh, coolness that surrounded Him and a powerful gentleness that I had not been aware of while sitting in the discourses. It was difficult to speak. He shone a small light on my forehead and in response my arms spread wide and shook. He gave me a meditation to do each night before sleeping, and said to report to him in two weeks as much had to come up.

Each night I did this new meditation and was expecting something really dramatic and 'spiritual' to happen to me, but I found that only happiness was 'coming up'. In my next *darshan* I told Osho and He said:

"More happiness will be coming, because once you have the opening for happiness, then there is no end to it. It goes on growing. Once you open yourself to unhappiness, that goes on growing. It is just a turning within you, a tuning within you...as if you tune the radio to a certain wave-length and it catches a certain station.

"Exactly like that, if you try to tune yourself towards happiness, you will become receptive to all the happiness that the world makes available. And it is tremendous; nobody can exhaust it. It is oceanic...it goes on and on and on. It knows no beginning and no end. And the same is with unhappiness; that too is unending."

He said that once you know how to turn your face towards happiness, then it goes deeper and deeper until a moment comes when you forget that unhappiness exists.

I have my own idea that possibly something like a honeymoon happens with meditation, because when I first came to Osho many strange experiences happened. I think it was because I was not expecting anything, and so I had a certain innocence about the esoteric.

Sitting in discourse one morning, not near the front, but close enough to make eye contact with Osho, I felt a surge of energy, like an atomic mushroom moving up inside my body and exploding around my chest area. For the next few years my 'heart center' was the area that was feeling most of the action.

When I first heard Osho speaking about awareness I did not understand. With my first few attempts at awareness, I found that whenever I tried to be aware my breathing would stop. I could not breathe and be aware at the same time. I must have been trying too hard.

I was beginning to understand what Osho was saying

about conditioning and about the mind being a computer, programmed by parents, society, teachers, television, and, in my case — pop songs. I had never thought about it before, but there were many things I began to notice about myself, my reactions to situations, my opinions. When I stopped to re-examine, I remembered that my teacher had taught me that...my grandmother thought this way...this is what my father believes in. "Where am I in all this?" I would ask myself.

Meditation happened for me naturally, from just sitting in discourse and listening to the sound of Osho's voice, and the pauses between his words. I sat and listened to the rhythm and in that way meditation came to me rather than me trying to do it.

Discourses became so important for me that I would wake up several times during the night and jump out of bed ready to go. After my emotional outbursts of crying in the bushes cooled down, discourse became a nourishing and essential beginning to my day.

I began to see how differently Osho moved from anyone else I had seen, and I became fixed sometimes for a whole discourse just watching His hands. Each movement, graceful and poetic and yet with a vitality and strength that emanated great power. He seduces us into meditation, to walk the spiritual path, offering His hand as though we are children.

He laughs with us and tells us never to become serious, that seriousness is a disease and life is playful. When He looked at us we immediately felt accepted, trusted and loved as never before. I use the word "us" because He was the same with everyone. He loves everyone equally, as though He is love itself.

His compassion is something I had never experienced before. I had never met anyone who spoke the truth about a situation, risking his own popularity in order to help others.

I sent a dream I had to Osho, as a letter. I thought it was a beautiful, colorful dream and wanted Him to see it. I received an answer that was: "Dreams are dreams, without any meaning." I was furious. After all, was it not because of a very important dream that I was here at all? I had been keeping a dream diary for years, and considered the meaning of dreams to be very significant. I wrote a discourse question asking, "Why did you say such a thing, that dreams have no meaning?" Part of the reply I got was:

"I am not only saying that dreams are dreams; I say that whatsoever you see when you think you are awake is also a dream. The dreams that you see with closed eyes in your sleep, and the dreams that you see with your open eyes in your so-called awake state — both are dreams and both are meaningless....

"Mulla Nasruddin was walking into town one evening when he suddenly came across a pile of cow shit on the path. He bent over slightly and looked at it carefully.

"'Looks like it,' he said to himself.

"He leaned closer and sniffed. 'Smells like it.'

"He cautiously put his finger in it, then tasted it:

"Tastes like it. I'm sure glad I didn't step in it!"

"Beware of analysis!" Osho said.

I was really hurt — how dare He say that my life is meaningless, so how can my dreams have meaning? Why couldn't He be nice about it, I wasn't asking Him anything to provoke this! But although I felt a little singed by the fire, I did have enough understanding to know that I wasn't yet in tune with existence the way He speaks of it. I didn't feel as fulfilled and blissful as He looked, so maybe I had been fooling myself that my life had meaning. I only had to look at Him and I could see in Him that there was another reality, a far deeper dimension, something I could see in Him but did not know for myself. I could see it in His eyes, and in the way He moved.

He had taken away a false notion I had about myself, and it left me space to explore the real.

Six months passed and Prabuddha needed to go to England to finish some business he was doing with his brother. He offered to take me with him, and as my sister was getting married and I knew I would be returning within a month, I agreed. I had another reason for going also, and although it was vague in my mind it was deep. I was feeling so secure in my new way of life that I wanted to test it somehow. My feeling to go was not clear to me, and when I saw Osho in *Darshan* to say good-bye and He asked why I was going, I cried and simply said, "I feel so secure here." He smiled and said "Yes, love is very secure."

I went back to England already feeling how I was changing. I felt more loving and open to my family than I had ever been. My sister is ten years younger than me, so when I left home at sixteen she was so young that we never really met. I was always the big sister who returned for holidays and was gone again, almost like a stranger. On this visit at her party on the eve of her marriage we danced together all night, and I felt for the first time that we had really met. On introducing Prabuddha to my parents, my father thought I said "poor bugger," and so that is what he was called. My parents were happily reassured that my new life was good for me, and so once again we said good-bye.

Prabuddha and I returned to India and landed in Goa. Goa is, to Pune, like Brighton is to London — the closest seaside resort. Behind the house in which we stayed was a high, steep cliff and one day we climbed over the cliff to the other side to explore the beaches there. Green fields and lush jungle spread out before we reached the beach and after a few hours we walked back. As we reached the top of the cliff I saw, moving through my mind like a movie, someone shooting at us, and we were lying in the grass to avoid the bullets. I said to Prabuddha, "Someone could easily shoot us right here."

The sun was low in the sky and just turning orange as we reached the top and began to climb down towards our house. It was very rough on this side with loose rocks, and extremely steep, and the path curved out of sight at many places.

I heard a sound behind us, turned, and thirty feet from us was an Indian man with a rifle. As I stood and looked at him, he placed the rifle on his shoulder, bent down on one knee, and aimed at us. I was in shock and reacted very slowly, considering the situation.

I tapped Prabuddha on the shoulder. He was in front of me, climbing down the slope, and when he turned I said:

"Look, someone wants to shoot us!"

"Fuck!!" screamed Prabuddha, and he grabbed my wrist and pulled me down the cliff. I swear that our feet did not touch the ground, running down that cliff.

We reached the bottom and our Goan neighbors ran towards us and took us into their house. They sat us down in a dark corner and "holy water" was sprinkled on us in a kind of ritual dance. (Goans are Catholics, but they add their own brand of voodoo to it.)

We explained what had happened and were told that only a few months before, two Westerners had been murdered on that hill.

I was fascinated. From where did my thoughts come of being shot at? Thoughts must be energy waves that travel, rather like radio waves, and all you need is to tune in to the right station. Radio waves are continuously in the air, but you need a radio to pick them up. Maybe thoughts are also in the air, just the same way. This explains to me how it is that lovers, or people closely related, will often have the same thought at the same time, and when staying in a new house, the "vibe" may be strange — thought waves left behind by the last occupants. I recently did an experiment with a friend, where he sat in one room and I in another and I sent him thoughts. We decided beforehand that the thought could consist of anything — a color, a sound, a word, a drawing — and he would write down whatever he received. He got six out of ten of my thoughts!

A few weeks after our return to Pune I was beginning to think that all this love and light was a bit much, a bit boring and maybe I would go to Bali and look for a bit of black magic. As a child in Cornwall I was intrigued by the idea of the devil. I had tried to provoke Jesus in churches late at night when no one was around, but had not come up with much. Just some light appeared in the church one time after I had called out "Show yourself, Jesus!" But calling up the devil was much more fun. Friends would freak out, furniture would rattle and glasses break. The darker side of life seemed to have more substance, seemed more real.

I wrote a discourse question to Osho: "You say take light into darkness and the darkness disappears. You are the light. Then where is darkness? And why do I long for darkness too?"

The first sentence He spoke in answer was enough for me. He said:

"When I say bring light and darkness disappears, what I mean exactly is: bring light and darkness becomes luminous."

Luminous darkness!! The search for luminous darkness! I was afire. I never again had the yearning to seek for anything less. Luminous darkness epitomizes for me the poetic majesty of the peaks of life that I yearn for. The peaks that I glimpse for a while and then are gone, leaving me drenched in an unforgettable sweetness.

Even though I had become a *sannyasin* in London, nine months before, I felt the first time I touched Osho's feet was my initiation.

One of the things that had shocked me the most around Osho was that after He left the meeting hall, Indians would go to the podium, bow down and put their heads where His feet had been. As a Westerner I had never seen such a sign of devotion and I found it quite shocking. When my day came it was Guru Purnima celebration. (The day of the full moon in July when all religious teachers and masters in India are worshipped and celebrated.)

Osho sat in His chair and surrounding Him were musicians, people in various stages of let-go, laughing, singing, swaying, and then a line of people who wanted to touch the feet of the Master. The auditorium was filled to capacity and with everyone in shades of the rising sun, the atmosphere was festive and quite overwhelming. I joined the end of the line, which stretched all the way through the overgrown garden and out to the gate. I could see, from the people before me, that all I had to do was touch His feet and move on. As I slowly shuffled forward from the garden into the auditorium, I was no longer thinking about it, because the celebration was so contagious.

Suddenly, I was there, in front of Him. I remember bowing down, but then there was a blank moment when I knew nothing. The next thing I knew, I was up and running. I ran, and I ran, with tears streaming down my face. A friend tried to stop me to comfort me, thinking something was wrong, but I pushed her aside — I had to run. I could have ran until I disappeared off the end of the world.

In those same months I did a few therapy groups. I found them very useful as a beginning to awareness. Becoming aware of emotions, as a separate experience from oneself, is invaluable. I was for the first time able to accept and express negative emotions freely. To feel anger pulsating throughout the whole body, and just be with it (without punching anyone else) is, in fact, a beautiful experience.

The energy of a group of people sitting together for days in a room with the aim to "discover themselves" is very intense. I remember hallucinating and seeing the walls move and the room change shape and size. It must be connected with adrenaline rushes because certainly fear was present at moments, the fear of being exposed. And then, the bliss when it is discovered that all the fears are just projections of the mind.

I became "possessed" by the lovable hunchback once more during a group in which I horrified the other group participants, and even the seasoned group leader was without any comment. And then once more, after a particularly beautiful *darshan* one night, while walking home from the *ashram*, I saw two Indian men having a fight. I was feeling vulnerable and the violence shocked me so much that as I walked away down the road I felt the hunchback taking me over, and I did not want to prevent it. I had enough sense to walk in the shadows of the trees, so no one would see me. I was not frightened by this gross distortion of my body because my physical body was nothing compared to the immense feeling of love that came with it. It was a fifteen minute walk and I watched myself, hobbling along in the shadows of the old banyan trees, eyes rolled up in my head, tongue hanging out the side of my mouth. Just before I reached home I was beginning to straighten up and "he" was fading. That was the last time we met. I didn't tell anyone though; I knew it would sound weird to them. And I never asked Osho about it because it didn't feel like a problem.

I have heard Osho say that the conscious mind is only the tip of the iceberg and the unconscious is full of repressed fears and desires. In a "normal" society, without the protective and understanding environment of Osho's commune, I would never have allowed such an experience to happen. It would have been kept suppressed, and instead of feeling cleansed by what was a natural expression of something unknown, anxiety would have built up. Why do so many people go mad in the Western world — especially sensitive and talented people, like artists, musicians and writers? In the East it has never happened, and this has something to do with meditation. In a series of talks called *The Beloved*, Osho has said:

"Madness is possible in two ways: either you fall below the normal, or you go above the normal. In both ways you become mad. If you fall below the normal you are ill; you need psychiatric treatment to be pulled back to normality. If you go beyond the normal you are not ill. For the first time you are becoming really healthy, because for the first time you are filled with wholeness. Then don't be afraid. If your madness brings you more sanity in life, then don't be afraid. And remember, the madness that is below the normal is always involuntary; that is the symptom: it is involuntary. You cannot do it, it happens; you are pulled into it. And the madness that is above the normal is voluntary — you can do it — and because you can do it, you remain the master of it. You can stop it at any moment. If you want to go further, you can go on — but you remain always in control.

"This is totally different from ordinary madness: you are going on your own. And remember, if you go on your own, you will never be neurotic because you will release all possibilities of madness. You will not go on accumulating them. Ordinarily, we go on repressing."

At a group *darshan* I mentioned to Him that I was about to do the encounter group for the second time. Osho said with a sigh, that, yes some people miss the first time. It proved to be true because by now I had the knack. I could provoke, detect and then express whatever emotion was happening.

I finished this process with a group in which you ask yourself the question, "Who am I?" for three days, continuously. This was really the group for me. Something happened in which my mind became a voice far in the distance and it (the mind) was unable to function, whereas, "I" was there, present and utterly fulfilled in each moment. I had been listening to Osho speak about no-mind in His discourses, but the words had not prepared me for this. To hear the word fulfilled is one thing, to experience it is something else. The experience lasted about six hours, and I was tickled pink that no one could see what was happening to me. We went for lunch and as I was eating, Prabuddha walked into the restaurant. Suddenly there was a "no" in me. I didn't want to see him, so I hid under the table. Either the food or the boyfriend broke the spell and at that point the experience started to fade. However, it took a few days to fade completely and I still have the memory dangling in front of me like a cosmic carrot.

I had a *darshan* in which I told Osho that I was worried that because I didn't do anything useful, I would be sent away. I told Him that I was worried that I did not trust enough. He explained to me that His love is in such abundance that He just gives and nobody needs to deserve it. He said that my being is enough, that I am not supposed to do anything to be worthy, that He loves me and accepts me in all my limitations.

"To have my love you need not deserve it at all; your being is enough. You are not supposed to do something, you are not to become worthy of it; those are all nonsense things. Because of those things people have been exploited and distracted and destroyed.

"You are already that which you can be; more is not needed. So you have to just relax and receive me. Don't think in terms of deserving, otherwise you will remain tense. That's what is your problem, your anxiety, continuously — that you are falling short, that you are not doing this, you are not doing that, that your trust is not enough. You create a thousand and one things.

"I accept all your limitations and I love you with all

your limitations. I don't want to create any sort of guilt in anybody. Otherwise these are all the tricks. You are not trusting me — you feel guilty; then I become dominant. You are not worthy, you are not doing this, you are not doing that — I will cut the supply of my love to you. Then love becomes a bargain. No, I love you because I am love."

I understood that this was one of the foundation stones of my conditioning, because this unworthiness would surface for years. So many times Osho has told me to just be, that I am enough unto myself.

And then He laughed and said for me to simply relax and enjoy and if I didn't trust, good. He needed a few *Sannyasins* who didn't trust Him — it made variety!

He has always had a way of dissolving problems like a magician, and I would be left standing in the present where there are no problems, and wondering what my mind would think up next. I was suspicious that maybe I made up problems sometimes just to go to *darshan*.

Lawrence came to visit. I hadn't seen him for almost two years and it felt as though no time had passed at all. We connected as though it had been only yesterday since he had put me on the plane to India. I think he came to check out the situation and confirm that I was well and healthy and not a cult victim, as he must have read all the negative press about Osho by then.

The journalists who visited Pune, or even the ones who had never visited wrote about violence in the group therapy and sex orgies, which I have unfortunately all these years never experienced!

Lawrence stayed for a few days and came to *darshan* to see Osho.

Not knowing the ropes, Lawrence got left behind as we all charged into the auditorium. The first to arrive sat in the front, you see, and as much as we tried to control ourselves and walk meditatively, the feet would move faster and faster and, turning the last corner along the garden path, we were running and finally kicking off our shoes in all directions, before skidding across the last few yards of marble floor. Osho came in after we were seated.

Because of my ungraceful entrance, Lawrence and I got separated. He was at the back and I was in the front.

His name was called for him to come and speak to Osho. Nobody knew we were together, and yet when Lawrence's name was called Osho turned in his chair and stared at me as though a flashing light and buzzer had gone off from me. Strange, I never understood how I sent out such a strong message without knowing it.

Osho gave Lawrence a gift, and told him to come back to make a film of the commune.

A year passed, as I marked off each month as another small miracle that I was still here. After spending most of the year sitting by the river trying to play a bamboo flute, I decided that to work in the commune would make me more vulnerable, or available to the Master and whatever "work" He had to do on me. I went many times to the office looking for a job but was told that there were enough workers and unless I could do something in the office (for instance, "An accountant arrived today from England" — this was Savita with whom I had changed clothes years before) then there was no space for me. I was not going to let anybody know that I had worked as a secretary for ten years for priests, psychiatrists, newspapers, hospitals, a veterinary surgeon and a casino. The office life did not appeal at all and so I worked as a gardener and spent most of the day watering plants with a hose, making rainbows. Gardening was considered a luxury and not a job.

Finally, I got caught with a proper job and I was screen printing book jackets. I took the job quite seriously for a while too, thinking that I might become boss of the department; until one day while traveling across town to get a film processed, I saw a man lying dead in an alley and I thought to myself, "Whoah there! you did not come to a Master to become the best screen printer in the world."

The first day I started work, Sheela, who was one of Laxmi's secretaries and who had also just started working, approached me and asked me if I would come to the office each day to inform her what hours my co-workers were doing and how many *beedie* (Indian cigarettes) breaks they took. I told her that I couldn't possibly do that as they were my friends. She replied that I had to, because it was for their spiritual growth. "How can they grow if they are lazy, and how can they be aware of their laziness if someone doesn't point it out to them?" she reasoned. At that point I could only say okay, but I never went to the office and when she came to see me to ask how my co-workers were doing I told blatant lies and enjoyed it. "*Beedie* breaks? No, never. Yes, every day they arrive on time and work hard all day." It is strange, looking back to that period to see how Sheela right from the beginning started a game of recruiting trustworthy spies. This shows that she had great ambitions and lust for power that later were to blow up in full.

I was by now living alone. Once again I was finished with men, as I had just been in love with two at the same time and it had driven me crazy. It climaxed one day when one was tearing up my clothes and when I reached home Prabuddha was throwing the furniture out in the street. I decided to be alone and moved into a house by the river. At night I would simply sit and listen to the sounds of cicadas and frogs, the ticking of the clock and the bark of a distant dog. I loved the dark.

It happened, though, that when I was with certain people, I would feel that they overpowered me and actually took possession of me. I would walk like that person, my face would take on their expressions and I would feel I had no will to stop them. It continued for a couple of months and I was trying to solve it on my own. I thought these people must be having stronger energy than me or something. It finally became too much for me and I wrote to Osho about it and He said to come to *darshan.*

It was quite obvious in *darshan,* that Osho could see right into the person He was talking to. He has said that He can see immediately whether the person is a new seeker or one who has been with many masters before in past lives. That night He called me forward and said I was to hold His foot. I sat and held His foot in my lap and cried. He said that my 'problem' had nothing to do with other people's energies; it was not that someone was overpowering me. It was because I was becoming open to Him and when a person's heart first starts opening, then anything can enter. Being open to Him meant I was open to everyone, and that is why most people decide it is safer to remain with their heart closed. He said that my heart was opening slowly, slowly, and it was beautiful, but then a stray dog would also enter sometimes. So chase the dog out!

"This is going to happen to many people here. Once they start opening up they will be flooded by anything. You are open: somebody passes by and immediately the vibe takes possession of you. But the reason is because you are becoming open to me, because you are becoming more and more possessed by me. So the doors are open and sometimes you may not like somebody's energy; it comes into you and you feel difficult with it. Just put the locket of the *mala* in your hands and remember my foot. You will be able even to touch it, to almost feel it. And immediately the feeling will be gone.

"That's why I am so interested in creating a commune as fast as possible — so that you need not go outside at all. Slowly, slowly, my people will start raising their consciousness higher and higher so nobody, even if you become flooded by anybody, will be felt as bad. It will be a joy. You will thank him, that he has given something beautiful to you by passing. That is what a commune means: where people are living a totally different kind of life, vibrating on a different plane. So each helps the other and everybody becomes a great tidal wave for each other. They can ride on each other's energies and can go on moving as far as they wish. And nobody needs to go outside." (*Let Go*)

Just a few more days, He said, and within three weeks it will all be finished.

A few days later Vivek, who was Osho's caretaker, came to me and asked if I would like to change my job. She needed someone to do Osho's laundry, as His *dhobi* (laundry man), who had been doing the job for seven years, was going on holiday.

Within three weeks I had moved into Osho's house and had started my new work.

CHAPTER THREE

Love Comes Faceless

ao Tzu House (Osho's house) used to belong to a Maharaja. It was chosen because of the gigantic almond tree that stands over the house, changing colors like a chameleon, from red, orange, yellow, to green. It's seasons change every few weeks, and yet I have never seen it with bare branches; as one leaf drops, the new shining green one is already waiting to take its place. Under the tree's foliage is a small waterfall and rock garden, created by a crazy Italian who has never been seen since.

Over the years, Osho's magic touch has turned the garden into a jungle, with bamboo groves, swan ponds, a white marble waterfall that at night is illuminated blue, and as the water runs into small pools, those pools shine with golden yellow light. The giant rocks, from a desert mine in Rajasthan, tower above and glisten in the sun, in contrast to the black granite walls of the library wing. There is a Japanese bridge and watercourse; and a rose garden that blooms out of season and is illuminated at night so that the roses stand and stare into Osho's dining room, with clown-like surrealism and dazzling colors.

There is, winding through the jungle, a science-fiction wonder of a walkway — air conditioned and made of glass. It was designed so that Osho could walk through the garden without being disturbed by the heat and humidity of the Indian climate. It somehow adds to the mystery of this strange garden, where there are white peacocks, and blue peacocks courting each other with their extravagant dance; swans, golden pheasants, cockatoos and the bird of paradise, all brought to Osho from around the world by disciples as their hand luggage. Imagine arriving at Bombay customs as a tourist: "Oh yes, I always travel with my pet swans!"

There is an abundance of birds that come and preen themselves in the reflection of Osho's dining room window, unaware that they are being watched by a Buddha on the other side. Osho's dining room is small and simple and He sits facing a wall of glass, through which He can see the garden.

There is the cuckoo that calls first in the morning, then half an hour later the rest of the orchestra wakes up and makes its declaration. Best of all is a recording of a rooster that is hooked into a loudspeaker at the gate and cockadoodledoo's everyone out of their skin every hour, on the hour!

"To remind everyone that they are still asleep," says Osho.

Osho has tremendous love and respect for any living thing. I have heard Him say, in regard to some trees being cut in order to build a house, that "The trees are living, a building is a dead thing. The tree is the first priority, and you must build around it."

Lao Tzu house is mostly library. The marble corridors are lined with glass-covered bookshelves. I remember on the day I moved in I crashed into them with my suitcase, and by some miracle, nothing broke. Still, to this day, every time I pass that spot in the corridor I remember the time I moved in.

When I started doing Osho's laundry, I was in shock. I have waited for that feeling of shock to wear off, but it never did. I felt the energy so strong in the laundry room that I would say to myself, "Whatever you do, don't close your eyes." I thought that if I closed my eyes I would be gone!

Everything was washed by hand and hung on a line on the roof. I used to splash around in the water like a kid at the seaside, and would end up drenched and dripping from head to toe. Many times I fell flat on the wet marble and, like a drunkard, would bounce and get up unharmed. The work would so totally involve me that at times it would feel as though Osho was in the room. Once I was suddenly overcome while ironing a robe and I fell to my knees with my forehead resting on the table, and He was there, I swear it!

Times changed and since visiting America I did the laundry in washing machines. I rarely got even my hands wet, as I wore rubber gloves for the handwashing. The amount of laundry always miraculously changed according to the amount of working hours. I have never understood how it was possible for one man's laundry to be someone's full-time work. But it was. My mother, on hearing that I was to stay in India and had the great job of Osho's laundry woman, wrote saying that she couldn't understand why I had to "go all that way, just to do someone's laundry. Your father says come home, and you can do his laundry."

I not only "came all this way to India to do laundry," but I moved all around the world to do laundry. My pristine, super-hygienic conditions in Pune were to be changed for a basement in a castle in New Jersey, a trailer in the Oregonian desert, a stone cottage in North India where we had to melt the snow in buckets for water, a hotel basement in Kathmandu where I worked with about fifty Nepali men, a bathroom in Crete, a converted kitchen in Uruguay, again a bedroom in a house in the woods in Portugal, and finally back to the place I started, in Pune.

My laundry room felt like a womb for me. The laundry

room was opposite Osho's room, and so it was a part of the house where nobody ever came. I was left entirely alone; sometimes the only person I saw all day was Vivek.

People sometimes asked me if I got bored doing the same job for years. But boredom was not something that I never felt. Because my life was so simple I did not have much to think about. Thoughts were there but they were like dry bones with no meat on them. Since I had been with Osho my life had changed in a way that I could never have imagined. I was so happy and fulfilled that to do Osho's laundry was my way of expressing gratitude. And the funny thing is, the more lovingly and carefully I did His clothes, the more fulfilled I felt and so it was like a circle of energy that kept returning to me.

He never complained or sent anything back even though during my first monsoon I sent the towels in to Him smelling of mildew. You will have to have been in India in monsoon to know what happens to damp clothes: the smell that they get cannot be detected until the towel is used, and so I was unaware of it. When Vivek told me that the towels were smelling of mildew I was surprised, but when she told me that actually they had been smelling for about a week I was really shocked. "Why didn't Osho tell me immediately?" I asked. He had waited for a few days to see if I would realize it myself, or to see if it would change without Him having to complain.

There were times when I would stop and sit still and feel overwhelmed by a feeling of love. Not thinking of anyone, and not even able to summon up a picture of anyone's face in my mind, it was a strange feeling. I had felt overwhelmed by love before only when there was someone around who had triggered it. And even then it was never as strong as this. I would feel as though I was extremely drunk, although it was a subtle and refined drunkenness. I wrote a poem about this:

"Memory can't recall your face,

So love comes, faceless.
Unfamiliar is the part of me
That loves you.
She has no name,
And she comes and goes
And when gone,
I wipe my tear-stained face
so that it remains a secret."

Osho replied:

"Love is a mystery — the greatest mystery there is. It can be lived, but it cannot be known; it can be tasted, experienced, but cannot be understood. It is something beyond understanding, something that surpasses all understanding. Hence, mind cannot take any note of it. It never becomes a memory — memory is nothing but notes taken by the mind; memory is traces, footprints left in the mind. Love has no body, it is bodiless. It leaves no footprints."

He explained that when love is felt as prayer, uncontaminated by any form, it is felt by the superconscious. That was why the way I was feeling love was unfamiliar. I had at this stage no understanding of my superconscious. So much of what Osho has said over the years was beyond my understanding at the time, but has slowly clicked into place as I have experienced myself more.

"...These are the three stages of the mind: unconscious, conscious, superconscious.

"...As your love grows you will come to understand many things in your being which have remained unknown to you. Love will provoke higher realms in you, and you feel yourself very strange. Your love is entering into the world of prayer. It is tremendously significant, because beyond prayer there is only God. Prayer is the last rung of the ladder of love. Once you have stepped beyond that, it is *nirvana*, it is liberation."

Working for Osho is a great blessing, whether a person

is making clothes for Him, or directing clean air through His air conditioners, plumbing all night so that He can take an ice cold shower in the morning, or any of the one thousand small tasks that disciples love to do. This blessing comes from one's own awareness and love. This will be difficult to understand for people who live and work for money, whose work does not fulfill them. Their day is divided in two parts — time belonging to the boss or the company, and time that is "free". I have always been very touched by the way people work around Osho, even though I can understand why they work with such joy. If someone works all night making something for Osho, the very quality of the way in which they have been working will create such a great feeling. The reward is just that — feeling great. And when you are around someone who makes you feel good, what can you do? — except say thank-you in whatever small way you can.

I have seen that Osho is in a permanent state of bliss. I never saw anything happen to put Osho in a mood or to change His calm, relaxed centeredness. He has no desires or ambition, and needs nothing from anyone. Because of this, there has never been a question of exploitation. He never told me what to do, or how to do it. At the most He would make a suggestion if I asked Him about a problem. Then it was up to me whether I accepted His suggestion or not. Sometimes I didn't. Sometimes I would want to do things my own way, but He never criticized that. He would accept that this was the way I chose to learn — the hard way! — because it always turned out that He was right. It became more and more obvious to me that His sole purpose for being here was to help us grow in awareness and discover our individuality.

As I said earlier, before I started meditating I thought I was my mind. The thoughts that ran constantly through my head were all I knew. I now begin to understand that even my emotions do not belong to me, but my emotional reactions come from conditioning that constitutes my personality.

A master has no ego, no personality. He has realized his essential "self", and in that realization the personality disappears. Ego and personality are given to us by society and people who made impressions on us as children. I see it in myself sometimes when my reaction to a situation will be "Christian", and I wasn't even brought up Christian! At least, I didn't go to church, and we didn't have a Bible in the house. I have been amazed with each discovery of my Christian conditioning and I can only presume that it is in the very air we breathe. Christianity is everywhere, in the way people think and behave, and yet what kind of religion is it now? All that is left are the morals and outdated ideas, which someone like me picks up. It is easy for anyone to see how people from different countries have different behaviour patterns. To be aware of all my conditionings is the greatest work that meditation does, because in meditation I am simply an unchanging silent presence.

I used to practice *latihan* in my room. *Latihan* is a meditation technique used in Subud, (an Indonesian religious movement) in which the meditator stands silently and "opens" to existence. Energy can flow through the person and can take any form — dancing, singing, crying, laughing — anything can happen but you are aware that you are not doing it.

I enjoyed this experience very much. It was a feeling of losing myself, and made me elated. I would stand in the same place every day (like someone having an evening drink, I guess, because I looked forward to my *latihan* time and missed it if I did not do it).

This continued for weeks, until a time came when I started to feel sick. I did not have any specific illness, but my energy was low and I cried very easily. I was worried that maybe I had been allowing the "possession" to happen too often and it was making me ill. One day I was crying and Vivek saw me and asked what was going on. I told her that I thought I was making myself sick because I was doing the *latihan* too much. She told Osho and His answer came back that I was to come to *darshan* and bring my *latihan* with me.

I went to *darshan* and Osho motioned to me to kneel at the side of His chair and then He told me to let the *latihan* happen. I closed my eyes and the feeling I used to get came to me, but not so strong. It was as though someone was standing behind me, somebody very, very tall, and then that presence moved into me and through me and I felt expanded and could see and feel myself across the whole of the Auditorium. A few minutes later Osho called me back and said that everything was good. After that *darshan,* my desire to go to that spot and be possessed faded away and I never thought about it again. The room was later converted to a dental room for Osho, and it was to be seven years later under different circumstances that I found myself back in the same place, once again possessed.

Vivek had been Osho's caretaker for about seven years at this time. Her relationship with Osho goes back through past lives, as He has talked about in discourses — and she can remember. She was a mysterious child/woman, Pisces, with all its qualities of Neptune, and large clear blue eyes. She had never been away from Osho for even a day, so when she announced that she was going to England for a couple of weeks and would I take care of Osho....

I spun dizzily in a confused state until, in an effort to stay in the moment I said to myself that, "Nothing is really happening, nothing is really happening. Just stay cool."

How could I possibly be clean enough to go into Osho's room? On *darshan* days, I used to take all day long in the shower before I felt ready. I almost washed my skin off.

The first thing I did for Osho was to give Him a cup

of tea. A cold cup of tea! I made His tea and took it to His room before He was ready for it. He was still in His bathroom, taking a bath. I sat on the cold marble floor staring at the tray of tea, wondering what to do. If I left the room to make another tea, then He might come out of His bathroom at that moment and wonder where His tea was; so I waited and waited. It is very cold in Osho's room. In the last years Osho liked the temperature at twelve degrees centigrade. Wherever Osho moves I can detect a subtle perfume of camphor, or mint. It was present in His room that day.

Osho was suddenly there! Walking across the room towards His chair,. He chuckled and said hello. At that point I completely forgot the situation of the tea, and passed it to Him. He drank it as though it was the best cup of tea He had ever had and didn't say anything until much later, when He pointed out that maybe I could pour the tea after He came out of the bathroom and not before, next time.

I was struck by His humbleness. He could easily have said, "Yuk! Cold tea. Get me another." Anyone else would have done. But He managed it so that I wasn't even embarrassed. In fact, I didn't even realize what had happened until afterwards.

"Beloved Master,
How does the man of Zen take his tea?"

Osho:
"For the man of Zen everything is sacred — even taking a cup of tea. Whatever he does, he does as if he is in a holy space."

Osho came to talk to us every morning at 8.00 a.m. I was always amazed that He did not need to prepare His talks, in fact I read the *sutra* or questions to Him about fifteen minutes before the talk began. He would simply choose the question and pick some jokes. Reading the questions and *sutras* I would sometimes get so touched that I would cry. He said of me once that I was the perfect crying and weeping type.

On a few occasions Maneesha, who always read the *sutras* and questions to Osho in the discourse, had been sick, and then Vimal, her stand-in, also got sick. Although at a loss for who should read the questions (Osho always liked an English voice for the reading), Osho said, "Not Chetana, and not Vivek — they always cry."

Knowing how close Osho and Vivek had been for years, I was amazed to see that her going away did not change Him at all. He continued as though nothing had happened. I had never seen a human being who was not changed by new situations happening around him. He had a vibrancy and aliveness that never changed. No moods, just a constant river of being.

I have seen it happen with many people, so I know it is not just me, that to do anything in front of Osho, one's self-consciousness becomes too much and it is difficult to even walk naturally. He is so still, graceful and present, that He acts as a mirror. Just to open a door, suddenly I was confronted with so many difficulties — timing it just right so as not to knock Him in the face, which hand, left or right, whether or not to lean in front of Him just as He reaches the door. At the same time, this does not cause tension, because Osho is so relaxed, it simply gives you a good look at yourself doing something for the first time consciously. When I first started to do each act consciously I felt a little awkward. The habit of doing a thing mechanically makes for a much smoother operation. Handing Osho a glass of water, consciousness is there, and that is the incredible gift of being close to Him. It might not sound like much, but a beginning to living a conscious life is for me the most valuable gift I have ever received.

On the day Vivek telephoned to say she was coming back, Laxmi rushed excitedly into Osho's dining room where He was having lunch and told Him that Vivek was on her way back. Osho was talking to me at the time; He turned and thanked Laxmi for her message, and then continued with what He was saying to me, without missing a beat. I was flabbergasted — no sign of emotion, no flicker in His eyes. He was a living example of what He talked to us about — love without attachment, and living in the moment.

How much can the Master see when He looks at us? Does He check out our auras? Does He read our minds? Would He want to read our minds? I guess not. But certainly He sees things that I can't see.

One morning I went to discourse with Osho. I collected Him from His room at 8.00 a.m., walked behind Him down the corridor to Chuang Tzu Auditorium and then I sat there while He spoke for an hour. I was aware that meditation was particularly strong for me that morning. The hour passed like two minutes and I could feel something more than usual had happened. I walked back down the corridor just ahead of Him.

As I opened the door and He walked towards me to enter His room, He said:

"Where have you been, Chetana?"

I thought to myself, "Oh! He has forgotten that I took Him to discourse. He must be spaced out."

I replied, "I've been to discourse."

He was just walking past me at this point and He chuckled.

As He laughed, I laughed. I remembered where I had been.

In those early Pune years Osho's days were busy. He read one hundred books a week. I use to see them going into His room on a trolley each day and every book was signed by Him and in many of them Osho painted exquisite enlightened art. He did work with His secretary, Laxmi, and apart from discourse at 8.00 a.m. there was always *darshan* at 7.00 p.m. He was never sick, and during those years He spoke on Jesus, Sufism, Zen, Lao Tzu, Chuang Tzu, Taoism, Yoga, Hindu mystics, Hassidism, and Buddha.

Osho spoke on Buddha's *Dhammapada* sutras over a period of six months. They were interspersed with talks on Sufis and questions from disciples. For a few weeks He didn't come out at all because there was an outbreak of chickenpox and it was thought too risky to expose Him. It was the day of the Buddha full moon, (full moon in May), when the last of Buddha's *sutras* was read; Osho said, "Buddha was born, became enlightened and died on the same day, and by coincidence today is that day."

For two years I rarely went out of the house. Just the laundry and morning discourses filled my day so much I was on overflow. Sometimes Osho would send me a message to come to *darshan*, because He was talking less and less at *darshan* and energy *darshans* were slowly becoming more frequent. When Osho gave *darshan* He used to answer anyone's problems. He would sit and listen intently to whoever was speaking, as though that person was the only person in the world for Him, and then He would talk for a long time to try to help with the problem. After a few thousand people have talked about their problems you realize that there are no problems, or rather, there are very few and those few are continuously repeated. The mind is the only problem, really. So for how many years can a person go on listening to the same thing again and again? Osho's compassion and patience with us always astounded me.

My last "speaking *darshan*" was the one that left the strongest impression on me. Still, many years later, I dip into that feeling I received then and feel cleansed and nourished.

I wrote to Osho about some great drama I was having at that time. I remember ending the letter by saying that

I was "screaming" for help. I received the reply, "Come to *darshan*."

I sat in front of Him. He looked at me and asked, "What is it?"

I looked into His eyes and everything disappeared.

I said, "Nothing," laughed, and touched His feet.

He chuckled and said, "Good."

Since that day, whenever I feel disturbed by something, I stop and ask myself what is *really* happening, what is it? In 'That Moment' nothing is happening, absolutely nothing.

Of course, I don't always remember this. The habit of the mind and its ability to create problems is deep. It is always a great mystery to me how many times we "get it" and then forget it. Sometimes I am as free as a buddha and then I slip right back and allow my mind to enslave me.

Almost two years passed and I had no interest in men. They were the happiest and smoothest years of my life. No problems. I was happy being alone. Sometimes going towards my room I would have a feeling of excitement, as though I had something waiting for me. I would think, "What is it? Am I in the middle of a gripping novel that I am about to continue?" But there was nothing, I was simply looking forward to being alone. I felt utterly fulfilled.

Sitting in discourse one morning I was surprised to hear Osho speaking of me with reference to discovering which path the seeker is on:

"The first thing is to decide whether you feel joy being alone. For example, Chetana is sitting here. Vivek always asks me, "Chetana remains alone and she looks so happy. What is the secret?" Vivek is unable to understand that one can live totally alone. Now Chetana's whole work is doing my laundry; that is her meditation. She never goes out, not even to eat in the canteen. She brings her food...as if not interested in anybody at all.

"If you can enjoy this aloneness, then your path is

meditation. But if you feel that whenever you relate with people, when you are with people, you feel joy, cheerfulness, bouncing, you feel more alive, then certainly love is your path.

The function of the master is to help you to find out what your real work is, what your type is." (*The Dhammapada*)

A few weeks after this discourse there was the chickenpox epidemic in Pune and the risk was too great for Osho to come out and speak.

For the first time in many years I was cut off from seeing Osho and I missed Him. I listened to the tape of the discourse, where I had been told quite clearly that my path was meditation and aloneness. I wanted to test what He had said about me. I wanted to see if I really was that centered in aloneness. As I walked out the gate, a man I had seen before and who was known as one of the worst flirts in the *ashram*, shouted to me, "Hey, how about a date?" and I said yes.

His name was Tathagat, and to me he looked like a warrior — muscular, with a battle-scarred face and long, dark hair half-way down his back. I "fell in love" with him and that opened the gates to all the emotions I had not felt for years, and had presumed finished. Jealousy, anger — you name it — I had it. I was back on the merry-go-round.

"Be in the world, but not of it," I had heard Osho say many times. Here was another chance for me to give it a try. I had virtually been living like a nun for the last two years. I was blissfully happy, but somehow, too safe, too easy. Now I wanted to try going through the old dramas again, but this time, watching them from the wings.

CHAPTER FOUR

Energy Darshans

Osho became enlightened on March 21st, 1953. Since that date He has helped hundreds of thousands of people along the path to self-realization.

For twenty years continuously He traveled in India visiting every village and town, talking to people, and later, holding meditation camps. He created new meditations for the modern man, whose mind, He says, is so busy that he does not find it possible to sit silently. These meditations usually include a cathartic stage where repressed emotions can be thrown out, and gibberish where the mind is given full rein to unravel all its madness, before sitting silently. Osho would help people to throw out all their madness. They would cry, scream, jump, go crazy and He would be there with them in the dust and the heat.

In 1978-79, energy-*darshans* started in the Pune *ashram*. *Darshan* was held in the circular Chuang Tzu Auditorium, and about two hundred people were present each night. Osho sat at one end and twelve mediums would sit on His right side.

As each person was called forward separately for their *darshan,* so Osho would arrange the mediums around that person. Osho called the mediums 'bridges'. We would kneel behind the person who had requested a *darshan*, one medium would sit in front, holding his hands, and usually someone would support the 'guest' in case he fell backwards. And then Osho's voice could be heard:

"Everyone close your eyes, and go totally into it."

Music began — crazy music — and everyone present in the auditorium would be swaying and allowing any feeling that arose to move through their bodies. It took a very determined 'guest' to resist being carried away on the tidal wave of let-go.

Osho would touch the energy center on the forehead (known as the third eye) of a medium and with his other hand the third eye of the person who had come for darshan. An energy transmission would happen that, to an outsider, might look as though people were being charged with high voltage electricity. There was a team of strong men to carry people out, if they were unable to walk, which was not unusual.

During this part of the *darshan*, the lights would be out throughout the entire *ashram* and so even people for whom there was no room inside the auditorium would sit in their rooms, or outside the gate, in the garden — wherever — and the whole six acres that was the commune would be joined with one energy phenomenon that was radiating from Osho.

Lights went on as the music reached a crescendo, and bodies danced, and swayed; screams and laughter filled the air, and for some people, silence.

Osho told us "Remember when you are joyous your energy flows into the other; when you are sad you start sucking energy from the other. So while functioning as mediums, be as joyous, ecstatically joyous, as possible; only then will it start overflowing. Joy is contagious. So you are not to be a medium out of duty; it has to be joyous celebration...

"This is not only a small experiment to help the guest; this is to transform the whole energyfield of the commune." (*Won't You Join The Dance?*)

To be on the receiving end of those high voltage hands was a psychedelic experience. It felt natural to be aware of energy shooting out of the heart center (like I had seen only in a superman comic book). At times, even amusing.

Riding downtown in a rickshaw one day the 'superman' beam suddenly appeared and struck a man walking by in the street. Not even a *sannyasin*, just a Pune citizen minding his own business. My rickshaw whizzed past him and before I could even see his face the episode was over. I never questioned what was happening because it felt so normal in a way. It was something that was happening and I was not doing anything.

Years later Osho said something to me that confirmed that I had not imagined it. It was in America, in Rajneeshpuram, where *sannyas* initiation meetings were held by one of the group leaders in our meditation hall. Osho said that the energy was not very high at these celebrations, and He was going to choose some mediums to juice it up, so to speak. He said that a beam of light would emit from the mediums' chest. He looked at me when He said it and I nodded as though to say, yes, I know that. But nothing more was said.

My body felt like a vehicle and I never knew what to expect next: a song in an unknown language, a flight into a nearby tree, the sensation of being pulled upwards into the sky: I sat there, simply aware of all the colors and dances of energy.

The feeling of expansion — that my body filled, not only the *darshan* area, but the whole *ashram* — was becoming an almost everyday experience. In answer to a question many years later, Osho explained that an ancient meditation technique is to feel the body expand until the whole sky is filled. He said many meditation techniques happen naturally to children and this is because in a past life that technique had been used and it is stored away in the unconscious.

As a child, I often had this experience while lying in bed, that my head would expand until it filled the room. Sometimes it grew so big that I felt as though I was outside the house in the sky. It seemed perfectly normal and I was surprised when I discovered years later that it did not happen to everybody. It became an enjoyable experience in *darshan*.

My parents had sent me a cheque, so one morning, I went straight to the bank from morning discourse. Sitting on a bench, awaiting my turn in the queue, my head started to expand until I filled the whole bank. An Indian bank is as chaotic and busy as an Indian street, but I felt perfectly relaxed.

I felt wonderful, but I couldn't move. A woman in the bank, sensing something was happening to me, took me by the hand and led me from counter to counter, and then stood in line for me and gave me my money. I was taken care of.

Mystic experience or not, money is for spending, and I wanted to go shopping immediately. I got into a rickshaw and went to Laxmi Road. This road is the busiest, most crowded shopping area in town. But strange, as I walked down the street, shopkeepers were closing up shop and pulling down the shutters. Slam! Slam! Street vendors were grabbing their wares and running off the streets. Cars, rickshaws and oxcarts disappeared. It was like a cowboy movie just before the baddies rode into town.

I was no longer spread all over the universe, but I did feel spaced out and too happy to feel any alarm, even though I was by now the only person on the street.

I walked along the empty street, turned, and saw that coming behind me, filling the street completely, were hundreds of men, shouting. It was a riot. An Indian riot was coming in my direction.

Suddenly, a rickshaw raced towards me and stopped.

"Get in," said the unknown driver, "and lie down in the back. Don't show yourself."

Without even asking where I wanted to go he took me straight to the *ashram*.

The strange thing is, everything felt as real, as normal and natural as any mundane activity of the day. That is why it was never frightening. I never felt the need to talk to anyone about it, or to have an explanation.

I tell you these things, simply to give an idea of my life at that time. Osho has said quite definitely that these type of experiences have no value spiritually, they do not help inner growth. Only awareness and meditation can do that.

I felt very protected and taken care of through these times. Vivek often came to me to ask, from Osho, how I was feeling, what was happening for me. This helped me to stop for a moment, and take note. That is to say I would become aware of where I could feel my energy moving. This deliberate 'look' into myself would act like a still shot in a movie and help me to recognize what was happening later.

As each individual *darshan* session ended, Osho talked us back very gently. "Come back now, slowly. Come back."

It was fascinating how different everyone felt. Even with closed eyes I knew which medium was close to me. Sometimes a man would have soft energy like a woman, and an old person might feel like a child. It was a light, playful, dance.

There were times, however, when the old habit of mind would penetrate and try to find a problem, such as: "Why does Osho use that medium, and not me?" Once, while "Why her?" was actually moving through my mind, He stopped and looked up at me, straight in the eyes, and I caught it, the thought was frozen — and still is.

I think Osho was not only sharing energy with us so that we might glimpse what is possible beyond what we know as life, but we were given the great opportunity to learn that we are the masters of our own emotions. Without suppressing an emotion, I could see it and take it higher, beyond jealousy into celebration and ecstasy. It was possible to turn a dark emotion into light. I only had to consciously drop the voice in the head and throw up my arms to the sky and I felt showered with golden rain.

It happened once that I felt I lost the 'knack' of meditation. Day after day I felt happy and as though I was flying, and then suddenly one day came when I felt I couldn't tune in. I had lost it! As energy *darshan* started I felt dull and closed, my celebration felt false and I could not feel any of the euphoric feelings I had known before. After this happened a few times I began to feel sad, and thought I would never meditate again.

My mind had been waiting like a vulture for this opportunity and jumped on me with full force:
"Of course, it (meditation) was all imagination anyway!" was the loud voice, and it repeated itself over and over — it was on to a good one! I was basically angry that I couldn't turn on the magic feeling. It seemed like it wasn't mine to turn on, and I felt cheated. I felt like it had been taken away from me. I thought Osho must be giving the magic to someone else and so I certainly was not going to ask Him for help. I decided to die.

I planned to walk to the mountains, and sit there until I died. Pune is situated on a plateau and is surrounded by mountains. You could see them from any place, on a summer night, black against the pinkish glow of the polluted sky.

I took the road to the black mountains, walked for about an hour and came to a dead end. I walked back to the *ashram*, chose another road — and arrived at the gates of a factory!

Getting desperate, I set off again.

The road I took finished in a pile of rocks, beyond which was wasteland, and in the distance I could see the lights of a village. Beyond that — the mountains.

I remembered hearing Osho say that the master takes away everything from the disciple and it struck me that He had even taken suicide away. This made me feel angry.

Standing in the darkness, nowhere to go, nothing to be done, I saw the absurdity of the whole performance and laughed at myself. I had stretched the whole drama to its ridiculous end and now there was only one thing to do — go home to bed.

Every night for two years I went to *darshan*. I was later to hear Osho say:

"I used to touch people's third eyes with my fingers, but I had to stop it for the simple reason that I became aware that stimulating the third eye from the outside is good if the person continues to meditate, continues to watch — then the first experience coming from the outside will soon become his inside experience. But such is the stupidity of man that when I can stimulate your third eye, you stop meditating. You rather start asking more and more for energy meetings with me, because you have not to do anything.

"I also became aware that for different people a different kind and different quantity of energy is needed from the outside — which is very difficult to decide. Sometimes somebody falls completely into a coma; the shock is too much. And sometimes the man is so retarded that nothing happens." (*The Rebel, 1987*)

My love affair with Tathagat was still fresh and exciting, and then Rishi came back into my life for a few weeks and for a while I was happy and overwhelmed that I was fortunate enough to be in love with two men. One day, at the time that in the East is known as *sandhya* — that gap when day is changing into night — as I was standing on the roof watching the cranes flying across the setting sun on their way to the river to nest for the night, I was struck by a sadness. I had everything I could possibly want and still I had that nagging feeling that, "No, this is not it — there is more."

As the months passed, Tathagat and I were not able to give each other what we wanted. I didn't know then that another person cannot supply what I am missing in myself. What I yearn for is inside myself, it is knowing myself — and the other will always fall short. The more time we spent together, the more I demanded and I became jealous every time he looked at another woman. I decided that with this man I was going to transcend jealousy, but I was simply stuck in a pattern that continually played the tape in my head called self-torture.

I wrote to Osho about my attempts to transcend jealousy and how I was becoming unhappy. I received an answer that, "This is not the way to go beyond jealousy. Drop him, and be alone." So, I finished my love affair and each night sat on the roof 'in meditation'. But, I couldn't meditate. I was expecting a *satori*. The line ran: "Well, I've dropped the boyfriend, where's my reward? Where's the bliss?"

After a week, Vivek brought me a message that Osho had seen my face in discourse and "I was obviously well pissed off with Him. So go back to the boyfriend." I went back with him, but with more awareness. What was I actually going back to?

Fortunately, his visa ran out and he had to leave. I took him to Bombay to catch the plane. I had to give him a good send-off.

This was the first time I had been away from Osho. We stayed in the 5-star Oberoi Hotel, and the same day we arrived, while in the lift, the lift attendant, noticing our clothes and *malas,* casually turned to us and said, "Oh! Someone threw a knife at your guru this morning!"

We ran to telephone the *ashram*. It was true. There had been an attempt on Osho's life during the morning discourse. Suddenly, the boyfriend, the holiday in Bombay, all seemed futile. What was I doing there in Bombay? Chasing dreams.

A Hindu fanatic had stood up during the morning discourse and thrown a knife at Osho. There were twenty policemen in plain clothes in the auditorium that morning. The assassination attempt had leaked out and the police had arrived to 'protect' Osho. At least, that was their story. It proved to be the opposite.

There were two thousand eye-witnesses to this attack, including the police. The man, Vilas Tupe, was arrested and taken away. He was then released, scot-free. The judge said that because Osho had continued with the discourse, then an attempt on his life could not have occurred!

That Osho did not stop His talk because a knife was thrown at Him says something of Osho's tranquillity and centeredness. I watched Him closely in a *darshan* once, when the person sitting at His feet, about to take *sannyas*, suddenly leapt up and, waving his arms threateningly, shouted that he had been sent by Jesus. Not a muscle in Osho's body flickered. He sat, relaxed, and chuckled "Very Good" at the raving crackpot.

During l980 I remember Osho speaking a lot about politicians and how corrupt and cunning they are. I could not quite believe that it was true. My conditioning had been such that I thought whoever ruled the country was a good man; maybe mistakes could be made, but basically he must be a good man.

I was to learn from my own experience. From November 1985 to January 1990 I was to witness an innocent man dying slowly of poisoning, administered by the United States government. And myself handcuffed and in chains in an American jail, for a fictitious crime.

Osho, like any genius, is years ahead of His time.

Whatever He says is difficult to digest. It always takes time. The patience of a Master must be phenomenal. How must it be to speak to people day after day and to know that they do not understand? To see on their faces that they are daydreaming, and can only understand one percent of what is said; and yet to keep trying to tell them. Osho has been speaking for thirty years. He used to give five discourses a day.

Towards the end of 1980 Osho began speaking of a new commune. We were at that time going to move to Kutch, in India. He told us that in the commune there would be a five-star hotel, two lakes, a shopping center, a discotheque, living accommodation for twenty thousand people.... We laughed heartily. It seemed so impossible. "In the new commune..." became a catch phrase, and even T-shirts and baseball caps were seen with these words. Lucky for us we were not made to eat our words, because it all came true!

In these early years (1975- 81) a lot of the people with Osho, like myself, were young 'flower children' of the sixties. Long hair, flowing robes, no underwear, our conditioning just beginning to crack, our consciousness growing, and we had a certain innocence. Maybe we were not very worldly, very grounded. We were children in a new world of spiritual dimensions.

In the beginning of 1981, I sat in discourse and without reason I wept and wept. I sat with my face contorted, beyond embarrassment and my eyes and nose streaming. I cried, not knowing why, for about a week.

This is always a mystery to me how some part of oneself is aware of an event before it happens.

Early in 1981 Osho developed severe back problems and a specialist from England came to treat Him. His back was not healing though, and He could not give discourse or *darshan* for several weeks. This was the beginning of a three-year period of silence.

When He could move comfortably again He sat with us each morning, while musicians played.

People tell me that the music was beautiful and it was a very special time. But it was lost on me. I was filled with fear and dread that something terrible was going to happen.

It did.

Osho went to America.

CHAPTER FIVE

USA — The Castle

1st June, 1981, New York City.

Osho left India with about twenty disciples. The corridors in Lao Tzu house and the road through the Commune were lined with tearful faces, hands folded in *namaste*, as it looked like the beginning of a long journey where we were never to know if and when we would see Osho again. He left in a Mercedes with Vivek and His doctor Devaraj.

Vivek, with her frail child-like quality that for moments camouflaged her strength of character and ability to take command of any situation, and Devaraj, tall, elegant and silver-haired, made an interesting couple.

I left an hour later, and this was to be my first experience of feeling that the death of the Commune had happened. In a way it had, because it was never to be the same again. How could it? The Commune had felt like one energy, one body; we had been joined together in our energy-*darshans* and our meditations. That we were now to be scattered all over the world saddened me. My path was not to be just blissful meditations in magical settings, dressed in long flowing robes, unaware and uncaring about what was happening in the rest of the world. The diamond of my inner world was having facets cut and the cutting felt like a surgical operation.

On the Pan Am flight Osho, Devaraj and Vivek, with

Osho's cooks, occupied the entire top floor, which was the first-class section. This was the only time Osho had been out of His near-sterile living conditions in Pune. We had done our best to clean the cabin and had covered all the seats with white covers, in an attempt to reduce any smells of perfume and cigarettes left from previous passengers.

The newness of the situation, to be sitting on a plane with Osho going to America, of all places, was exciting, despite the tearful farewell to India and all my friends. Two brothers, who taught karate in Pune, turned out to be photographers. They kept us informed of all the gossip from above as they raced back and forth, snapping Osho doing all manner of unimaginable things, such as drinking champagne. Well, at least, holding the glass.

Sheela was there. She was to be Osho's secretary while He was visiting America. She insulted one of the stewards, and then moved on to one of the stewardesses, and within a few minutes the entire crew of the tourist-class section were our enemies. She tried to explain that she didn't mean to insult the steward by calling him a Jewboy; that she had been married to a Jew, was herself a Jew...too late. Her rough tongue had done its work. For me this was typical of Sheela's character, or personality. She was a rough diamond. My understanding of Osho and how He works with people is that He sees beyond the personality. He sees our potential, and He puts His trust in our higher capabilities. "I trust my love," I have heard Him say; "I trust that my love will transform you."

We were met at the New York airport by Sushila. Both her personality and physical appearance earn her the description of earth-mother; on the periphery she is outspoken and quite a tough cookie. I have only ever met her at airports. On this occasion she seemed to be in charge of the whole customs and luggage department. All the porters were working for her, and when it came to declaring goods, she was everywhere. What a worry it was to move Osho through a chaotic airport and try and protect Him from smells that might bring on an asthma attack. I had known Him in Pune to develop an asthma attack from the slightest smell of perfume or, on one occasion, the smell of new curtain fabric. He was tremendously fragile in the body, and especially now with His back pain. What would we do if an official stopped Him and kept Him waiting around? These worries did not reflect on Osho though. He walked through the airport calmly, looking neither left or right. I think He was so content and at ease with himself that His surroundings never touched Him.

Out of the airport. New York! — I couldn't believe it!

The drive to New Jersey was quite a shock. There were no people in the streets, not even a stray dog; miles and miles of houses and cars, but no sign of life. The sky was still and grey, no clouds, no sun. It was the opposite to India, where in the midst of overpopulation and poverty beats a heart full of life and color. I looked at the deserted streets of New Jersey and for a moment was panicked with the thought that maybe there had been a nuclear explosion and everyone was dead.

We took a winding road up a hill through a pine forest and arrived at a castle. It stood on the top of a small hill and was surrounded by lawns, then forest; it had a tower and balustrade, round leaded windows and stained glass windows. Along the same winding, forest road was a monastery, just before entering the gate to the castle, and the monks roamed in the forest wearing white habits. It was straight out of a Grimms fairy tale, right in the middle of suburban New Jersey.

Tired and disorientated, I sat on the lawn with a group of about thirty *sannyasins* who had arrived a week before us in order to clean and renovate the castle. People had been working all night and as we waited for Osho to arrive we all keeled over in a heap and fell asleep. Then someone shouted that He was coming and we raised our sleepy bodies and our hands in *namaste*. Everything felt so new. I was hardly aware that I had also traveled with Osho on the plane; I was sitting on the lawn awaiting His arrival and seeing Him for the first time.

For years in Pune we had only seen Osho wearing one style of robe, white and straight up and down. I used to spend hours pressing the knife-sharp creases on the sleeves, as it was the only detail. Now He was wearing a long, knitted jacket over the robe with a black and white border, and a black knitted hat. He always looked so thrilled to see everyone; His eyes sparkled and He smiled as He *namasted* us all and walked so graciously towards the stone stairs leading to the entrance. He sat for a few minutes with us on the lawn with closed eyes... I was reminded that in India or America, when my eyes are closed, I am in the same place. I was carrying the silence of my meditations in the *ashram* in India inside me. When my mind is still there are no countries, not even a world.

Osho's rooms were still being renovated, and as a temporary arrangement He was to live in two small rooms at the very top of the castle, which He could reach in a lift.

I had been spoiled in Pune with my immaculate laundry room, so quiet and cut off from the rest of the hustle and bustle of the Commune. In fact, no one was even permitted to enter my laundry room. I must have been a bit of a *prima donna*, because now I was horrified to discover that my laundry room was in the cellar! Although one area had been cleaned up, the cellar was still a cellar, full of junk and cobwebs. Periodically the pipes which lined the cellar would burst and send out a shower of steam or gas.

I went into a catharsis when I saw that I didn't even have a bucket, but was duly amazed by the wonders of the modern world when not only bucket but washing machine arrived that same day.

I arranged my washing line on the castle tower. Walking

up its winding staircase I was reminded of the many times I had climbed the tower of Notre Dame Cathedral in Paris (no, not as the hunchback!). At a certain point, while climbing up or down stairs like these (there are also a few underground stations in London that have the same effect) a voice in my head says, "These stairs are to eternity; they are never going to end." And always, for a moment, I believe it and see my life stretched out before me, forever on the stone staircase. But then the last turn in the winding narrow stairs is there, and I burst through the heavy wooden door and stand on the top of the tower. Below me is a sea of green fields and houses and then a great mist, and floating in the mist is another planet called New York City. I can see it clearly, and the sky is pinkish orange, smoldering behind it.

Osho explored and experimented with this new American way of life with child-like enthusiasm.

He had for years eaten the same food — rice, *dal* (lentils) and three vegetables. His diet was always strictly watched to ensure that the diabetes with which He suffered was kept under control. Devaraj would sit in the kitchen and weigh each gram of food to calculate the calories. Osho's fragile health was difficult for me to understand. I remember when in London, sitting in the white tunnel at the meditation center, and I first saw a photograph of Osho's hand. I remarked that He couldn't be enlightened because He had such a short life line. Some misunderstanding born out of Christian conditioning must have made me think enlightenment meant a person became immortal.

So it was a big deal for us that Osho was experimenting with new foods — American cereals, omelettes, and once even spaghetti, which He returned untouched saying it looked like Indian worms. He watched television for a while and made trips to New York City.

Osho explored the whole castle and turned up in the most unexpected places, beaming, as we would shriek with shock, never having seen Him go anywhere except to sit in His chair in Buddha Hall. He visited my laundry in the cellar. When I turned and saw Him standing in the doorway I was so surprised that I put the hot iron down on my hand. Italian Anasha, who had not been fortunate enough to be in the right place at the right time to see Osho on His castle walks, wrote to Him and asked, "Was He avoiding her?" When He visited her as she was cleaning, He affectionately put His arm around her.

Osho had always been so far away for us, always the Buddha who talked to us from the podium or helped us move into unknown realms in energy-*darshans*, and so this was extraordinary for us. He continued to appear unexpectedly, anywhere, and I found I was becoming more aware during the day, and was reminded of the Zen stories of masters who would suddenly appear with a stick and hit the disciple — except Osho did not carry a stick, just a loving smile.

But I have never been able to surprise Him, and I asked Him once if He had ever been surprised.

Osho: "There is no one to be surprised. I am absent, as I will be when I will be dead, with only one difference... that right now my absence has a body, and then, my absence will not have a body."

However, I was certainly surprised, or rather, in a state of permanent shock at the change in my environment. I missed the Commune even though I was fortunate enough to be with Osho. America always seemed to me to be unborn; it has always felt unformed, like a foetus not yet with a soul, whereas India feels ancient and steeped in magic.

I sat alone on the tower with closed eyes, but meditation did not happen so deeply for me. It was more in the air to fall in love. Almost everyone fell in love at the castle. Vivek and I had a love-affair with the same man, but there was no fight, no jealousy. In fact we used to laugh about it. I know that it is 'normally' thought to be strange, even suspected that a person does not really love if jealousy is not there. But I was learning that the opposite is true. Where there is jealousy, there is not love. It was here that Anando, whom I first met in the meditation center in London, and Devaraj, Osho's doctor, were to meet and fall into a love that lasted many years.

I had been wearing shapeless, orange robes for the last six years, as had everyone else. Now it was time to adapt to our new environment. Our clothes were still to be the colors of the rising sun, and we wore our *malas*, but now we wore 'American' clothes. In my case it was a punk outfit from which my knees, shoulders and many other parts of my anatomy could be unzipped. I am sure we looked pretty weird as we explored our new terrain in small groups, excited and laughing about everything we saw. We were actually coming from another world.

Osho began driving lessons. Sheela and her new husband, Jayananda, arrived one day in a black, convertible Rolls Royce. Osho came down the steps of the castle with Vivek, and placing black Russian hats à la Gurdjieff on the three passengers, He took the wheel. Off down the hill they went with the car hood going up and down, up and down, as He tried out all the buttons as they drove along. We, the spectators, were shocked, as we had not expected that He would drive Himself! It must have been twenty years since He had driven a car, and that would have been a small Indian one, and on the other side of the road, in India. But, what a wonderful sight!

Each day Osho invited two people for a drive in the car with Him and Vivek. For some of the passengers it was rather more than they expected, and they came back white-faced and shaken. On more than one occasion Vivek, on her return to the castle, would ask for a stiff whiskey to calm her nerves.

Osho liked to drive fast. Forgetting that He was the only

person driving on the road who was actually "awake," and therefore, safer than anyone else, His passengers could not contain their gasps and muffled screams as corners were taken in wide sweeps. And He always made for the fast lane. On more than one occasion Osho said that there was too much fear in the car. Once He stopped the car and said that if people didn't relax then He would stop driving altogether.

A back-seat driver exclaimed, "You just missed that car!" and He replied, "That's your judgment!"

Nirgun, a spunky sixty-year-old who cooked for Osho, describes her ride on a dark, stormy night as the most exhilarating experience of her life. Afterwards Osho sent her a message that she had been the only person so far who had really been present.

As Osho left twice a day for the car ride we used to sit on the lawn next to a hydrangea bush, rich in blue flowers, at the bottom of the stone stairs, and send Him off with music. There was Nivedano, a dark and mysterious Brazilian, who was then a new sannyasin. Years later, still playing music for Osho, he was to show his other talent — building waterfalls. There was Govinddas, a pale German who played sitar as well as any Indian, and Yashu, a Spanish, gypsy woman who played two flutes at once, accompanied by Kavia, her three-year-old daughter, on bells. Rupesh (Osho's tabla player) was a dynamo of energy and I was so happy to see him when he arrived that I jumped on him with such enthusiasm I knocked out my front tooth on his head. Our neighboring monks heard the music and freaked out. They accused us of practicing black magic and having "sacrificial rites."

Sheela was now well established as Osho's secretary and Laxmi, who had done this work in India, was now on holiday and Osho told her to relax and do nothing. In fact, a year later He was to tell her that had she listened to Him she would by now be enlightened.

Around a Master when situations change there is nothing to be done except go with it, because everything is changing all the time in existence, and with a Master the emphasis is on accepting change. A few people who in Pune had jobs with a certain amount of power or prestige, were to find it impossible to adjust to their new positions. Some went their own way and the group around Osho changed, just as great winds come and dead branches fall from the trees.

I understood from talking to Devaraj that Sheela did not simply become Osho's secretary because of the convenience. Although she was Indian she had become an American citizen through her first marriage and had spent a lot of time in America. It was more involved than that, and had in fact begun four or five months before in Pune.

Devaraj has written a book and in it he says:

"...Sheela, with the active or passive help of us all, became the 'boss'. It wasn't that Bhagwan said one day, 'You are the best person for the job'; He merely confirmed that she had in fact taken the job. Any other choice would have been an imposition by Him on us. In the Buddhist context this is what is called 'choiceless awareness.'

"To have simply 'selected' somebody would have been against the whole way He worked. He was living in this experimental community, and for it to remain alive it had to have an integrity of its own. To just select His choice against the flow of events was not his way. He always went with the flow, surrendered totally to what existence offered to Him, and gave it one-hundred percent of His support to help it work. If existence had brought Sheela to the top, there must have been some reason for it; there must have been something we needed to learn from it — and how!

"Just as Bhagwan put His life in the hands of His physicians with total trust, so He put His life's work in the hands of His administrators with total trust. And while he is always aware of the potential for unconsciousness and ugliness in all unenlightened people, He is also aware of the potential for consciousness and beauty in all unenlightened people. He has total trust that one day, in all of us, however long it takes, consciousness will eventually disperse unconsciousness as light disperses darkness." (*Bhagwan: The Most Godless yet the Most Godly Man* by Dr. George Meredith)

I don't think Osho 'chose' anyone. It is not as though He sat in *darshan* or discourse, looked around and found the person with the brightest aura or most potential and said, "That one can do my laundry, or that one can cook for me..." I think whoever came His way, He accepted that person in total trust. For instance, I will never know because I never asked, whether Osho or Vivek decided to give me the opportunity of doing the laundry and thereby become part of Osho's household — but I suspect it was Vivek. It seems as though 'just by chance' I was in the right spot at the right time.

The forest surrounding the castle was filled with pines and blue spruce trees, and at night the cicadas sang so shrill and loud that it seemed the windows would break. I saw a cicada one time on a tree trunk; he was six inches long and luminous green. I thought, no wonder he sings so loud.

I liked to sleep in the woods. The alertness that became entwined with sleep was animal-like. There were always so many sounds and rustling of leaves. It was a little frightening, but I liked that too.

A woman, unknown to anyone, came from Germany. She was a Christian fanatic and she spread rumors through the town about Osho.

Soon hooligans started to come to the castle at night. They spray-painted the walls telling us to "go home..." and exploded paper bombs. These made a tremendous noise, and we jumped out of our beds thinking real bombs were exploding. They threw rocks through windows, shattering glass.

We started to take turns guarding, and I stopped sleeping in the woods. What with the monks drifting through the morning mists in their white habits and cars full of shouting hooligans, I was beginning to feel uneasy. We had been minding our own business, disturbing nobody and yet people did not like us — we were different.

We stayed at the castle for three months. Most of this time Sheela was away looking for land. She came up with "The Big Muddy Ranch," in central Oregon, 64,000 acres of barren desert that had been overgrazed and left to die over the last fifty years as a tax write-off.

Sheela purchased "The Big Muddy" because she found it on the anniversary of her late husband's death, and signed the papers for it on his birthday! At least, that is what she said.

CHAPTER SIX

Rajneeshpuram

Rajneeshpuram was not in America.
It was a country on its own, without American
dreams.
Maybe that is why the American politicians went to war
with it.

We flew across America, me, Asheesh, Arpita and
Gayan.

Asheesh is a wood wizard. He is not only a master
carpenter, he makes Osho's chairs and fixes anything
technical or electrical. It's always, "Asheesh, Asheesh!
where's Asheesh?" when anything needs fixing or inventing.
And he has a great way of speaking with his hands, because
he is Italian.

Arpita has always made Osho's shoes. She is eccentric,
paints Zen pictures and has a zany personality which was
later to be expressed in helping design Osho's clothes.

Gayan arrived in New Jersey after Vivek telephoned her
in Germany and said, "Come." On her arrival, Vivek picked
her up at the airport and said, "I hope you can sew." She
could, and has sewn Osho's clothes for all the years of His
"fantastic" wardrobe. She is also a dancer, and you can see
her in the videos made on celebration days at the ranch,
with her long dark hair flying, as she dances playfully
around Osho on the podium in our meditation hall,
Rajneesh Mandir.

So we flew across America together and landed in Oregon, just twelve hours before Osho was due to arrive. I remember nothing of the flight, but will never forget the long, long, winding drive down the mountain to the Big Muddy. Mile after mile of dusty, tall, spiky dried flowers and cacti by the side of the road, lit up by the car's headlamps. Spooky, yellow, white and grey.

Osho's trailer and the adjoining one which was to be our home, was a hive of activity, because as usual we were working in a race against time. We stayed up most of the night, putting the finishing touches to curtains and cleaning. Outside grass lawns were being laid like carpets.

The trailer was completely made of plastic — I had never seen such a thing. If it caught fire it took only ten seconds to burn down to the ground! Osho's trailer was the same as ours, but instead of carpet (because of His allergies), there was white linoleum all over the place. The walls were covered in plastic that was made to resemble wood.

There were to be eleven of us living in the one trailer, plus the sewing room. Devaraj, *le docteur*, and Devageet, Osho's dentist, were together in one room. They are the best thing in humor to come out of Britain since Monty Python. There was Nirupa, the pre-Raphaelite in the group with her waist length golden hair, and Haridas, tall, German and looking fifteen years younger than his forty-five years, who was one of Osho's first Western disciples. And sixty-year-old Nirgun who surpassed us all with her endless dancing in the sitting room to the new Western music we found. Vivek would have her own room in the adjoining trailer, and then Osho had a sitting room, bedroom and bathroom.

It was too dark to see any of the surrounding scenery, so, tired and grumpy, I went to sleep. While taking a shower the next morning, I looked out of the window. The trailer was in a small valley and behind us was a rock so huge, so majestic, that I ran outside naked and wet and bowed down on the earth.

Osho arrived that morning to find a handful of *sannyasins* sitting on the instant lawn singing songs. He sat with us in meditation, and His silence was so overwhelming that the music softly petered out, and we were all silent at the foot of the rugged mountains. This was the beginning of Osho's four years of silence. He stood up and looked around, and then walked up the steps to the trailer and we could see Him on the front porch, hand on His hip. He was to say that He was shocked that there were no trees at all on so much land, and He had never seen a house "standing naked" before, meaning the absence of any garden or plants of any kind. It was indeed the complete opposite of the exotic and lush jungle that surrounded His home in India.

There were only two buildings on the land of Rajneeshpuram when we arrived. The first few months there was a great pioneering spirit. We had arrived in August and there was a race to have everyone living in a trailer with central heating by the winter. Most of the people were in tents, and temperatures in the winter could go as low as twelve degrees below zero.

We ate together on tables arranged outside one of the ranch buildings, and as the winter progressed we had to first scrape the ice off the table, or our plates would slide into our laps. We kept a barrel of beer submerged in a pond, because we lacked a fridge, but our meal times were great. Men and women were dressed alike, in fat quilted jackets, jeans, cowboy hats and boots. If I had thought *sannyasin* men were too feminine years before, now it was the reverse.

The roof of Osho's sitting room leaked when it was raining and it was a miserable thing to see Him sitting there with a bucket either side of the chair, to catch the water. The room was empty except for a low oak table and chair.

His rooms have always been simple and without the usual clutter of furniture. There were no pictures on the walls, no ornaments, no possessions at all except a cassette player, but the emptiness of a plastic room did not have the grandeur and Zen-like quality of a marble room. It hurt me to see Him in this setting, although I noticed that it made no difference to Him. He was at home anywhere and I have never heard Him complain about how or where He lived. He accepted that this was what existence had come up with and I always felt He was grateful, knowing and trusting that in our love this was the best we could do.

But it wasn't the best we could do and work was started on an extension to the trailer, which was to be an emergency living space and medical facility. When the extension was finished about nine months later it was so beautiful that Osho moved into it rather than His plastic trailer. This caused a lot of friction between Sheela and Vivek, because for some reason Sheela did not want Osho to move. The extension had been built by Richard, Vivek's boyfriend, and the bedroom and sitting room were panelled in wood; the bathroom was the nicest bathroom Osho has ever had — large, with a jacuzzi. A long corridor led to an Olympic size swimming pool and in the medical facility there was a fully-equipped operating room with all the latest hospital equipment.

Vivek didn't like the ranch from the beginning and she was often unhappy, and would get sick. She wasn't shy about expressing herself either, and one day announced on the motorola for the whole commune to hear, exactly how she felt about this "barren desert." She announced that she would like to burn the whole fucking place down. When she was happy she was the most totally ecstatic, childlike person I had ever seen, but when she was unhappy — phew! look out. She had a knack of discovering problems, and seeing a person's failings. I found it impossible to argue with her because I always had the impression she was right.

I think that when a criticism is made then it holds more weight than a compliment.

Nirupa or I accompanied Osho on car rides if Vivek did not want to go. He enjoyed to drive and each afternoon He drove out of the ranch for about two hours along the almost empty highways and back again. In the early days there would be no armed escort and it was exhilarating to be sitting with Him in the middle of nowhere, going nowhere, only the vastness of the sky, the empty road and His silence. I always felt to respect his privacy when we went out in the car and never spoke unless He asked me something. My aim was to still my mind, and I would give myself a goal like, "okay, no thoughts between here and the old barn," and so on.

In the first year everything was going well, people were arriving in the hundreds, and a city was appearing in the desert with fantastic speed. Within the year there were living accommodations for a thousand residents and ten thousand visitors, the beginning of an airport, a hotel, disco, a farm producing vegetables, medical facilities, a dam, and a canteen big enough to feed everyone.

When He asked me how "Sheela's commune" was, (He always called it Sheela's commune) I said that I felt as though I was in market place of the world. That was not a complaint, it just showed how different it was from the days when meditation was the main event in our lives. Sheela was not a meditator and her influence on the commune was that work, and only work, mattered. Through work she could dominate people, because she had her grades of "good" workers and rewarded them accordingly. Meditation was considered a waste of time and even on the rare occasions that I did meditate, I sat with a book in front on me, in case someone came in the room and "caught" me. I had lost perspective of the importance of meditation, and all the years Osho had been talking of it were lost for a while. Having taken great flights into the sky in India, I now felt grounded and earthbound. I was thinking that another dimension of my being had to develop, that maybe if we had all stayed in Pune in our robes and almost 'airy fairy' existence, then we might have all become enlightened, but of not much use to the world in a practical sense. I didn't know yet how hard the lessons would be. My journey as a disciple had started though, and there was no going back.

The years of silence that were to follow, somehow made Osho seem more translucent, more fragile and less in His body. He had always said that talking to us kept Him in His body and as time passed His connection with the earth seemed less. His day changed from quite a busy one in Pune — up at 6.00 a.m., morning discourse, painting, reading books and all the newspapers, work with Laxmi, evening *darshan*, giving *sannyas* and energy *darshans*. Now He sat silently in His room, alone. He still got up at 6.00 a.m. and took long baths and swam in His pool, listened to music; but He had no contact with His people, except for the car ride once a day.

How must it be to just sit silently in your room for years? This is how Osho described it in one of His earlier discourses:

"When He (the mystic) is not engaged in any activity, when He is neither speaking nor eating, nor walking, breathing is a blissful experience. Then just to be, just the movement of the breath, gives so much bliss that nothing can compare with it. It becomes very musical; it is filled with *nada* — the uncreated inner sound. (*In Search of the Miraculous*)

I was leading my own secret life that no one ever found out about. My washing line was about five minutes walk into the mountains at the back of the house. I arrived at the washing line, hung out the washing, put down the basket, threw off my clothes and ran like a wild woman naked through the mountains. The mountains stretched for miles and I followed an old dried river bed, or deer tracks through the long grass in summer. I had my own bed and a garden way into the mountains. I worked hard on the garden and at one point had seventy-two flowers in bloom!

When I first stood still in the hills, the silence was so immense that I could hear my own heart beating and the blood pulsing in my ears. At first I was frightened, I didn't recognize the sounds. And when I slept out in the hills I felt as though I had been wrapped in the womb of the earth herself. This was the summer, and in the winter, I ran in the snow, and sat under the juniper trees for shelter.

I fell in love with a cowboy. He had blue eyes, blonde hair, tanned skin and a deep Virginian accent and was called Milarepa. Most of the men were dressed as cowboys — after all this was cowboy country — and Milarepa was no exception. He sang country and western songs and played a banjo, and I was enveloped in the magic of this mountainous terrain colored only by sage brush, junipers, pale grasses and wide open spaces. There were deer and rattlesnakes, and one day while returning home over the mountains, I came face to face with a coyote. We were only twenty feet from each other and he was a proud and handsome specimen. His coat was thick and silky and his eyes stared straight into mine. We stood and looked at each other for several minutes in wonder, and then he turned his head and slowly, so slowly and with great dignity, he walked away.

There were two lakes, just as Osho had promised there would be in 'the new commune', Krishnamurti Lake which was huge and Patanjali Lake, tucked away more in the hills, smaller and for nude bathing. It was here at the beginning of the ranch that I used to take off in a borrowed pick-up truck with a few of the boys, to go fishing. Being vegetarians this was not the thing to do! We hurtled across the dirt roads in the dark and, like outlaws, we swooped down onto the lake where we went off in different directions to see who could catch the biggest fish, or any at all. I had no interest in eating fish but I enjoyed the adventure and we laughed a lot. We were never discovered, but one day it was over. The fun was gone, and it seemed gross and cruel to pull fish out of the water. So that was that.

Rajneeshpuram was in a valley surrounded by mountains and hills and from the top of the property you could see the rolling hills, blue colored in the haze of the horizon. To reach to the top took good driving, because the road was steep and curving and had not been repaired for years, and many winters' worth of snow and rain had washed half of it away.

Once off the dangerous mountain road we would be confronted by rednecks in their pick ups aiming their rifles at us, just for fun, or standing by the side of the road giving the finger or throwing stones. The roads were icy and hazardous, and the odd rock from an avalanche in the middle of the road made extra business for the Rolls Royce repair shop more than once. The land was flat and desolate, not a tree or building would stand between the road and the horizon in some places. Every few miles I would see an old wooden barn or house, blackened by the harsh weather and leaning over as though it had been hit by a hurricane; and there were billboards that read, "Repent ye sinners. Jesus saves." And in this Christian land, Oregonians hung rotting corpses of coyotes on their barbed wire fences along the roadside until nothing was left but the head and empty hide.

Walking across the frost-covered lawn one night as I approached the house, I saw Osho getting into a car alone. Someone always drove with Him, so this had never happened before. I opened the passenger door and asked Him if I could go with Him and He very sternly said, "No." I went to Vivek and told her and we both ran for her car to give chase. Osho had five minutes on us and He was in a Rolls, we were only in a "Bronco," and one that had a weakness for turning over on its back, though we didn't find that out until later.

The road was slippery that night with ice and as we skidded around one of the corners of the mountain road, Vivek told me that she had never taken a driving test, in fact she couldn't really drive. She had only had one lesson, twenty years before in England and only driven once after that. When we arrived at the ranch she wanted a car so she told Sheela that, yes, she had a license. Looking back, I realize I must be crazy because the thought that came into my head was that "I can really trust this woman, because she has guts!"

It started hailing and through the storm we broke all speed limits and tried to catch up with Osho. We had to guess which way He had gone and then we realized that once on the open road, we would never catch Him. We stopped by the side of the road and waited, hoping that He would turn around and come back to Rajneeshpuram. As each car rushed towards us, headlights blinding, and rain soaking us, we had a tenth of a second to see if it was Osho or not. After a few false chases after the wrong cars, there He was! We jumped into the Bronco and moved up close behind Him and started honking and flickering the lights. He saw us and all seemed well; in fact, all seemed wonderful as we followed Him safely back to Rajneeshpuram. On arriving back at the house nobody spoke, we simply parked the cars and went inside. The incident was not mentioned again.

Although I have never been with another enlightened master, I am sure there are similarities and one of them must be that you just don't know what He is going to do next. However, you do know, that He will do ANYTHING if it will wake you up. Why He took off like that into the night in the middle of redneck country, I will never know.

During these winter months while the roads were treacherous, Osho drove into ditches five times. Each time He went into a ditch, Vivek was with Him. She had to climb out of the car, once with an injured back, go to the road and flag down a car, hoping it wouldn't be one of our redneck neighbors. Leaving Osho sitting in the car, unaccompanied, was the difficult part for her. But she said He just use to sit there with His eyes closed, as though meditating in His room.

Osho would go out driving twice a day and one night Vivek returned home very shaken and told us that a car had been tailgating them, and going too close to the bumper of Osho's car. This was quite common and always scary. Pick up trucks with two or three cowboys in them shouting insults found it a great sport to try and send Osho off the road. But this night as Osho approached the ranch two *sannyasins* were coming towards Him and He stopped the car and asked them to help. The man who had been following took off in the other direction at the sign of help and the *sannyasins* followed him. He drove into his yard, parked the car, jumped out with a gun and started shooting. He was clearly quite mad, and was threatening that he was going to "Get the Bhagwan." The sheriff was called, but he refused to do anything about it, because a crime had not been committed — yet!

The next night, at exactly the same time and taking the same route as always, Osho wanted to go for His drive. Vivek refused to go, so I went, but tried to persuade Osho to at least go on a different route because this madman knew exactly where Osho would be and at precisely what time. He refused. He said that it is His freedom to drive where He likes and when, and He would rather be shot than give up His freedom. And, He continued, "What if they do shoot me? It is okay." I gulped at this. It certainly was not okay with me.

It seemed darker than ever that night and Osho stopped

the car in the middle of the wasteland to take a pee. I didn't know whether I was shivering from fear or cold, but I got out of the car and walked up and down the road staring out into the darkness, not understanding why freedom should come before security.

The madman didn't show up that time. There were other times when we received threats that there were gangs out on the road waiting for Him, but He always drove exactly where and when He wanted to.

Osho said in discourse that it was no joy to drive within the speed limit if the car can do 140 m.p.h., and anyway, who is looking at the sides of the road to see what the limit is? He said it's better to keep your eyes on the road. It was my responsibility to look right and left at crossroads and to say when it was safe to go, because Osho never turned His head when He drove. He just looked straight ahead. Having never driven a car, I did not have a clear perception of distance and speed, and I also didn't know the rules of the road. Maybe I would have been more nervous had I known, but as it was I trusted that whatever happened would be happening in awareness and that was all that mattered.

The First Annual World Celebration came in July 1982, with more than ten thousand people arriving from all over the world. It was the first time we had all met since being in India together. In the valley a huge temporary Buddha Hall was built, and when we all met and meditated together it was very, very high energy, and Osho came and sat with us. On the last day of the festival Osho beckoned to Gayan to come on the podium to dance. Twenty people thought He was looking at them, and so they all got up; and then hundreds of people followed them, and Osho disappeared from view. It could have resulted in Him being mobbed, but it was just an overflow of high energy. He said afterwards that everyone was so gentle with Him and so respectful that when He walked, people simply stepped back and made room for Him. Even those who touched Him, did so with care, He said. At that time everything seemed so perfect, and there seemed to be no reason why our oasis in the desert should not bloom and be an example to the world that thousands of people can live together without all the ugliness that society, religions and politicians bring.

It was a beautiful festival. There was a full moon eclipse, which I watched from my bed in the mountains, and as the moon turned red and sank in the morning sky, I felt I was not on planet Earth.

CHAPTER SEVEN

Rajneeshpuram cont.

I t seems to be a sad fact of human nature, that if a person, or group of people, are different from you — then you fear them. I was brought up in a small town in Cornwall, England, where even the people living in the next village were called "them strangers." It wasn't even enough to be born in the town, at least one parent had to be born there before you were accepted. So I wasn't surprised at the local Oregonians' reaction to us, although it was certainly excessive and violent. The shouts from their local church minister of "satan worshippers go home," the T-shirts that read "Better dead than red," with the sights of a gun on Osho's face; and the bomb that exploded in our hotel in Portland, were definitely excessive.

I did not realize, though, that a whole government would react in such a prejudiced and irresponsible way.

Our commune was a successful ecological experiment. Rajneeshpuram was a barren desert when we arrived and every effort was being made to transform it. Water was being collected in dams and distributed in the fields, and we were growing enough food to make the commune self-sufficient. The commune recycled seventy percent of its waste — a normal American city at the most recycles five to ten percent, and most cities don't bother at all. We cared for the land and the earth was not polluted in any way. The sewage system worked in such a way that after being pumped into a lagoon, it went through a biological breakdown and was sent down a pipe right through the bottom of the valley, through a multiple filtering system, until finally it irrigated the fields. The deeply eroded land was being saved, and ten thousand trees were planted in the valley. Many of the trees are standing there now, ten years later on, in the once again deserted land, and I have heard that the fruit trees are so laden that their branches are breaking.

In 1984, Osho commented:

"They want this city to be demolished because of their land use laws — and none of those idiots have come to see how we are using the land. Can they use it more creatively than we are using it? — and for fifty years nobody was using the land. They were happy — that was 'good use'. Now we are creating out of it. We are a self-sufficient commune. We are producing our food, our vegetables...we are making every effort to make it self-sufficient.

"This desert...somehow it seems to be the destiny of people like me. Moses ended up in the desert, I have ended up in a desert, and we are trying to make it green. We have made it green. If you go around my house, you cannot think it is Oregon, you will think it is Kashmir.

"And they don't come to see what has happened here. Just sitting in the capital they decide that it is land use and it is against land use laws. If this is against land use laws then your land use laws are bogus and should be burned. But first come and see and prove that this is against land use laws. But they are afraid to come here...." (*The Rajneesh Bible*)

The issue of land use laws went back and forth between the high court and the lower courts, until we did finally win the case, but it was too late. The commune had been destroyed one year before. All the *sannyasins* had left and it was now safe for the government to say that our city had been legal.

While we were waiting for decisions to be made in the

court, it was not possible to establish any business or have enough telephone connections without being in a "commercial zone." The nearest town was Antelope, and it had just forty residents, and was situated in the middle of nowhere surrounded by a grove of tall poplar trees. It was eighteen miles away, and we moved a trailer there to enable us to conduct business. One trailer and a few *sannyasins* and we were accused of trying to take over the town. In fear, the local residents "disincorporated" their town and we took them to court and won. This escalated into a very ugly drama, that appealed to the American masses more than their latest soap operas.

Newspapers and television stations were becoming very interested — Sheela appeared as the big bad witch and the townsfolk of Antelope represented everyone's fears, and stirred up the pioneer-defending-his-home drama.

The drama grew and grew and finally more *sannyasins* moved into the town, elected their own mayor, rebuilt houses, renamed the town "City of Rajneesh," and then turned around and went back down the valley to Rajneeshpuram and dropped the whole thing. Meanwhile the residents of Antelope were still there but their lives had meaning now. They were interviewed on television and the fight was on.

Sheela was getting a taste of stardom. She was asked to go on many TV programs, I think because her gross behavior, such as giving the finger as an answer to a question, helped the ratings.

There were, by now, many new *sannyasins* from Europe who had never seen Osho. To them Sheela was The Pope. At her meetings held in Rajneeshpuram for the whole commune, she was always surrounded by young people with adoring faces, fresh from the communes in Europe, eager to clap their hands at anything she said. These meetings used to frighten me. I used to think how they must have been like Hitler's youth movement.

Rajneeshpuram cont. — 83

I retreated more into the mountains.

As Sheela increased her fight with the 'outside world,' so a battle began within. Vivek and Sheela gave a meeting together in Magdalena cafeteria one night to assure commune members that there was no rift between them. Although the meeting seemed genuine and was touching, it did in fact confirm everyone's suspicions that there was indeed conflict between the two of them. Otherwise, why the meeting?

Vivek didn't trust Sheela one inch, and she was not allowed a key to Osho's house. When she came to see Osho, Sheela first had to telephone Vivek, then the door would be unlocked for her at the exact right time and locked behind her. Sheela was also forbidden to walk through our house to get to Osho's trailer, she had to use a side door. This was because she always caused trouble when she walked through our trailer, but of course, it pissed her off because she felt insulted. It was a matter of who had the power.

Sheela would never have told Osho about these seemingly small squabbles, because she had enough sense to know that His solution would diminish her power. I never told Him, because in comparison with how Rajneeshpuram was growing it seemed petty. I was under the illusion that at least if Sheela was angry and nasty to us (meaning the people who lived in His house), then we would be her outlet for anger and she would behave well with the rest of the commune. I was being naive.

Even though I was working twelve hours a day, seven days a week and the rules about what we could and could not do were increasing I was very happy. I remember Osho asking me if I was tired and I replied that I couldn't even remember what it was like to feel tired.

I thought everybody was blissed out. Excuse me, but I never had the feeling that it was a difficult time. In our sleepiness we were allowing ourselves to be ruled by a group of people who were undermining our intelligence and in some instances creating fear in order to control, but that took time to surface and in the meantime, we were enjoying ourselves. If you put a group of sannyasins together, the common denominator will be laughter.

Vivek suffered a lot though. It was the beginning of a hormonal and chemical imbalance that manifested in bouts of depression. I also think that she was so sensitive that her intuition about Sheela and her gang was driving her crazy. She was prone to depression and would sometimes be in a black hole for two or three weeks. We tried every way we could to help her and nothing helped, except to leave her alone, which is what she was asking for in the first place.

She decided to leave the commune. John, a friend, and one of the "Hollywood Set" — a small group of *sannyasins* who had been with Osho in Pune, and had now given up their luxurious lives in Beverly Hills to join this great experiment — was asked if he would drive her to Salem about two hundred and fifty miles away so that she might take a direct flight to London. They drove for eighteen hours through a snow blizzard, visibility nil, and roads slippery with ice. She caught the plane though.

John made his treacherous trip back to the commune, and before he arrived Vivek had called from England where she had visited her mother for a few hours and decided she wanted to come back to the commune. Osho said, yes of course, and John was to meet her at the airport, as he had been the one to see her off. John arrived back at Rajneeshpuram, just in time to turn around and do the trip again. The snow was so thick by now that many roads were closed down and the snow was still falling. They made it, and Vivek was welcomed back with open arms. As usual she carried no guilt or embarrassment and walked back into our lives, head held high as though nothing had happened.

Driving down the winding road to Rajneeshpuram one

day with Osho, as we approached a corner, instead of going around with the road He drove straight towards the edge. The car stopped with its front, which was one third of the car, sticking out in space. Below us was a drop of about thirty feet, and after that it was all down hill to the bottom of the valley.

Osho said, "There, you see what happens...?"

I sat rigid, not daring to breath in case the slightest movement would tip the balance and send us hurtling down. He sat for a few seconds before restarting the engine. I was praying to a non-existent god, "Please, let it be reverse gear!" Then slowly the car backed on to the road and we were driving towards home. I didn't understand, so I continued the conversation: "What happens...?"

He said: "I was trying to avoid that muddy puddle back there, because it would have been a trouble for Chin who cleans my car."

Sheela surrounded Osho's house and garden with a ten-foot-high electrical charged fence.

"To keep the deer out of the garden?"

"Pardon?"

Anyway, we were fenced in. My washing line was outside the fence and although there was a gate and I was assured that the gate was not charged, every time I tried to get through the gate I got a shock that felt like a horse had kicked me in the stomach. The first time it happened I fell to my knees and vomited. That was the end of my mountain days. Instead of running through the mountains to the canteen twice a day I now walked down the path to the bus stop like everybody else, observed by the guards in the watchtower. Oh, yes, there was a watch-tower that was manned twenty-four hours a day by at least two guards armed with sub-machine guns. Paranoia was growing on both sides of the fence.

In April 1983 the commune received a message from

Osho. He had been informed by Devaraj of an incurable illness called AIDS that was spreading throughout the world. Osho said that this disease would kill two-thirds of humanity and the commune had to be protected. He suggested that condoms and rubber gloves be used while making love, unless a couple had been together in a monogamous relationship for over two years. The press delighted in this news and ridiculed the protective measures for a practically unknown disease.

When Osho remarked on the absence of trees, He was told by Sheela of a pine forest that existed on the far side of the property. He loved trees so much, and He was often asking me, "Have you seen the pine forest? How many trees? How big? How far away is it, and could I drive there?"

I went one day on a motorbike and there was no road at all. It was about fifteen miles across country and was situated in a small valley on the border of the property.

It was becoming increasingly dangerous for Osho to drive outside Rajneeshpuram, so a road began to be cut to the pine forest. It was a slow process. No sooner had the first cut been made than the men would be called off to work somewhere else, and then it would rain and the road would be washed away. Ten miles were completed by 1984 and each day Osho drove along the road getting closer and closer to the elusive pine forest. It was a magnificent drive, but the forest was not even in sight.

Osho left before the road ever reached the forest that He wanted to see so much. Milarepa and Vimal had been working on the road since the project began. They were close friends and Vimal's sense of humor and innocence was yet to come to its full glory — years later he would create great laughter for Osho and us by coming to our evening meeting place (Buddha Hall) dressed as a woman in a sari one night (imitating Maneesha) and another night he came to discourse dressed in a gorilla skin. But before this was to happen, they were working together building a small highway, miles from anywhere, for their Master to see the forest. They had worked so long and determinedly on it that when the time came to give up they continued — just the two of them. While everyone else was bringing back the machines to sell them, they were trying to reach the pine forest "just in case Osho came back."

As the weeks and months passed the energy of the *sannyasins* could be contained no longer. It was not enough to stand by the side of the road and simply *namaste* Osho as He drove past. One afternoon, as Osho was taking His car ride, a small group of Italian *sannyasins* stood by the side of the road and played music to Him. He stopped for a few minutes to enjoy them, and within a week the road through the valley was lined with red-clad musicians, dancing and singing — from Lao Tzu gate, across the small dam and Basho Pond, along the dusty road past Rajneesh Mandir, through "downtown" Rajneeshpuram, and up into the hills. This was the beginning of a wild celebration that was to happen every day for the next two years, through blistering heat and falling snow. It was a spontaneous explosion of joy, of people who wanted to express their love for Osho in the only way they could.

Musical instruments started arriving from all over the world, the most favored being huge Brazilian drums; but there were also flutes, violins, guitars, tambourines, shakers of all dimensions, saxophones, clarinets, trumpets — we had them all; and those without an instrument sang or simply jumped up and down on the spot.

Osho loved to see His people happy and He drove so slowly that the Rolls Royce engine had to be specially tuned. He moved His arms to the music and stopped at certain groups and musicians. Maneesha, who had been one of Osho's mediums and was to become His "recorder" (as Plato was to Socrates), would be there with her small group of celebrators. Osho would stop opposite her, and I could see her disappearing into a wild, ecstatic cyclone of colored tambourine ribbons and joy. Her long dark hair would fly around her face, her body leapt in the air, and yet her dark eyes were fixed silently and still on Osho's. Osho especially spent a lot of time with Rupesh, His bongo player, and to see Osho playing drums through Rupesh was something other-worldly. Despite the mixture of music, from the Indian *kirtan* group to the Brazilians, there was immense harmony. It would sometimes take two hours to drive past the line of celebrators, because Osho would not be able to resist anyone who was really going for it. The car would bounce up and down as He moved His arms and I was always amazed how He had the strength in His arms to last that long.

Drive-by was as intimate and high as any energy *darshan* and I was sometimes in the car with Osho and so could see the peoples' faces. If ever there was reason to save this planet this was it. Even those people in the line up could not imagine how beautiful they looked. I was often overwhelmed with tears and once Osho, hearing my sniffling said:

"You have a cold?"
"No Osho, I'm crying."
"Mmmm. Crying? What happened?"
"Nothing, Osho, just that it's so beautiful.
They can't destroy this, can they?"

Back at the house, Osho was having a lot of trouble with His teeth. He had nine root canals and while this treatment was happening He, of course, made the best of it, and while under the influence of the dentist's gas, He talked. It was not an easy task for Osho's dentist, Devageet, to work on a mouth that is most of the time moving. Osho talked three books worth. We realised that something was worth recording here, and so recorded all He said. The three books, *Glimpses of a Golden Childhood, Books I Have Loved,* and *Notes of a Madman* are extraordinary.

While we were out on a car ride one day some cowboys threw stones at Osho's car. They missed, but I got a good look at them. At that time Osho's car was followed by our "security force," but none of the five security people saw what happened, even though I called to them on the motorola.

After the ride I was asked to go to Jesus Grove (Sheela's house), and give a talk to the security force. I was the hero of the day! My ego was puffed up and I felt a rush of intense energy, like adrenaline. Everyone in the room was listening to me, and I was giving advice and telling people how to do their job better. The meeting ended at lunch time and I went to catch the bus to the canteen. While standing at the bus stop I felt so high; I couldn't stop talking and I was quite carried away with myself, when suddenly with a sickening thud, I saw — this is power. This is what power feels like. This is the drug with which people are bought, and for which people sell their souls.

Sheela controlled her group by giving or taking away power from them. I think power is an intoxicant and like all drugs it destroys a person's consciousness. Lust for power does not happen to someone who is meditating and yet it is strange that we allowed Sheela complete power over the commune. The people in Rajneeshpuram wanted to be there because of Osho and to live in His presence and this was the threat — of expulsion — that gave Sheela her power. I think that we were not yet ready to take responsibility for ourselves also. It is much easier to leave decisions and organizing to someone else, and not claim responsibility for anything that happens. Responsibility means freedom, and responsibility needs a certain maturity. We were to learn, in retrospect.

"When I am gone, remember me as a man who has given you freedom and individuality." ...Osho

...and He has, He really has.

Although our house was guarded round the clock by

Sheela's security force in the watch tower, at night everyone in our trailer, on a rota system, had to get up, get dressed — that meant full gear because it was below zero outside, and usually raining or snowing — and walk around the house with a motorola. It was pitch dark, slippery and scary. Climbing up the slope at the end of the swimming pool, creeping through the bamboos, I would jump over the small stream that babbled like strange voices — and often at this point the motorola let out a loud static screech. Standing as stiff as a corpse, heart thumping, I would stare into the darkness with a silent scream frozen on my face. This was the beginning of Sheela's revenge on us, for existing. Her jealousy was to grow beyond all sane proportions, because we were close to Osho.

We, in turn, were to ensure that there was no way Sheela could get into the house without our knowing. She would send her workmen up to the house to change a lock on a door, and Vivek would send Asheesh off to the tool shop to steal (no other way) a bolt and fix it to the other side of the door with the changed lock. This was to save Vivek's life when Sheela sent four of her gang to Vivek's room with chloroform and a syringe of poison. Rafia, Vivek's boyfriend, was sent away from the Ranch "on business," for the night and the murder attempt was foiled only because they couldn't get into the house. We did not find out about this plot until after Sheela had left, and some of her gang were questioned by the FBI.

It was in June 1984 I received a telephone call from Sheela. She sounded very excited, like someone who had just won a lottery and she was screaming so loud I had to hold the receiver two feet from my ear.

"We've hit the jackpot. We've hit the jackpot!" she screeched.

Thinking something great had happened, I asked what, and she replied that Devaraj, Devageet and Ashu, who was

Osho's dental nurse, had been found to have the infectious eye disease, conjunctivitis.

"And that proves," she said, "that they are dirty, filthy pigs and shouldn't be allowed to take care of Osho."

I put down the telephone, thinking, "Oh, my God, the woman has lost it."

Next step was that she wanted Puja to come and test Osho's eyes. Puja, lovingly known as Nurse Mengele, was not liked or trusted by anyone. Something about her swarthy, puffy face and the way her eyes — mere slits — were always hidden behind tinted glasses. I told Osho that Sheela wanted to send Puja to examine Him and He said that as the disease had no cure and patients were simply isolated, what was the point?

Sheela insisted that everyone in the house go to get their eyes tested, so, except Nirupa who stayed to take care of Osho, we all went to the medical center. And, would you believe it, we all had the disease. Vivek, Devaraj, Devageet and I were put into a room together and were then joined by about twelve of Sheela's people, including Savita, the woman I had met in England and who was now in charge of the accounts. The inquisition that followed was so ugly that I resolved on that day that should Osho die before me then I would surely commit suicide. Everyone in the room had something nasty to say, as though they had been brewing vile thoughts and jealousy for a long time and now was their opportunity to unload on us. Savita kept repeating that love is hard and not always nice, and we were attacked for our inability to take care of Osho properly. They spoke of Osho as though He didn't really know what He was doing and He needed someone to think for Him.

I saw the doctor hesitate when he examined Vivek's eyes and he was nervous as he was taken aside and spoken to by one of Sheela's gang and although we had no symptoms of a disease, we didn't feel we could argue with the doctors' findings.

The next day Osho developed a toothache and asked for Raj, Geet and Ashu to attend Him. Sheela tried to send her own doctor and dentist but Osho refused, He said He wanted His own people, irrespective of the risk. So the trio went back to Osho's house, where they were duly disinfected, and allowed to treat Osho.

The whole commune was then tested for the "bogus disease," as Osho called it, and everyone was found to have it. The medical center was overflowing with people, and there was no one left to take care of the commune. Finally, a doctor spoke with an eye specialist and learnt that what had actually been seen under examination were small dots on the cornea that were common to anyone living in a dry, dusty climate such as ours.

We were allowed back to our house after three days. On walking up the driveway, I was appalled to see our belongings strewn all over the lawn and pathway. A team of cleaners under Sheela's orders had gone through the house and thrown everything out as contaminated.

We were stripped and sprayed with alcohol as we entered the house and were then greeted by another inquisition, and this time there was a tape recorder set up so Sheela could get an accurate report of what was said. This was too much, and Vivek went to Osho's room to tell Him what was happening. When she returned with the message from Him that they should stop all this nonsense and go home, nobody believed her. It was like trying to call off the hunting dogs once they had the smell of the lair. They said Vivek was lying, so we all got up and walked away, leaving everyone sitting there, and Patipada, who was one of Sheela's team, was on her hands and knees screaming abuse into the tape recorder, because she had no one else to shout at.

The next day Osho had a meeting in His room for a

few of us, including Savita, Sheela, and some of her followers. He said that if we could not learn to live in harmony then He would leave His body on July 6th. There was enough fighting going on outside the commune without internal fighting. He talked about the abuse of power.

A few days after this Osho gave a list of twenty-one people, living in the commune, who were enlightened. This really caused a stir!

And, if that stir was not enough, next came three committees (*sansads*), composed of *Sambuddhas*, *Mahasattvas* and *Bodhisattvas*. These people were to take care of the commune, should anything happen to Him. Sheela was not on any of the lists, nor were any of her cronies.

By doing this, Osho took away all possibility of Sheela becoming His successor. She no longer had any power.

A story that can explain how a mystic lives and works happened one day when I was in the car with Osho.

There was a fly in the car buzzing around our heads, and I was swinging my arms around trying to catch it. We stopped at crossroads and were waiting for the traffic to move and I continued to slap at the windows and seats. Osho sat motionless, looking ahead, while I worked myself into a sweat trying to squash the fly. Without turning His head, or even moving His eyes, He quietly pressed the button on the automatic window. The window on His side slid down and He sat silently and waited. When the fly flew close to Him, He ever so slightly moved His hand and the fly flew out of the window. Then He touched the button and the window closed. He never took His eyes off the road, and He didn't say anything.

So Zen, and so graceful.

This was His way with Sheela too. With grace He waited until she made her own exit. He was still her Master too, He loved her and trusted the Buddha in her. I know Osho trusted Sheela because I have been watching Him closely for fifteen years, and the man is Trust. The way He lived His life was pure trust and the way He died shows His total trust.

I asked Him what the difference was between a person who trusts, and one who is naive, and He said that being naive is being ignorant, but to trust is intelligent.

"Both will be cheated, both will be deceived, but the person who is naive will feel cheated, will feel deceived, will be angry, will start distrusting people. His naiveness will sooner or later become distrust.

"And the person who trusts is also going to be cheated and deceived, but he is not going to feel hurt. He will simply feel compassionate towards those who have cheated him, who have deceived him, and his trust will not be lost. His trust will go on increasing in spite of all deceptions. His trust will never turn into distrust of humanity."

Vivek went to Jesus Grove for a meeting with Sheela. After drinking a cup of tea she became sick and Sheela brought her home. I saw them from my laundry room window; Sheela was supporting Vivek as though she could hardly walk. Devaraj examined her and her pulse beat was between one hundred and sixty and one hundred and seventy, and her heart was abnormal.

A few days later Osho broke His silence, and started giving discourses in His sitting room. There was room for about fifty people, so we attended on a rota system, and the video of the discourse was shown to the whole commune the next evening in Rajneesh Mandir. He spoke on rebellion, as against obedience, freedom and responsibility, and He even said that He would not leave us in the hands of a fascist regime.

He said that at last He was speaking to people who could accept what He had to say, that for thirty years He had to disguise His message amongst sutras of Buddha, Mahavira, Jesus, etc. Now He was going to tell the naked truth about religions. He emphasized again and again that to be enlightened you need not be of virgin birth; in fact, all the stories surrounding enlightened people were lies invented by the priests.

"...I am just as ordinary as you are, with all the weaknesses, with all the frailties. This is to be emphasized continuously because you will tend to forget it. And why am I emphasizing it? So that you can see a very significant point: if an ordinary man — who is just like you — can be enlightened, then there is no problem for you either. You can also be enlightened...."

"I have not given you any promises...any incentives...any guarantee. I don't take any responsibility on your behalf, because I respect you. If I take the responsibility on myself then you are slaves. Then I am the leader and you are the led. We are fellow travelers. You are not behind me but by my side — just together with me. I am not higher than you, I am just one amongst you. I don't claim any superiority, extraordinary power. Do you see the point? To make you responsible for your life is to give you freedom."

"Freedom is a great risk...nobody really wants to be free — it is pure talk. Everybody wants to be dependent, everybody wants someone else to take responsibility. In freedom you are responsible for every action, every thought, every movement. You cannot dump anything on anybody else."

I remember that once when things were chaotic and Vivek was being difficult, Osho said to me, looking slightly surprised:

"You are so calm."

I replied that it was because He was helping me. He didn't say anything, but I felt my words freeze in the air and then fall splat at my feet. I couldn't even take responsibility for my own serenity. Osho had to be the cause.

He was to ask me how the commune felt. The same question He asked years before when He was in silence.

I answered that now He was speaking again it felt like His commune. It didn't feel like Sheela's commune anymore.

Sheela was losing her stardom. She was no longer the only person to see Osho, everybody saw Him, and not only that, we could ask him questions for discourse. What Osho was talking about was opening people's eyes.

His talks on Christianity were outrageous, even to someone who had been listening to Osho for many years. He was calling a spade, a fucking spade.

It was these talks that must have stirred fear in the hearts and stomachs of the fundamentalist Christians, not the possibility that He didn't have the right tourist visa.

Sheela called a general meeting for the whole commune, and it was to be held in Rajneesh Mandir. Vivek suspected that Sheela was going to try and stop Osho talking, so we made a plan that a few of us would spread out in the Mandir and call out "Keep Him Talking." This way people would understand what was going on and everyone would start chanting to keep Him talking!

I sat at the back of the Mandir and switched on my tape recorder, hidden in my down jacket, just to record the meeting correctly. Sheela started to say that with the coming festival there was so much work that there was a "backlog" and it was going to be impossible to prepare for the festival, and go to discourse. My cue.......

"Keep 'im talking. Keep 'im talking!" I bellowed out. Silence.

Where were my fellow anarchists?

"Keep 'im talking!" I continued to shout, as people turned around to see who the idiot was disrupting the meeting. I saw their faces incredulous — Chetana, Chetana? — but she is such a quiet type. Must have gone mad.

Everybody knew that there was no backlog of work, but nobody could understand what Sheela was getting at, so the meeting turned into total confusion and ended up with a compromise being made. Our Master — who says never, never compromise — and we, unknowingly, made our compromise which meant that Osho would talk to a few people each night and the video would be shown after everyone had done twelve hours' work and had their dinner. Even the most devoted disciple fell asleep during the video. Not only were His words not heard, people felt guilty into the bargain for not being able to stay awake!

While Vivek was out driving with Osho on the Ranch they passed a group of people in the creek who were picking up stones and dead branches.

"What are they doing?" asked Osho.

"They must be picking up the backlog," said Vivek.

Searching for the backlog became a great joke among *sanyasins*.

A few days passed and Osho became very sick and a specialist was called in to attend Him. He had an infection of the middle ear and was in tremendous pain for about six weeks. Discourse and car rides were cancelled.

I had been working in the garden for almost a year and Vivek had been doing Osho's laundry. I had not been without my own traumas and difficulties and working with plants and trees had been a great solace to me. Osho's house now had hundreds of trees surrounding it, pines, blue spruces, and redwoods had been planted and some were already sixty feet high. There was a waterfall that ran past His window, around the corner of the swimming pool, and cascaded a second time into a pool surrounded by weeping willows. Blossoming cherry trees, high pampas grasses, bamboos, yellow forsythia, and magnolia trees were either side of the small stream. There was a rose garden directly in front of Osho's dining room window and in His car porch was a fountain in which sat a life size Buddha statue. Poplar trees lined the driveway until it reached a grove of silver birch trees. The lawns were by now lush green and spreading, and wild flowers had been sown over the surrounding hills.

There were three hundred peacocks in the garden, dancing with their psychedelic colors. Six of them were pure white, and these six were the naughtiest. They used to stand in front of Osho's car with their tails fanned out like giant snowflakes, and wouldn't let Him drive past them.

Osho has always liked to live with gardens and beautiful birds and animals. He wanted a deer park to be created at Rajneeshpuram, and we were to grow "alfa-alfa" for the deer, to attract them away from the hunters. He told a story of a place in India He used to visit near a waterfall where there were hundreds of deer. At night they would come to the lake to drink, "and their eyes would shine like a thousand flames, dancing in the dark."

At the bottom of the garden, before Basho Pond, where black swans resided on one side of the bridge, and white on the other, there was the garage in which were the famous ninety-six Rolls Royces. In India Osho's one Mercedes created an uproar, but in America it took almost a hundred Rolls Royces to achieve the same effect.

For many people these cars were a barrier between them and Osho. They could not see past the cars.

It is said that Sufi masters create disguises so that they may go about their business unrecognized and do not have to waste time with people who are not seekers.

"There was no need for ninety-six Rolls Royces. I could not use ninety-six Rolls Royces simultaneously — the same model, the same car. But I wanted to make it clear to you that you would be ready to drop all your desires for truth, for love, for spiritual growth to have a Rolls Royce. I was knowingly creating a situation in which you would feel jealous.

"The function of a master is very strange. He has to help you come to an understanding of your inner structure of consciousness: it is full of jealousy.

"...Those cars fulfilled their purpose. They created jealousy in the whole of America, in all the super-rich people. If they were intelligent enough, then rather than being my enemies they would have come to me to find a way to get rid of their jealousy, because it is their problem. Jealousy is a fire that burns you, and burns you badly." (*Beyond Psychology*)

"Everything that I have done in my life has a purpose. It is a device to bring out something in you of which you are not aware." ...Osho

The Fourth Annual World Celebration began and Osho came to meditate with us in Rajneesh Mandir. Devaraj was reading passages selected from Osho's books, interspersed with music. Masters' Day, July 6th, was upon us and I was sitting in the celebration feeling very bad. I said to myself that I was sitting in front of Osho, and this was a celebration day, so what was the matter? When the morning celebration was over I waited in the car with Maneesha for Devaraj. I felt sick and so undid my buttons and put my head between my knees. We waited until there was no one left in the Mandir, and yet he hadn't passed us. Only an ambulance had shot past us.

Maneesha drove home and as we were walking up the driveway someone came running and told us that Devaraj had been injected with poison during the celebration, and was dying.

My mind raced, why would anyone want to come to Rajneeshpuram to kill Devaraj, and how come such a maniac was allowed in to the Mandir? I was imagining a group of Charles Manson type characters dressed in black leather and chains.

The world had turned upside down.

The medical facilities built for Osho were being used to test Raj's blood, and I overheard the doctors saying that, "By all rights, this man should be dead."

Devaraj was taken to an intensive care unit in the nearest hospital, a plane ride away. He was coughing blood, which indicated his heart had gone into failure and he now had pulmonary oedema.

It was twenty-four hours before we were to know that he was going to pull through.

That afternoon I was standing with Maneesha by Basho's Pond, to greet Osho in drive-by. Before Osho's car came, Sheela, with Shanti Bhadra, Vidya and Savita cruised by. The four of them leaned forward to stare defiantly at Maneesha and I. It was a weird moment

They stopped the car and stared, then they called Indian Taru (Taru who had been Osho's singer during Hindi discourses for many years) over and asked something. I found out later that they asked her if she had seen anything during the celebration in the morning.

She had indeed seen something, as was to come out later. She saw the puncture wound on Devaraj's backside made by the injection, and she was told by Devaraj just before he passed out that Shanti Bhadra had injected him.

Taru did not tell this to the car full of would-be murderesses, as she was obviously in fear for her own life.

I heard it whispered that Shanti Bhadra, Sheela's closest aide, had tried to kill Devaraj, and in the same moment it had been denied and I was told that Devaraj was confused and very sick — maybe even a brain tumor.

Nobody was prepared to believe such an outrageous story, that he had been injected with poison by a fellow *sannyasin*, and Devaraj, instead of shouting it to everyone in sight — including the doctors who tended him in the hospital — had enough awareness to see the implications: police descending on the commune. There were already rumors, confirmed by an official memo, that state troopers were being kept on hold, awaiting orders to attack the commune. Rumors had spread out of all proportion that we had many guns in the commune, and no one had stopped to investigate that it was our own state-trained security force that had the guns, just like any other police force in America.

Devaraj was in fear that he might be knocked off while

lying in the hospital bed, and also he was aware that if he did survive he was going to have go back to Rajneeshpuram.

So Devaraj told only Maneesha, Vivek and Geet and they decided to keep quiet until they obtained proof. Some of us thought Raj had lost his faculties. He was left utterly vulnerable to another attack and yet he continued living day to day as though everything was normal. Imagine what trust Devaraj had, on one side surrounded by his friends who thought he was nuts, and on the other side, surrounded by people who had tried to kill him, and might try again.

On the same day that Devaraj returned home from the hospital, Osho began giving press conferences in Jesus Grove. This was the long bungalow where Sheela and her gang lived, and a large room was kept at an exceptionally cold temperature for Osho to speak at night. Journalists from all over the world had interviews with Him. Music accompanied Osho as He arrived and left Jesus Grove and He danced with the people filling the corridors and driveway to the house. Any of Sheela's people who had been in doubt as to who their Master was, now had the opportunity to see.

Osho danced with us in the Mandir; He would call to people to come up on the podium and dance, and He visited our discotheque, offices and the medical center. He graced everywhere in Rajneeshpuram with His presence. He was showing people, "Look, I am not a God, I am an ordinary human being, just like you."

It was difficult for me to see Osho as an ordinary man. It was not until after He left His body that I was flooded with memories of how human and ordinary He was. His humbleness and frailties became clear only after I no longer could be dependent on Him.

While I saw Him as a godly figure, then I didn't have to take responsibility for my own enlightenment. My own realization was as far away as He appeared to be, and I could continue to snore and dream.

Devaraj began to recover his health and for a few weeks Sheela was away from the commune. She was visiting centers in Europe, Australia, and other places. Anywhere where she was still a star, in fact. She wrote a letter to Osho saying that she no longer felt excited whenever she returned to Rajneeshpuram. Friday, 13th September, 1985, He answered her letter publicly in a discourse and said:

"Perhaps she is not conscious, and this is the situation for all — she does not know why she does not feel excited here any more. It is because I am speaking and she is no longer the central focus. She is no longer a celebrity. When I am speaking to you, she is no longer needed as a mediator to inform you of what I am thinking. Now that I am speaking to the press and to the radio and TV journalists, she has fallen into shadow. And for three-and-a-half years she was in the limelight because I was silent.

"It may not be clear to her why she does not feel excited coming here and feels happy in Europe. She is still a celebrity in Europe — interviews, television shows, radio interviews, newspapers — but here all that has disappeared from her life. If you can behave in such foolish, unconscious ways even while I am here, the moment I am gone you will be creating all kinds of politics, fight. Then what is the difference between you and the outside world? Then my whole effort has been a failure. I want you to behave really as a new man.

"I have given Sheela the message that this is the reason: So think it over and tell me. If you want me to stop speaking just for your excitement, I can stop speaking."

"To me there is no problem in it. In fact, it is a trouble. For five hours a day I am speaking to you, and it is creating unhappiness in her mind. So let her do her show business. I can move into silence. But that indicates that deep down those who have power will not like me to be here alive, because while I am here nobody can have any power trip. They may not be conscious about it; only situations reveal your power trip."

The next day Sheela, with about fifteen of her followers, boarded a plane and flew out of Rajneeshpuram, out of America, and out of our lives.

Sheela's departure from the commune did not make me happy. I felt worried and sad. It meant she was leaving Osho. But why?

I was soon to find out, as stories poured in from commune members of their mistreatment by her, and even worse. She had committed many crimes, from attempted murder, to wiretapping, to planning to poison a nearby city's water supply.

Osho immediately called in the FBI and CIA to investigate. They moved into the main ranch house and from there interviewed everyone. They did not interview Osho although appointments were made; but then the officers would cancel them.

I heard a few (much less significant) stories about myself, also. How Sheela told people that I was a spy, so not to speak to me — I never noticed! The guards that had been watching over Lao Tzu house where we lived had been warned that one day they may have to shoot us, so not to become friendly with us. Instinctively I had always been careful on the telephone, so I was not too surprised to hear that our 'phones were bugged. But I was astounded to know that Osho's room was bugged.

At least a hundred journalists came to Rajneeshpuram and stayed for weeks. It was the first and only time I have felt relieved to have them around, because I felt they were in a way our protection.

If I hadn't been so shocked by the catastrophic turn of events I would have realised what danger Osho was in.

The press and neighboring farmers had seen that when Osho drove in His car He was flanked by guards carrying guns. It is not an unusual sight in America to see a person guarded, and yet it started rumors that the commune was stockpiling weapons.

Charles Turner, US Attorney, made a statement to the press a few months after the dissolution of Rajneeshpuram when he was asked why Bhagwan Shree Rajneesh was not charged with any crimes:

He said that there was no proof that Bhagwan had committed any crimes, but that the government's main objective had always been to destroy the commune.

Our commune, where people were working twelve or fourteen hours a day, celebrating together at lunch time and dancing in the discotheques at night. The atmosphere in Rajneeshpuram was very alive and happy.

For instance — the buses. Whenever I took a bus ride I could not help but compare how a bus ride is in, say London — long faces, everybody arguing with the conductor about the lateness of the bus or the price of the ticket; people shouting at the driver, and pushing each other; elbows in the ribcage, and the odd pervert grabbing a tit as he lurches off the bus. In Rajneeshpuram I always left the bus feeling elated, because to start with the driver/conductor seemed to be having a great time. He would be playing music and greeting everyone as they got on the bus. The passengers were most often laughing and enjoying themselves and it was an opportunity to meet people that you may not have seen for a long time.

Taking a plane trip was like sitting at home in your own sitting room with all the comforts, plus a friend bringing you snacks and drinks. In fact, I always got the impression when I looked around our city that we were children playing at being firemen, truck drivers, farmers and shopkeepers. It never felt serious and "grown-up", though it certainly was sincere and heartful.

The huge cafeteria where we ate together was tremendously alive and buzzing, and the food was so good that everyone became big. When *sannyasins* were working or eating together, or dancing, the energy was very high in spite of Sheela's fascist regime.

That she was listening in to every phone call we made and even our conversations in our rooms, shows to what degree her paranoia had developed.

Sheela's tremendous energy had helped build a city in the desert and that cannot go without admiration; but she had gone mad. Her lust for power had corrupted her and she had no understanding of Osho's teachings. Under Sheela's house were found secret tunnels and rooms. A laboratory was discovered in the hills for making poisons. This was Nurse Mengele's department.

When Sheela left I think some people felt foolish and that they had been taken for a ride. Foolish because so much had been going on under their noses and no one had the guts or even the awareness to say, "Hey, wait a minute...." And taken for a ride because everyone had worked so hard towards a dream, a vision and it was being destroyed. Some people were to only remember the negative aspects, and their joyful moments, which I had seen on their faces, were to become faded dreams. We had all enjoyed making our contribution to creating an oasis in the desert, nobody can deny that. Otherwise, for what other reason were we there? And, of course, there were the people whose money Sheela had run off with. At least forty million dollars were stolen from donations and shifted into a Swiss bank account.

Certainly we had behaved blindly. But what an opportunity to live all this and see it, and have a chance to begin all over again with sharpened awareness. It's as though we lived many lives in that short time.

During the month that followed Sheela's exit flight, Osho talked three times a day (about seven to eight hours) to disciples and journalists. For such a self-acclaimed lazy man He was doing a tremendous amount of "work," and was obviously getting tired.

When asked by a journalist how was it possible that He did not know everything that was going on if He was enlightened, Osho replied:

"To be enlightened means I know myself, it does not mean that I know my room is bugged."

September 26th, 1985. It takes a diamond to cut a diamond, and I recognized that what was coming was going to hurt when in discourse Osho said:

"And today I would like to declare something immensely important — because I feel perhaps this helped Sheela and her people to exploit you. I don't know whether tomorrow I will be here or not, so it is better to do it while I am here, and make you free from any other possibility of such a fascist regime.

"That is, from today, you are free to use any color of clothes. If you feel like using red clothes, that is up to you. And this message has to be sent all over the world to all the communes. It will be more beautiful to have all the colors. I had always dreamed of seeing you in all the colors of the rainbow.

"Today we claim the rainbow to be our colors.

"The second thing: you return your *malas* — unless you wish otherwise. That is your choice, but it is not a necessity anymore. You return your *malas* to President Hasya. But if you want to keep it, it is up to you.

"The third thing: from now onwards, anybody who wants initiation into *sannyas* will not be given a *mala* and will not be told to change to red clothes.

"So, we can take over the world more easily!" (*From Bondage to Freedom*)"

These words from Osho had an ominous feel to them, but it was the clapping and cheering that frightened me. It was like a stupid mob; like the clapping that had accompanied Sheela's meetings. Many people left Rajneesh

Mandir very happy and went to buy new color clothes in the boutique. I saw Vivek, we were both wary of the change, and she said to me, "He may disband the commune next."

October 8th, 1985, Osho said in discourse:

".....You have been clapping because I have dropped red clothes, *malas*. And when you clap, you don't know how it hurts me. That means you have been a hypocrite!

"Why have you been wearing red clothes if dropping them brings you so much joy? Why have you been wearing the *mala*? The moment I say, 'Drop,' you rejoice. And people rushed to the boutique to change their clothes, they have dropped their *malas*.

"But you don't know how much you have wounded me by your clapping and by your changing.

"Now, I have to say one thing more, and I would like to see whether you have guts to clap or not: that is, now there is no Buddhafield. So if you want enlightenment, you have to work for it individually, the Buddhafield exists no more. You cannot depend on the energy of the Buddhafield to become enlightened.

"Now clap as loudly as you can. CLAP!...

"Now you are completely free: even for enlightenment only you are responsible. And I am completely free from you.

"You have been behaving like idiots!...

"And this has given a good chance to see how many people are really intimate with me. If you can drop your *malas* so easily....Even in my own house there is one *sannyasin* who immediately changed to blue clothes, with great joy. What does it show? It shows that those red clothes were a burden. She was somehow managing to be in red clothes against her will.

"But I don't want you to do anything against your will.

"Now I don't want even to help you towards your enlightenment against your will. You are absolutely free and responsible for yourself."(*From Bondage to Freedom*)

When He shouted "Clap!" it was as though a bomb had exploded and we were all sitting in its fallout, frozen. After the discourse I walked away from the Mandir, red, raw and sobbing. The first two friends I saw, I went to them saying "Help, help," and we went together to drink coffee in the sunlight. I felt that we had all let Osho down. It seemed that our behavior throughout the last four years had culminated in this moment. We all shared the responsibility for Sheela's actions — myself for simply not saying anything. It is not enough to be a nice loving person, I also had to grow in intelligence, understanding and the courage to say how I felt.

It was the end of October, and one night I dreamt that Osho was leaving the house in a hurry. The house was in pandemonium and I was running through the rooms carrying a robe of Osho's on a hanger. This particular robe — grey and white — funnily enough, turned out to be the robe He was wearing when He was arrested. Savita, Sheela's partner, was in the dream and was trying to block my way.

That night I must have picked up, in my unconscious, the vibrations of the events that were to follow. This must mean that the future is already in the present in some form.

The next afternoon I was told that Osho was going to take a holiday in the mountains and I was to accompany Him with Mukti, His cook, Nirupa, Devaraj, Vivek, and Jayesh. Jayesh had come to Rajneeshpuram just a few months before; one look into Osho's eyes as He passed by in His car and Jayesh walked back to his hotel, made a telephone call to Canada, where he was a successful businessman, and cancelled his life there. Someone with no understanding of a seeker recognizing his Master would say he was hypnotized. Jayesh is a handsome, sophisticated, 'worldly' *sannyasin*, and has a sense of humor matched well by his determination and clear insight. He has set the foundation stone for Osho's fast growing, and last, commune, and many times I have heard Osho say that without Jayesh the work would have been very difficult. Jayesh was introduced to the work by Hasya, who Osho selected as His new secretary. Hasya was the total opposite to Sheela. She hailed from Hollywood and was elegant, charming and intelligent.

As we drove towards the airport the sky was bright orange with the setting sun. There were two jets awaiting us, and I boarded one with Nirupa and Mukti. We pressed against the window and waved to our friends on the tarmac. Within minutes we were in the sky, tilted upwards, and climbing higher. We did not know where we were going and this made us laugh.

CHAPTER EIGHT

USA — Prison

O ctober 28th, 1985.
The Lear jet was just coming in to land at Charlotte, North Carolina, and I looked out into the darkness and saw that the airport was deserted. A few thin tall bushes were blowing in the wind gusts created by the jet as we touched down, and as the engines were switched off Nirupa saw Hanya. Hanya, with whom we were going to stay in Charlotte, was Nirupa's extremely young mother-in-law. She was standing on the tarmac with her friend Prasad.

Nirupa called out excitedly to Hanya, and almost simultaneously from many directions loud shouts of "Hands up" threw me into another reality. I was in that terrible gap for a moment, from where the mind surfaces to say, "No, this can't be real." Within a couple of seconds the plane was surrounded by about fifteen men pointing their guns at us.

It was real alright — darkness, flashing lights, screeching brakes, shouts, panic, fear, all spun around me, but I was too aware of the danger to be anything but calm. "Don't even sneeze," I said to myself, "because these men will shoot." They were scared — and no wonder.

A freelance reporter interviewed the authorities three years after the event and was told, and shown evidence, that the message that these men had received was to arrest the occupants of these two planes — they were told we were escaped criminals fleeing from justice and that we were terrorists, armed with submachine guns.

The men were dressed in lumberjack shirts and jeans. I thought they were Oregonian rednecks and nillbillies come to kidnap Osho. We were not told that we were under arrest, or that they were FBI agents.

I was looking at professional killers. They looked perverted and inhuman; they did not have eyes with any expression in them, they had only glistening holes in their faces.

The men were shouting for us to get out of the plane with our hands up, but although the pilots opened the door we could not get out because Osho's armchair was a third the size of the jet, and stood in the doorway. We tried to call to our captors that we couldn't get out and they must have thought it some kind of ploy while we were maybe loading our machine guns. They got very agitated and a light was shone into my face through the window. I turned and twelve inches from my face was the barrel of a gun, and at the end of the gun was a very tense and frightened face. I realized that he was more frightened than me, and that was dangerous.

After a scene that would befit Monty Python, with the gunmen shouting contradictory orders at us to "Freeze," "Get down from the plane," and "Don't move," Osho's armchair was removed, and men jumped on board the plane and almost shot Mukti in the head for bending down to put her shoes on.

Outside on the tarmac it was arms up and legs spread as we were searched, with our bellies pressed up against the jet. As we were being roughly handcuffed, I turned to Hanya, who was looking frightened, and said, "It'll be alright." We then sat in the airport lounge, surrounded by gunmen behind desks, cupboards and potted plants, aiming sawn-off shotguns at the entrance, waiting for Osho's plane to land.

There was the sound of heavy boots running, arms rubbing against plastic bullet-proof vests, hissed messages on walkie-talkies. And then the sound of a lone jet coming in to land. The next five minutes were terrifying. We did not know what they were going to do to Osho. Nirupa tried to walk over to the glass doors that looked out onto the landing strip, hoping to give a warning signal, but she was ordered back to her seat at the point of a gun. I felt the deathly stillness of waiting, the helplessness of being in the hands of violent men. The tension in the deserted waiting room was suffocating and then there were panicked shouts from the armed men. They couldn't understand why the jet had landed and yet the engines were still running. This was only to keep the air conditioner running for Osho but they did not know this and they became more freaked out. Moments passed and I felt a sickly emptiness.

Then Osho walked through the glass doors, handcuffed and flanked on either side by men with their shotguns at the ready. Osho walked in as though He was walking into Buddha Hall to give a morning discourse to His disciples. He was calm, and a smile crossed His face as He saw us all sitting waiting for Him, in our chains. He walked on stage in the drama — quite a different drama than we had ever experienced before — and yet He was the same. Whatever happened to Osho on the periphery never touched His center, such a deep and tranquil pool it must be.

Next followed a fiasco, as our captors read out a list of names of which I recognized none. The drama was becoming more confusing.

"You've got the wrong people," said Vivek.

Wrong movie, wrong people — it was all bizarre to me. The man reading the list of names looked to me like an albino who dyed his hair red. He had a strong sexual vibe that made me think, "I bet he enjoys hurting people." We asked repeatedly if we were under arrest but received no answer.

We were all pushed outside and at least twenty police

cars were waiting with red and blue lights flashing. At this point Osho was separated from us and put in a car alone. My heart fell to my stomach; and as I was seated in one of the cars, I bent my head, put my hand over the empty place where my heart use to be, and it flooded into my shocked mind that something really terrible was happening.

At no point did the police take a good look at us. If they had, we would not have been put in chains or treated like mass murderers. They would have seen four extremely feminine women in their mid-thirties, about as dangerous as kittens, two mature, intelligent men, with an elegance and gentleness that they would not have come across before, and Osho ...what to say of Osho?...just look at His picture. During the whole episode of the arrest I just couldn't believe that Americans were watching the arrest of Osho, and were not able to see the contrast between Him and His captors, between Osho and any other human being they have ever seen on their TV screen. I was watching TV in the jail and saw the film footage as we were carted from jail to courthouse and back again. The television programs were loud, vulgar and violent and then suddenly on the screen was an ancient sage, a holy man, smiling at the world with His hands and feet in chains. He would raise His manacled hands to *namaste* the world that was trying to destroy Him. But nobody was able to see Him.

We were driven at breakneck speed to the marshal's jail, and I wondered whether these people were insane, or what. The streets were empty and quiet and yet they drove in such a way that we were thrown around in the back of the car and bounced off the walls and doors, hurting knees and shoulders in the process. Osho was in the car in front, being driven in the same way and I thought of Him with His delicate body and disjointed spine. Later Osho was to say:

"I am myself a reckless driver. In my whole life I have committed only two crimes, and those were speeding. But this was not speeding, it was a totally new kind of sudden stop — for no reason at all, just to give me a jerk. My hands were cuffed, my legs were chained, and they had instructions where to put a chain on my waist, exactly where my back is giving me the trouble. And this would happen each five minutes: suddenly fast, suddenly stopping, just to give as much pain to my back as possible. And nobody said, "You are harming Him."

Arriving at the prison, Jayesh, surprised at the new turn his holiday had taken, exclaimed in mock anger: "Who booked these hotel accommodations?"

We spent the night on steel benches, and were given nothing to eat or drink. The toilet was in the middle of the room so that the electronic "eye" in the doorway could watch every move. Osho was in an identical cage-type cell on His own, and next to Him, Devaraj, Jayesh, and the three male pilots.

Devaraj to Osho through the cell bars:

"Bhagwan?"

"Mm?" Osho replied.

"Are you alright, Bhagwan?"

"Mm mm," came the reply. There was a pause, and then from Bhagwan's side came His voice, "Devaraj?"

"Yes, Bhagwan"

"What is happening?"

"I don't know, Bhagwan."

There was a long pause, then Bhagwan's voice:

"When are we continuing?"

And Devaraj responded, "I don't know."

There was another pause, then Bhagwan's voice again:

"There must be a mistake or something.

It has to be cleared up."

Third in the row of cages were we four girls, and a woman pilot who was crying and screaming. I looked at the contrast between our centeredness and the woman who was pacing up and down and shouting and I felt grateful that even in this situation I could feel the meditative quality in me that Osho had been teaching me for years. I had not had the opportunity to experience it before so clearly.

I had my moments of rage though. It was obvious that the prison system is designed to break a person, to humiliate, frighten, and then reduce a person into an obedient slave. During the first few hours we were told that it was against the rules to give a prisoner coffee. This is because it is often thrown into the face of the guard. I was shocked when I heard this and couldn't understand how anyone would throw hot coffee over the very person who was giving it to him. A few hours later I understood perfectly, and I knew exactly who would be wearing my hot coffee, should I be given the opportunity.

All night and all day we remained in our cages and then we went to the courtroom for the decision to be made about our bail. It would take only about twenty minutes, we were told, just the usual procedure.

In order to move us to the courtroom we had to be put in leg irons, as well as handcuffs that were joined by a chain to our waists. Two men went into Osho's cell and I watched them through the bars. They were very rough with Him and one of them kicked Osho as they pushed Him to face the wall. He kicked Osho's legs apart and then pushed Him around. To see this kind of brutality done to a new born child could not have been more repulsive. Osho does not have even the smallest fraction of resistance in Him. To pluck a flower is violence as far as Osho is concerned. His frailty and gentleness is awesome.

I saw the man who did it. I can still see his face. I was so enraged and helpless to do anything that whenever I saw the man I used to stare at his head and will it to burst.

The question of bail was a lie from the very beginning. I took note that the judge, a homely looking woman called Barbara De Laney, never once looked at Osho throughout the whole court proceedings. At one point during the "trial" our lawyer, Bill Diehl said:

"Well, your honor, it seems your mind is already made up. We might as well all go home."

Osho was accused of unlawful flight. It was said that He had knowledge of a warrant for His arrest on immigration charges and He was trying to avoid it. We were charged with aiding and abetting unlawful flight and concealing a person from arrest.

We were sick with worry that if Osho had to spend another night in jail, He would become dangerously ill. For many years His diet had been specially controlled because of diabetes, and He took medicine at set times. His whole routine was strictly scheduled and never broken. If He didn't eat the right food at certain times then He could become sick. He was asthmatic and allergic to smells of any kind. For years He had been watched over and even the smell of a new curtain, or someone's perfume could bring on an asthma attack. His back condition of a prolapsed injured vertebral disc was still present, and in fact never did heal.

It was requested that Osho be looked after in a hospital facility.

"Your honor," began Osho, " I ask you a simple question..."

He was interrupted by the judge and arrogantly told to speak through counsel.

Osho continued: "Your honor, I have been sick the whole night on these steel benches and I have been asking those people continuously — not even a pillow."

"I don't think they have a pillow," said Judge De Laney.

"Sleeping on the steel benches — I cannot sleep on the benches," Osho continued, "I cannot eat anything that they can give."

It was asked that Osho at least keep His own clothing as He could be allergic to materials provided by the jail.

"No, for security reasons," said the judge.

The hearing was to be continued the next day and we were to be transferred to Mecklenberg County Jail. At least we were out of the Marshal's cell. In the last few days of Osho's life He was to say to His doctor that:

"It all started in the Marshal's cell."

We were taken to Mecklenberg County Jail, and again our hands and feet were chained. The chains on my feet cut into my ankles very badly and it was difficult to walk. Osho never lost His graceful way of moving, even with the leg irons on, and the first time Osho saw that Vivek and I were chained together, He laughed!

When a prisoner is moved in or out of the prison he waits in a windowless cell about eight feet long, with room for a single steel cot, and there is about six inches of space before the knees touch the wall.

Vivek and I sat on the steel cot side by side choking on the smell of urine. There were shit and blood stains smeared on the walls and the heavy door was pitted with scars, obviously from past occupants going crazy and pitifully throwing themselves against it. We looked at each other wide eyed when we heard two men on the other side of the door, discussing us in their Southern drawl. They were talking about the four Rajneesh women and what they would like to do with them. How they looked, "and one is having her period," they said (how did they know that?). We waited for two hours, with fears of rape attacks and abuse, not knowing whether this was to be our permanent place or not. But the most devastating thing was knowing that Osho was being treated the same as we were, and we couldn't see Him.

Throughout the jail experience the worst thing was knowing that Osho was not getting any better treatment than anyone else, and if He was treated like this...!

Our clothes were taken away, as were Osho's, and we were given prison clothes. They were old and obviously washed many times, although the underarms were stiff with old sweat, and when they warmed up with my own body heat I had to endure the stink of the many people who had worn the clothes before me. It was so gross that when offered a change of clothes three days later I refused, because at least I hadn't caught crabs or scabies, and who knows, next time — ?

I heard from Nurse Carter, who was helping to care for Osho, that when Osho was given His clothes He simply said in a joking voice, "But they don't match!"

The bed linen was far worse than the clothes, so I went to bed fully dressed. The sheets were torn and stained yellow/grey; the blanket was full of holes and made of wool. Wool! Osho is allergic to wool. Niren, our lawyer, took new cotton blankets to the prison for Osho, but He never received them.

The prison is a Christian establishment. A priest visits the cells with a bible and talks of Christ's teachings. I felt as though I had gone back in time five hundred years, it all seemed so barbaric.

Ninety-nine percent of the inmates were black. Can it be that only black people commit crimes, or is it that only black people are punished?

I entered my cell, that I was to share with about twelve junkies and prostitutes. "Help," I said to myself: "What about AIDS?" The women stopped what they were doing and all heads turned as I crossed the floor to the empty bunk, carrying my flea-bitten mattress. For a moment I was in the gap. Then I walked over to the table and benches, where some of them were playing cards, and asked them if I could play. I also wanted to learn how to speak with a Southern accent before I left the jail.

I enjoyed the prisoners and found them more intelligent than people I met outside the prison. They said that they had seen me on television with my guru and they couldn't understand why we had been arrested and put in jail with so much fuss, for an immigration charge. They couldn't understand what was going on, why we were being treated like big criminals. I thought that if it was so obvious to these girls, then surely a lot of Americans were going to be outraged at Osho's arrest and someone with intelligence, courage, and power, would step forward and say, "Hey...wait a minute...what's happening here?" I was totally convinced that it would happen. This is called hope, and I was to live on hope for five days.

After a few hours my cell was changed, but I didn't ask why, because I was relieved to see I was to join Vivek, Nirupa and Mukti. We had a cell with two other prisoners which consisted of three sets of two bunks in a row, a table and bench, a shower and a television set that was only switched off at sleeping time.

Sheriff Kidd was in charge of the prison, and I believe he did his best for Osho, under the circumstances. He said to Vivek and I while we were having our mug shots taken that, "He (Osho) is an innocent man." Nurse Carter was sensitive to Osho also, and she brought us messages each day such as, "Your boy ate all his grits (a Southern version of porridge) today." Looking through the bars of my cell one morning, I saw Osho greet Deputy Chief Samuels in a way that stopped time for me, and changed the prison into a temple. He took Samuels' hands in His and they stood looking at each other for a few moments. Osho looked at him with such love and respect. The meeting was not taking place in a jail, although in reality it was.

Osho gave a press conference and was seen on television in prison clothes, answering questions from the press. The first time I saw Osho in prison clothes I was shocked by a beauty that I had never seen before. As I walked away with Vivek, we looked at each other and simultaneously exclaimed "Lao Tzu!" He looked like the ancient Chinese master, Lao Tzu.

The prison warders warmed to us and had respect for Osho, and I saw that there were good people there, but the system is inhuman and they don't realize it. One of the guards, while taking us down in the lift on our way to court, turned to us and said, "God bless you people." She quickly turned away, embarrassed or not wanting anyone to overhear.

We were allowed to visit the exercise yard each day for about fifteen minutes. Osho's second floor cell had a long window overlooking the yard and an inmate arranged it so when we went to the yard, we would throw up a shoe and Osho would appear at the window and wave. It was difficult to see Him clearly, but we could recognize Him and His gently waving hand was clear. We danced and wept with joy, once in the pouring rain, and it was *darshan* for us. The misty figure in the window reminded me of saints on stained glass windows in cathedrals. On our way back to our cell the guards used to exclaim that we went down to the yard with long faces and came back laughing — what happened?

Over the next four days in the courtroom I watched as American "justice" revealed itself as a farce. Government agents lied on the stand, evidence was produced against Osho from *sannyasins* who had been blackmailed into telling lies. Crimes committed by Sheela were produced even though they had no relation whatsoever to Osho's case. Day after day passed as I saw that there was no sense in this world, no understanding, no justice.

My hopes were in vain, that there would be someone in America who would come forward to say that what was happening was inhuman and insane. There was nobody out there. Osho was alone. He has said that a genius, a man of the calibre of Buddha, is always ahead of his time, that he will never be known by his contemporaries. In this country called America Osho was in a barren and barbaric land, and there was nobody with the guts to hear what He was saying or to try and understand.

The trial lasted five days and on the day they took our chains off, a reporter shouted to us as we left the courthouse

"How does it feel without your chains?" I paused, put my hands in the air and said, "It feels the same."

No bail was to be given to Osho. He was to travel to Portland, Oregon, as a prisoner and a decision would be made there. It was a six hour flight. I saw Him on the television news being escorted up the steps of the prison plane. Even though His feet and hands were in chains He moved with such grace, as only a man of awareness can move. The way He moved broke my heart.

We were allowed to say goodbye to Him through the cell bars. Mukti, Nirupa and I went and put our hands through the bars and wept. He got up from the steel cot, walked towards us, and holding our hands, said:

"You go. And no need to worry. I will be out soon. Everything will be okay — you go happy."

Waiting in the office of the jail to be released, while watching Osho on the television, I heard a policeman say:

"That man really has something. No matter what is happening to him, he remains relaxed and peaceful."

I wanted to tell the whole world that here is the Master, arrested and accused of false crimes, abused by the American judicial system, physically suffering, and about to be dragged across the States at the point of a gun — and He says for us to "go happy." Couldn't they see from this small statement what kind of man He is?

My energy turned, I stopped crying and I looked at Him. Happiness has a strength and happiness is His message. "I will go happy and I will be strong," I vowed to myself. I found an inner strength, but my happiness was superficial. It was like a band-aid on open heart surgery.

We all returned to Rajneeshpuram and left Osho in the hands of the people who were to kill Him.

The journey from North Carolina to Portland which should have taken six hours took seven days and Osho was put in four different prisons. During His incarceration He was exposed to radiation and given the poison, thallium.

We waited in Rajneeshpuram for ever. On November 6th nothing had been heard of Osho since the evening of November 4th, when it was said that He had landed in Oklahoma. The journey should only take six hours! and already it had been three days since He left Charlotte.

The prison authorities would not reveal His whereabouts and it took a lot of shouting by Vivek to start a search. Bill Diehl, who had taken such care with us in Charlotte as our lawyer, and who had worked so lovingly for Osho, flew to Oklahoma. Osho was found, after He had been moved twice to different prisons and had been forced to sign Himself in under a false name — David Washington. This was obviously so that no trace could be found in the prison records of Bhagwan Shree Rajneesh should anything "happen" to him.

Osho arrived back in Portland twelve days after the arrest and was granted bail.

Osho rested, sleeping twenty hours a day for the next few days. There was to be a court hearing on Thursday 12th November. The night before, I was told that after the court hearing Osho would be leaving America for India.

Laxmi, was now on the scene again, having been away from the commune for four years, and I was present at a meeting with her and Osho when she was telling Him of a place she had found in the Himalayas where a new commune could be started. She told Him of the magnificent river, with an island in the middle of it. "That," said Osho, "is where we will build the new Buddha Hall." There were many small bungalows and a large house for Osho, she said, and added that she saw no difficulty in getting planning permission for extensive building.

Osho was ready to start all over again. Despite being betrayed by some of His *sannyasins*, and despite His ill health, His work had to continue. I was astounded at the total enthusiasm with which He discussed details for our new commune.

I packed at least twenty huge trunks, as I had the idea that if we were to be miles up in the Himalayas, then how were we going to get supplies of warm clothes, toiletries, special foods, etc., and I wanted to take as many of Osho's clothes as possible. The sewing room might not be in operation again for a long time.

The next day Vivek and Devaraj left before Osho, leaving me to accompany Him to Portland. I was already feeling the pain of separation from the commune, even though, if Laxmi was to be believed, we would be together again soon. Still, the pain was there.

While packing the few things in Osho's room, He picked up His Shiva statue that He had talked about many times in discourse and said, "Give this to the commune, they can sell it." He then walked across the room to His Buddha statue that He loved so much and said the same. I stuttered, "Oh, no! Please not these, you love them so much," but He insisted. Then He said that when His watches came back from the Federal Agents they were to be placed on the podium in the Meditation Hall so that everyone could see them. He then said to tell His people that, "These watches will be your air fares to India."

We did not know, nor could have imagined, that the government would steal all His watches. When we were arrested in Charlotte all our belongings were confiscated. Some of them were returned after a legal battle, one year later, but they kept Osho's watches. This is sheer piracy.

I said goodbye to my friends, and I went outside and bowed down to "my" mountain, that I had slept under, climbed over, and simply sat and looked at for the last four years. Then I called Avesh in the garage to bring the car up, just like I had done many times before.

Avesh drove and I sat in the back with Osho. From Basho's Pond, past Rajneesh Mandir, winding through downtown Rajneeshpuram, and out to the airport were people. People dressed in red, playing musical instruments, singing, dancing, waving goodbye to their Master. Musicians followed the car all the way to the airport, some running all the way carrying their Brazilian drums. I saw such beautiful faces, some of the people who years before had looked dull, and now were transformed, shiny and alive. Osho sat and *namasted* His people for the last time in Rajneeshpuram. I felt rigid with pain but wouldn't allow myself to break down. It was not the time for emotional outbursts. I was there to take care of Osho, and I said to myself, "Later I will cry, but not now."

We reached the small plane on the runway and Osho turned around on the steps to wave to everyone. The runway was filled with people, optimistic, beaming faces, playing music and giving their Master a good send off. I took one last look out of the small window as the plane took off, and looked at Osho as He sat silently, leaving behind His people, His dream.

CHAPTER NINE

Crucifixion American Style

I t was getting dark as we drove through the rain-soaked streets of Portland on that afternoon in mid-November. A police escort the size of a president's motor cavalcade flanked the Rolls Royce. There were at least fifty policemen, looking like giants in shiny black clothes, their faces covered with helmets and goggles, riding powerful Harley Davidson bikes. All the roads were cordoned off at each junction, and the bikers did an impressively choreographed maneuver as two on each side of the car would be smoothly replaced by another pair — they drove in and around the traffic like stunt men.

It was in this fanfare of sirens and giant bodyguards that Osho stepped out of the car, untouched as always by anything happening on the "outside," and glided smoothly into the courtroom, accompanied by six or eight plainclothes policemen. I stepped out on the other side of the car into chaos — hordes of pushing people, press, and television crews. I wasn't allowed to follow Osho through the same door and so for a moment I stood watching Him disappear into a sea of grey and black suits that filled the courthouse corridor. I pushed my way through the crowds and found another entrance, and after much fuss I was sitting beside Osho in the courtroom.

Osho sat relaxed and peaceful, watching the drama from the wings.

Later, Osho was to say: "The government blackmailed my attorneys. Ordinarily it never happens that the government takes the initiative in negotiating, but just before my trial they called my attorneys for negotiations and hinted in many ways... They made it clear that, 'We don't have any evidence, any proof: we know it and you know it — that if you go ahead with the case, you will win. But we have to make it clear that the government will not like to be defeated by a single individual; we will not allow an individual to win the case. The case can be prolonged for twenty years, and Bhagwan will remain in jail. And there is always a risk to Bhagwan's life — that you should understand clearly.'

"Niren was crying when the attorneys came out of the meeting. He said, 'We can't do anything, we are helpless; we feel ashamed to ask you to say that you are guilty. You are not guilty and we are asking you to say that you are, because from what the government has said, they are making it clear that your life will be at risk.'

"They told me," Bhagwan continued, "that if I accepted two minor crimes I would be released and just deported. I was ready to remain, to die in jail — there was no problem — but when they started saying, 'Think about your people,' then I thought that this (saying he was guilty when he was not) was not a point to take seriously."

Osho was accused of thirty-four immigration violations — two were accepted. What happened to the other thirty-two? The judge must have been a criminal, because negotiations took place, but can crimes be negotiated? Is crime a business?

Even the two crimes that were accepted were bogus. One that He had arrived in America with intent to stay and two that He had arranged for a foreigner to marry an American citizen.

1. Osho had been writing to INS to apply for immigration status for years and they had not replied to any of His letters. Why?

2. He was accused of arranging thousands of marriages and "at least one was certain" — is this a joke? — one was certain! What happened to the other thousands, and anyway that one was not proved.

My mouth fell open as I heard the judge read out that Osho had come to America in order to create a place of meditation for many people, because His *ashram* in India was too small. This was a crime!

Osho did not stir, He was humble and yet He was a king. His childlike innocence and vulnerability somehow made Him untouchable. He was totally accepting, but not turning the other cheek. Opposites meet where emptiness is vast enough, and I have heard him say that:

Judge Leavy asked Osho, "Do you plead guilty or not?"

Osho answered, "I am."

Our lawyer, Jack Ransome stood up beside Osho and said, "Guilty." This happened twice, and when I asked Osho later about His response to the plea He said to me, laughing:

"Because I am not guilty! My answer simply states that I am.

"Our lawyer answered, 'Guilty' immediately. It is his problem whether he is guilty or not."

The court imposed a sentence of ten years imprisonment, with suspension of execution. Also, Osho would be on probation for five years, under the condition that He leave the United States and agree not to return during the five-year probation period without permission of the attorney general of the United States.

When the judge asked Osho if He understood that He could not re-enter America for a further five years, Osho said, "Of course, but you don't have to limit my entry to five years — I am not going to step on this land again." The judge said, "You may change your mind," but Osho just remained silent and smiled. Later I asked Him why He had remained silent and smiling, and Osho replied:

"For the same reason that Jesus remained silent when Pontius Pilate asked him, 'What is truth?' I also remained silent and smiled because this poor fellow does not realize that I don't have a mind to change."

Osho was fined half-a-million dollars for two minor charges of the sort usually punished by a twenty-five dollar fine and deportation.

Hasya, with help of friends, produced the fine within ten minutes and Osho was out of the courtroom, and driving through the wet streets of Portland. Crowds of people lined the streets, some waving their hands, and some waving a finger. The lights of the shops were reflected in the puddles and I looked out of the car window and saw that the shop windows were filled with Christmas decorations. Life had been beyond bizarre these last few weeks — but this! This hypocrisy called Christmas was too much.

We drove straight to the airport where a group of *sannyasins* and reporters were waiting at the steps of Osho's plane, with Vivek standing in the doorway to meet Him. As He reached the top of the steps He turned around to wave. I watched Him, as rain fell and the wind blew His beard in the night air. I was mesmerized by His gentle beauty and paralyzed by the awful significance of the moment. Goodbye America. Goodbye World. The door was closing as I realized that I was also leaving and I propelled myself forward, through the crowd, up the steps and into the warm, crowded cabin. Vivek was settling Osho down on three seats as a makeshift bed. His pillows and blanket were nestled around Him and He lay down and closed His eyes. This unfamiliar sight was to become much too familiar over the next year, when at times, the cabin of a plane, flying over the planet, was to be our only "home."

Flying out of America was the best feeling I had had in a long time. We opened a bottle of champagne and celebrated as Osho slept peacefully. Osho slept from take-off to touch down, always and everywhere.

On the plane were Vivek, Devaraj, Nirupa, Mukti, Hasya, Asheesh, and Rafia. It was a small jet — the large plane we were expecting had cancelled on hearing who their passengers were and so most of the party, including Osho's family, had been left behind in Portland to follow on commercial flights.

We landed in Cyprus because we did not have permission to fly over the Arab countries, and there was a Muslim holiday so there was nobody to give us permission, either.

We were a hilarious sight in Cyprus airport. We had flown out of the Oregon winter into the sweltering heat of the Mediterranean dressed in boots, fur-lined coats, scarves and hats. Eight of us, dressed entirely in red, with Osho wearing His long robe, knitted hat (studded with diamonds, as the press were to say) and His long flowing silver beard. The airport officials were agog as they tried to figure out what was going on and what they should do. The situation was not helped by a stray reporter who happened to be in the airport and shouted out for the officials to hear "Bhagwan Shree Rajneesh! He has just been deported from America." However, after an hour of filling in forms while Osho sat in the dirty, smoke-filled waiting room, we were allowed into Cyprus and took off in taxis for the "best" hotel.

It was about two in the morning and we were too hyped up to sleep, so I sat on the balcony of my hotel room. I looked out into the night and wept. I had been witness to a modern day crucifixion and I was flooded with memories of seeing Osho in chains, prison, unreal court scenes, and the end of Rajneeshpuram and all the beautiful people there. I knew the truth of what we had been trying to create in America, knew the innocence and joy of all the people, and I felt as though existence itself had turned against us and there was no chance in the world for people like us.

The next afternoon, with permission to fly over the Arab countries, we were on our way to India. India! My last hope. America had proved to be barbaric and had no understanding of Osho, but India will be different. Indian people understand what enlightenment is, they know the search for Truth, and they respect "holy" men. Even if only out of superstition, Indian people have a respect for a man who is a great teacher and certainly they know Osho. He had spent thirty years travelling in India, sometimes giving lectures to crowds as large as fifty thousand. I was certain that India would welcome their "Godman" home with open arms. The treatment Osho had received in America would confirm their suspicions that the West had no understanding of inner riches. "They will give Him land, and a place to live," I thought.

We arrived in Delhi at 2.30 a.m, twenty-four hours later than expected because of our stay in Cyprus. That gave thousands of people time to reach the airport, and it must have created a tremendously tense atmosphere as people waited and waited, and waited. When we arrived at the immigration counters and I looked out at the mob beyond, I was frightened. There were hundreds of reporters and TV crews with cameras and they were standing on chairs and tables as the sea of excited and frantic looking people pushed and shoved each other, all wanting to touch 'The Guru.'

Laxmi was there, all four feet ten inches of her, and Anando, who had travelled with Laxmi from America a few days before (Anando whom I met in the white tunnel at the beginning of my *sannyas* journey). The rest of our party were held up in customs, and that left Vivek and Osho to reach the exit and get in the waiting car, through the crazed mob. I followed, despite Vivek shouting at me to "go back, go back." I still can't understand why she said that, it was an impossible situation. People were pulling at Osho's clothes, one woman jumped on Him from behind with her arms wrapped around His neck, others were throwing themselves at His feet, banging His legs, hurting His feet, and almost knocking Him to the ground. The people at the back were pushing hard to join in the action and reporters were springing in front of Osho trying to ask questions. There was only one way through this, and I wasn't going to go back to the immigration counter and watch. I grabbed people by their arms, or hair — anything I could get hold of — and tried to clear the path. Anando was doing the same, and Laxmi, despite her size put up a good fight. Osho smiled at everyone and with His hands folded in *namaste*, glided serenely along the treacherous path. When we finally reached the car it took a good five minutes just to open the door against the crush of people, and an immense amount of strength to keep the door open while Osho got in.

I stood trembling as the car moved away, and I started to relax. We were in India and Osho was safe!

CHAPTER TEN

Kulu

The flight to Kulu Manali took off from Delhi at 10.00 a.m. It had already been a full morning as Osho had given a press conference at 7.00 a.m. in the Hyatt Regency Hotel, in which He spared no bones while expressing what He thought of America.

I had snatched a couple of hours sleep, before a hair-raising and chaotic race through Delhi on a lorry, with the trunks that the Indian press had described as "silver and encrusted with jewels." These were the very same trunks that I had packed two nights before that had been bought at a hardware store in the middle of redneck country.

Osho's mother, Mataji, had joined us with some of her family, and close behind was Haridas who had been living with us in Rajneeshpuram. Ashu, young, red-haired and with porcelain skin and a wicked laugh, was Osho's dental nurse, and she traveled with Haridas and Mukta. Mukta was one of Osho's first Western disciples and hails from a Greek shipping family. She has a mane of silver hair and has been Osho's gardener for many years. I was happy to see that Rafia was traveling with us. He had been Vivek's closest friend throughout the last two years. He emanates a strength that is centered deep inside and yet he is light and playful and always ready to laugh. We filled the plane, but the trunks would not fit and so they were to follow — we hoped!

Aah! what joy it was to finally sit in a plane that was taking off — nothing more to do. I looked down the aisle of the plane and saw Osho sitting next to the window drinking a juice. Osho had spoken so much about the Himalayas and I felt thrilled that He would see them, and I would be able to see Him looking at them. However, these were not the romantic snow capped peaks, this was only the foothills of the Himalayas, but still....

Hasya and Anando were to stay in Delhi and work. Osho suspected that the government would make it difficult for Western disciples, and there were contacts to be made and arrangements regarding the purchasing of property.

It was only a two hour flight, and then we were driving along winding roads, up into the hills. The local people we saw along the way were very poor, but had a grandeur that the poverty-stricken souls in Bombay did not have. They had beautiful faces that told of mixed blood, maybe Tibetan? The property, called Span, was about fifteen kilometers away and the road for most of the way ran parallel with a river, then across a rickety bridge past miles of primitive looking stone walls, and winter landscape.

The cars suddenly turned right and we drove into a totally different world. Here was a rather nice looking holiday resort, with about ten stone cottages centered around a large building of stone with two walls of window overlooking a river. One of the small bungalows nearest the river was to be Osho's and the big house was where we would eat, watch movies and shout into the telephone in many hopeless attempts to speak to Hasya.

But there was something about the place that didn't quite click. The management in the large house never treated us as though we were the people who had bought the property, and I wondered! Maybe they didn't know that we were the new tenants yet.

Osho was out the next morning looking over the property and saying to Rafia that the mountain over the river would be purchased, and a bridge built across to it. He walked around, hand on hip and told Rafia of His vision of the place and its possibilities. This touching and inspiring scenario was to be repeated whenever Osho arrived somewhere. Immediately, He would have a vision of it and would be pointing to buildings and pools, and gardens, yet to be built. For Osho, wherever He was, was 'The Place.'

The Indian press came to interview Osho, sometimes twice a day, either in His living room, or on the porch overlooking the river.

The river bed was very rocky and so the water made a tremendous noise as it rushed past. It was a small river though, and how anyone ever imagined an island in the middle of it was beyond me. Osho walked each day along the river, and past the cottages to a bench where He sat and looked at the Himalayas. Each day the approaching snow could be seen as it covered the mountains. Many old friends came to visit Osho and they would meet on His walk and chat. Sometimes I accompanied Him on the walk and we sat together on a bench as the river roared past and the pale winter sun turned the tops of the mountains golden.

News of Rajneeshpuram filtered in and I heard how the American government had frozen the assets of the commune and declared it bankrupt. Hundreds of *sannyasins* were leaving the commune and going out into the world with no money. It felt to me like a time of war, when families and friends are separated and lost. I had always presumed that the commune would be there for ever, and now I thought of all the times I had been miserable because my boyfriend had chosen to be with another woman. I could have used those times to enjoy myself, if I had only known how temporary it all was. I reflected that death would come one day, just like the American government, and I vowed that I would not look back and regret. There is no time to be unhappy.

A reporter asked Osho:

"Do you feel any kind of responsibility towards your *sannyasins* who have lived in your commune, invested money, sometimes their inheritance, and their working powers into the projects of the commune...?"

Osho:

"Responsibility according to me is something individual. I can be responsible only for my acts, my thoughts. I cannot be responsible for your acts or your thoughts.

"There are people who have given their whole inheritance. I have also given my whole life. Who is responsible? They are not responsible because I have given my whole life to them, and their money is not more valuable than my life. With my life I can find thousands of people like them. With their money they cannot find another me.

"But I don't think that they are responsible for it. It was my joy, I loved each moment of it, and I will continue to give my life to my people, to the very last breath without making anybody feel guilty that he is responsible..."

Sarjano came to visit during the first week in December and to interview Osho for a magazine. He is one of Osho's wild Italian disciples, and quite unusual in that he has always been able to keep contact with the magazine world with his talent for photography and his writing, and also has spent years sitting at Osho's feet. To follow up on the article he arranged for a television company to come and make a documentary about Osho. He contacted Enzo Biagi, who represented Italy's national television. Biagi was a well-known film maker in Italy, who had his own show, "Spotlight." The Indian Embassy refused to grant visas, and for me this was the first indication that India was as unable to recognize a Buddha as any other country. The US Attorney, Charles Turner, had made it quite clear the US government's intention was that Osho should be isolated in India, cut off from foreign disciples, restricted in access to foreign press, with no freedom of speech. Clearly Osho's work, or message to the world, was to be finished, and obviously India was not beyond the reach of powerful American pressure.

Meanwhile we lived one day at a time, and my days were filled with the laundry — which was quite different from my set up in Rajneeshpuram! I washed clothes in a bucket in an Indian-style bathroom, which consisted of one tap through which came rust-filled water. The adjoining bedroom was where I ironed on the bed, and hung the clothes to dry with buckets and bowls to catch the dripping water. Osho's beautiful robes soon started losing their shape, picking up the damp smell of Kulu, and the whites turned brown. But I was lucky, for within a couple of weeks the snow would be coming and then there would be no electricity and no water at all — only snow to melt.

Osho was often speaking to the press twice a day and we sat outside listening to Him with the background sound of the rushing river and the thin pale sunlight on our faces. I heard Him say that, "Challenge will make you strong." His patience with his interviewers was immense. Many of the Indian press would interrupt Him as He was speaking, to agree or disagree. I had never heard such a thing and sometimes these interactions were hilariously funny.

Neelam and her daughter, Priya, arrived from Rajneeshpuram. They had been with Osho for fifteen years, since Priya was born, and are beautiful women who look like sisters. They are two of the many Indian disciples of Osho who are a perfect blend of East and West.

Neelam gave Osho His lunch and accompanied Him on His walk, the day that all nine of us went off to get our visa extensions from Mr. Negi, the police superintendent in Kulu. We had a very pleasant meeting with him as he supplied us with countless cups of *chai* and seemed very pleased to have such a lively audience to whom to tell his stories of tourists who had been eaten by bears. He assured us that there would be no problem, we shook hands and drove back happily to Span.

The next day, December 10th, I was in my room when Devaraj came to tell me that our visa extensions had been canceled. I felt nauseous and sat on the bed. How was it possible? The efficiency of the Indian immigration office was, in itself, worrying. I thought to myself that it must be an urgent and serious case for them — I had never experienced Indian authorities getting anything done quickly. It was difficult at that time to even make a telephone call because winter was closing in. The weather conditions were worsening and the plane flights to Delhi were being canceled regularly. Trying to connect with Hasya in Delhi had been so difficult that on one occasion she found it quicker to take the plane and visit us than to try and speak on the telephone.

That same day the police arrived at Span, asked for all the foreigners and stamped in our passports, "Ordered to leave India immediately." Vivek, Devaraj, Rafia, Ashu, Mukta and Haridas missed them by minutes as they had gone to Delhi to re-apply for visa extensions.

The day before Vivek left for Delhi I heard her talking to Neelam, telling her that Osho had said that if we were all to be deported, then He would come too. Vivek was asking Neelam, "Please, don't let Him follow us, because at least in India He is safe."

Hasya and Anando had been busy in Delhi making appointments to see officials there. Arun Nehru was the Minister for Internal Security then, the man at the root of this problem, but their appointments with him were continually canceled. When they did see an official they were to be told "confidentially" that we should look within our group to see from where the trouble came. It appeared that Laxmi had written to the Home Office giving full details of all the foreign disciples and her words were to be repeated to us that "it was not necessary that Osho needs foreigners to see to His welfare." It was necessary actually, because more important to Osho than life itself was His work, and Westerners were needed for that. Osho was to say, "My Indian disciples meditate, but will not do anything for me. My Western disciples will do anything for me, but will not meditate." I didn't understand this at the time, but was soon to learn.

That afternoon, just before Osho was to take His walk along the river, there was a great commotion at the main gate of Span. I went to investigate and the staff of Span were in a desperate struggle with a busload of drunken Sikhs who had arrived and were shouting aggressively about Osho and wanting to see Him.

I ran across the lawns and zig-zagged through the cottages to where Osho was already standing on the porch waiting to go for a walk. He was visible from the road and I said to Him to please go inside, there was a busload of drunken Sikhs who were becoming violent. We went inside and I closed the curtains of the sitting room. Rain started to fall outside and the room darkened as I looked at Osho and He said:

"Sikhs! but I have never said anything against Sikhs. Such stupidity! What do these people want?" And then, as He sat on the edge of the sofa with His shoulders hunched He said, "This world is insane, what's the point in living?"

I had never seen Osho anything other than blissful. Throughout jail and the destruction of the commune He had remained untouched. He was not sad now, or angry, just tired. He looked tired as He sat there looking at nothing and I stood a few feet away from Him unable to move. Anything I could have said would have been superficial, any gesture I could have made would have been meaningless. It went through my mind that it was His freedom to feel like this and there was nothing I must do to interfere. We remained frozen in our stances as the sound of the falling rain filled the room and I felt as though I was standing on the edge of a precipice, looking into a dark abyss.

After how long, I will never know, out of the corner of my eye I saw a chink of sunlight coming through the curtain. I moved across the room and opened the curtains — the rain had stopped. I went outside and it was silent. The Sikhs had left.

"Osho, would you like to go for your walk?" I asked.

As we walked along the river I felt such overwhelming joy I could barely contain myself from dancing around Him like a puppy dog as He walked. He was smiling, and waiting near the lawn were some *sannyasins* to greet Him. Among them, two old friends, Kusum and Kapil who were two of the first people to take *sannyas*, with their grown-up child, who Osho had not seen since he was born. He touched the boy lovingly and chatted in Hindi to them for a long time. I was walking on air. This was the first day of my life, everything was so new and fresh.

Since that day whenever I feel surrounded by darkness and hopelessness, I stop still and wait. I simply wait.

At night I would read to Osho. I read the Bible to Him, or rather *The X-Rated Bible*, by Ben Edward Akerley. It was a newly published book that consisted of three hundred pages, untampered with, straight out of the Bible. These pages are pure pornography and it is one of the biggest jokes to me that probably even the Pope does not read the Bible, otherwise he would freak out.

When we left Rajneeshpuram everyone in our small group left their jewelry behind for sale. Osho had given me a necklace, ring, and watch, and looking at my naked wrist in Kulu one day He asked me where my watch was. A few days before, Kusum and Kapil had given Osho a gold chain bracelet as a gift, and He told me to go and get the bracelet from His bedroom table, it was mine. I was touched, because He also did not have anything, and this was the first gift He had received since He left everything behind in America. He said that, "Please don't let Kusum see, because it may upset her." My eyes filled with tears when He then went on to say that, "One day, when we settle, I will be able to give everyone a present."

I saw the police arriving one morning, and as they entered the manager's building, I ran to tell Osho, and with a great flourish I announced their arrival.

"What are they here for?" He asked.

"Oh, they are just more players in the drama," I said with a theatrical wave of my arm.

He looked at me in a way that told me He definitely did NOT need an esoteric answer from me. He wanted to know what was really happening, so feeling a bit foolish I ran to Neelam to get the bad news. We had to leave — now.

The police left and Asheesh, Nirupa and I packed our bags. We would be in time for the plane to Delhi. I went to say good-bye to Mataji, Osho's mother, and Taru, and all the family. I wept so much I was a little worried that I had overdone it and upset Mataji. This felt like good-bye forever.

Before approaching Osho I looked at Him for a few minutes. He was sitting on the porch, with the Himalayas in the background, peaks now covered in snow. The robe He was wearing had always been one of my favorites; it was dark blue and one of the few that really washed well. His eyes were closed and He looked far, far away. I had been here before — *deja vu* — the disciple leaving his master in the mountains. It was all so familiar as I touched His feet and rested my forehead on the ground. He bent down and touched my head, and with tears streaming I thanked Him for everything He had given me. I said good-bye and dragged my numb body to the car and we drove away. As we drove out of the gate I turned my head and looked back.

Two hours later we were at Kulu airport and with more

tearful good-byes we approached the plane carrying our suitcases. The pilot from the Delhi-Kulu flight handed us a letter that Vivek had given him in Delhi, telling us that they had not got the extensions arranged, but as it was a weekend (today was Friday), then stay with Osho until Monday. Anyway we had until Tuesday officially to be out of the country.

We drove straight back to Span and I was in Osho's sitting room, my drama of a few hours before light years away. He woke up from his lunch time nap and walked in:

"Hello Chetana," He chuckled.

The police arrived again and were furious with us. They had seen us at the airport and wanted to know why we did not get on the plane. Were we trying to trick them? Neelam, with enough charm to stop a hurricane, explained the situation. It was the weekend; the plane was gone; the roads were full of ice; anyway, we couldn't leave India today, etc. They stormed off and said they would be back in a few hours but they didn't return.

Osho spoke about going to Nepal, and Indians do not need a visa for Nepal, so it would be easy. His work would not grow here in the back of beyond with only a few devotees, who would love Him and take care; but it wasn't for Him to just live happily ever after with a few disciples. His message had to reach hundreds of thousands around the world. He said in Crete a few months later:

"In India I told *sannyasins* not to come to Kulu Manali because we wanted to purchase land and houses in Kulu Manali; and if thousands of *sannyasins* had started coming, immediately the orthodox, the old-fashioned people would have started freaking out. And the politicians are always looking for an opportunity...

"Those few days that I was not with my sannyasins, not talking to them, not looking in their eyes, not looking at their faces, not listening to their laughter, I felt undernourished."
(*Socrates Poisoned Again After 25 Centuries*)

Thus began a few days which I am sure Asheesh will never forget. The message had to get to Hasya, Anando, and Jayesh, who had now joined them in Delhi. They were to make arrangements for Osho to go to Nepal. The telephone wires were down, there were no planes during the weekend, and that meant a twelve-hour journey by taxi for Asheesh to take the message, receive an answer and come straight back. The roads were hazardous with ice and snow falling so thick that many roads were completely blocked. The distance between Kulu and Delhi is seven hundred kilometers.

The first night Asheesh took off in the car with instructions such as, "make contact with the cabinet ministers in Nepal." One was in fact a *sannyasin* and it was said that the King read Osho's books. But we didn't know at the time the full situation, and that is that the King had a brother who was wicked and in control of the army, the industries, and the police.

Asheesh reached Delhi at 6.00 a.m., had breakfast and was back in Kulu in the early evening. Ah Ha! Another message. Find a house in Nepal — a palace on the side of a lake.

Asheesh ate a quick supper and told us how the fog had been so dense on the road that it had been necessary for him to get out of the car and walk in front to avoid the driver going into a ditch. He then took another taxi to Delhi, and returned the next day with a reply, but he was staggering a little and bleary eyed. On this trip the car was lost in the fog, and when Asheesh explored his surroundings, he was in a dried up river bed. Silhouetted against the moon, that broke through the clouds for a moment, were three camels.

He could not sleep in the taxi, and now it was two nights and days that he had not slept. One more message, very important. Asheesh was delirious. He staggered out into the cold night with his missive and was back again just in time to catch the plane to Delhi with Nirupa and I.

Driven by extremely demanding situations, Asheesh blooms. When in Pune he had worked all day and all night without a break making a new chair for Osho, it was said by Osho that he (Asheesh) had a psychedelic experience when the chair was completed.

Asheesh, Nirupa and I touched Osho's feet, said good-bye and left Span, once more.

The police escorted us to the plane and on arrival in Delhi we met up with the rest of our group in a small hotel. Vivek, Devaraj and Rafia were to fly to Nepal first and look for the palace. We were to follow the next day and stay in the commune in Pokhara, about one hundred and eighty kilometers from Kathmandu.

A few days later Hasya's visa extension, which had been granted without any trouble a few weeks before, was canceled and police called at her hotel and took her to the airport at the point of a gun.

The Calcutta paper, The Telegraph, of December 26th, 1985, reported that: "The government has imposed a blanket ban on the entry of Bhagwan Rajneesh's foreign followers into the country." It went on to say that the decision had been taken by Arun Nehru of the Union Home and External Affairs Ministries. In addition, Indian embassies and foreign regional registration offices had been instructed not to grant visa extensions to any foreigner "if he or she was identified as a follower of Bhagwan Rajneesh. Such a person would not get any visa, even as a tourist." To justify the government's action, it was suggested that Osho was a CIA spy!

A very tired Asheesh, Nirupa, Haridas, Ashu, Mukta and I were at Delhi airport about to board the plane for Nepal, when one of the officials saw that I was missing one of the many papers that had been issued to us by the authorities. He said that I couldn't leave the country! I pointed to the page in my passport that read: "Ordered to leave India immediately," and asked him what the hell was he talking about, and if he didn't stop messing around I would miss my plane. He then called everyone back from the exit lounge, wrote our names down, let everyone go again, but kept me. He had by now called in three other officers and I was reeling with the insanity of the situation.

I was carrying a rose that I intended to place on Nepalese soil as some kind of symbolic offering. I gave him the rose, he took it, and with great embarrassment, laid it down quickly on his desk and told me to go.

CHAPTER ELEVEN

Nepal

I could feel the magic of Nepal before the plane landed, and I whispered, "I'm coming home!" The airport officials were gentle, smiling people, the people in the street had the most beautiful faces I had seen anywhere in the world, and although Nepal is poorer than India, they have a dignity and bearing that denies this.

The road to Pokhara wound through lush green jungle and when I got out to take a pee I walked into a grove where a small waterfall cascaded down to a pool surrounded by rocks, orchids wrapped themselves around trees like huge spiders, and a small stream curved out of sight into a mysterious looking dell. "Chetana! Chetana!" My name was being called and I was torn away from the magic spell. The van we were in, driven by two Nepali *sannyasins* who had met us at the airport, climbed up and down mountains that overlooked neatly layered rice fields, bamboo groves and gorges with fierce rushing rivers.

It was dark when we arrived at the commune in Pokhara fourteen hours later. Very dark — there was no electricity! We entered the dining room carrying a bottle of vodka and asked that it be put in the fridge, please. Maybe alcohol had never been on the premises before. I looked around and saw that the twenty or so *sannyasins* who lived there were either Indian or Nepali, and mostly men. The dining room was sixty feet long, with bare concrete walls and floor. It was empty except for the serving pots at one end and at the far, far other end was a table and chair where Swami Yoga Chinmaya sat. He was the commune leader and very much respected by the residents, who made certain that nobody entered the dining hall by "Swamiji's" entrance. We were told that in respect no one said his name, but called him Swamiji. But to us he was Chinmaya, just as he always had been and he had no objection to that. He had no objection to anything that we did actually. He was treated as a guru and he just said yes, and when we came along and treated him like anyone else, he said yes to that too. Chinmaya certainly has a presence; he always moves very slowly and his face shows a serene and tranquil expression. To me he represented the holy man of maybe one thousand years ago. He has been a disciple of Osho's since the early Bombay days when he worked as Osho's secretary. I noticed him ten years earlier in Pune, when he and his girlfriend shaved their heads and declared they were celibate.

Osho's *sannyasins* are from every country in the world; here there are no nations. And every religion in the world has been dropped at His feet; here there are no Hindus, Christians, Mohammedans, Jews. Every type of individual possible is here, all mixed up in the cosmic cooking pot, from punky teenagers to old *sadhus*; from young revolutionaries to ancient aristocracy; the simple person to the jetsetter, business man to artist...every color of the rainbow meets here and disappears in a prism of white light.

When I saw the diners sitting on the floor facing each other with a distance of twenty feet between each other, and the communal showers and bathroom, open air and with no hot water, followed by the rooms we were to sleep in, so small, bare bricks and mattresses on the floor — I saw that this was a completely different gig to what I was used to, and would demand all the meditation I could muster.

Next morning, as I found my way to the toilets across a small patch of grass, I turned and saw the Himalayas. From where I stood three quarters of the horizon was mountain peaks. They were not on the horizon actually, they were neither of earth or heaven, but in between. The snow-covered peaks were suspended in the sky and they looked so close that I felt I could touch them. As the sun rose it touched the highest mountain first and turned it pink, then gold before it moved on to the next. I watched the sun rising on the Himalayas one by one and shook my head in wonder — why had no one ever told me ? I had always thought the Himalayas were just a range of mountains, but they are not! I watched, spell-bound, as the mountains in the sky changed colors and threw my senses into new dimensions. Without any doubt, I knew I was going to be very happy here.

Days passed without any news of Osho. I would look at the mountain range and think of Him on just the other side. A plan went through my mind to take a bus into India through the mountains to Kulu and arrive just in time for Osho's walk around the Span garden, *namaste* Him, and return to Pokhara. Asheesh and I talked of our concern for Osho's safety, even though we were happy that He was in the gentle and capable hands of Neelam. Our fear was that we might never see Him again.

Weeks passed without any news, but we were well into the swing of our monastic life. The land around the commune was fascinating, and we went on walks passing places where the land had been washed away by rivers, leaving cliffs three hundred feet high. Carefully approaching the edge I could see cows grazing below, and rocks that had once supported great waterfalls standing still, marked forever and worn away by the once rushing water. A gash in the ground would reveal, hundreds of feet below, a small trickle of a stream. It would be so easy to fall into one of these holes and never be found, as indeed, had happened to one German visitor.

I soon began to enjoy the morning ritual of washing clothes and body in the open air, and even became accustomed to a diet that included chillies for breakfast. The *sannyasins* at the commune were innocent, gentle people and we made a few very good friends. Chinmaya was a genial host, and though he was very spiritual, his sidekick Krishnananda was a wild Nepali man with a flowing mane of black hair, flaring nostrils, and a great love of speed on his motorbike.

The challenge that I was facing of being in the unknown, uncertain whether I would ever see Osho again, made me realize that I had to *live* Osho. I had to live as He had been teaching me to — totally and in the moment. This brought a great feeling of acceptance and peace and I might well have been living there today, in a village maybe, quietly, alone, if it hadn't happened that:

One evening while we were having dinner Krishnananda rushed in and throwing himself in the air shouted out the news that Osho was coming to Nepal! — tomorrow! We didn't even take one more bite of dinner, but rushed to pack and the whole commune crowded into two vans and we were on our way to Kathmandu.

The next morning, having moved into the Soaltei Oberoi Hotel with Vivek, Rafia and Devaraj, where they had been based while trying to find a house or palace for Osho, we all made for the airport. Arun was the Nepali *sannyasin* who ran the meditation center in Kathmandu, and he had gone to great lengths to arrange a spectacular greeting for Osho. It was Nepali tradition to line the streets with brass pots filled with local flowers, for royalty. The local police were in fact miffed, saying that we should not use the pots and flowers because only the King should receive such a welcome. *Sannyasins* in red and hundreds of onlookers lined the streets and the airport entrance. The plane touched down, a white mercedes pulled up in front of the exit for Osho: the crowd pushed forward, everyone got very excited and started throwing flowers in the air, and then Osho walked through the glass doors of the airport, waved and disappeared into the car.

We all raced off to the Oberoi where Osho was to stay in a suite on the fourth floor, with Vivek and Rafia in the room opposite Him. Rafia had performed an intricate operation of wiring up an alarm system in Osho's room, so that if He should want anything, He could call Vivek. It was about midnight when the hotel security guard came across Rafia on his knees, in the corridor with the carpet pulled up, wiring the two rooms together.

Mukti and I shared a room on the floor below that was to become half kitchen and half laundry room. There were three big kitchen trunks and bags of rice and *dal*, baskets of fruit and vegetables, and that was only half the room. The other half was full of the whole laundry paraphernalia.

We arranged with the very accommodating hotel staff that Mukti would cook for Osho in the hotel kitchen. She had her own portion of the kitchen where no meat would be left around and it would be kept especially clean for her. I would be washing Osho's clothes in the hotel laundry with about fifty Nepali men. They were great people and used to clean out the machine for me before I arrived and wait, even after their work hours, to see that everything was okay. Then I would take the robes, carrying them up in the lift, high in the air on large teak hangers, to the amusement of guests and the staff. In our bedroom I used to iron on the bed, amidst the increasing baskets of fruit and vegetables that *sannyasins* were bringing as gifts for Osho. The food in Nepal was inferior in quality because of the poverty of the land, and Mukti, now assisted by Ashu, was making plans for importing vegetables and fruits from India. Meanwhile, the Nepali *sannyasins* shopped at the crack of dawn in the vegetable markets and with great joy, arrived each day with the best of everything they could buy for Osho.

The day Osho arrived He called us to His room to see Him. He asked us how we were, and said that He had heard there had been a bit of unrest between us. Mukta and Haridas had left the day before for a holiday in Greece, having given up the hope that Osho would be coming, and it was true that Ashu and Nirupa had also been unhappy in the Pokhara situation. When Osho heard the words, "Well, it was not up to the standard that I am used to living," He said that He also had not been living quite the way He would have liked, and reminded us that He had been in jail and living in Span without electricity or water for a lot of the time. I felt so ashamed, even though I had not said it myself.

We learnt that Jayesh had been making intricate plans to get Osho safely out of India and to Nepal. Two days before take-off, Osho walked out of Span, got into an old Ambassador car with Neelam, drove to the airport and took a commercial flight to Delhi. Even the fact that there was a flight that day was unusual, and that there were two spare seats was a miracle.

The police had arrived a few hours after Osho left to detain Him and confiscate His passport. He would have been in prison awaiting a trial that had suddenly manifested itself, both unexpectedly and ridiculously. The income tax department (F.E.R.A.) wanted Osho to pay tax on the half a million dollar fine paid to the United States government. They did not believe that the fine was paid by friends of Osho, and thought that somehow India deserved a share in the booty.

Laxmi had confused the situation even more by spreading rumors with the *sannyasins* who lived in Delhi, that Hasya and Jayesh were trying to kidnap Osho. In a valiant attempt to save their master the Delhi *sannyasins* tried to snatch Osho back, but were thwarted by Anando. Osho took the plane to Nepal, just in time to avoid arrest by the Indian police. The Span property that I had heard

Laxmi telling Osho about, had not been purchased by her, it was not even for sale!

Some *sannyasins* arrived a couple of days later in Kathmandu with an offer of a palace in India in which Osho could live. They didn't understand that at this point He could not go back to India, but Osho talked to them. A video of the palace had been made for Osho to see, so He agreed and to my surprise invited all of us to watch the video with Him.

We sat at Osho's feet in his living room and the film began. After ten minutes of footage of trees in the driveway of the palace, we saw a row of five or six stone huts with the roofs completely fallen in. These were the servants' quarters, and obviously a lot of work had to be done on them — but that was nothing, we have worked before on buildings. The camera then scanned up and down a few more trees and I thought to myself that someone must have told the cameraman that Osho loved trees.

Osho asked if there was any water in the palace. "Yes, yes," was the reply from the bearer of the video. After five more minutes travelling up and down the trunks of trees, we saw the "palace." It had only four rooms, and they were in an advanced state of dilapidation. "Is there any water on the property?" asked Osho. "Yes, yes," came the reply. The four-roomed palace must not have been lived in for at least fifty years. "What about the water?" began Osho... Aah! there it was! A thin trickle of water ran down some moss covered stones in the garden. "And do we have rights to this water?" asked Osho. "The water belongs to the girls' school, next door," was the reply, "but, no problem."

Now I understood. This is why Osho wanted us all to watch the video with Him, so that we could have some idea of how difficult the situation was when trying to get anything done with some of His *sannyasins*. That their hearts are with Osho is without question, but they must be crazy to want to take Him back to India, and even crazier to think He could live in the remains of what was a four roomed house, and without water!

Osho said to them that their asking Him to remain in India was out of love, but it was absurd. He said that it would create trouble for Him and trouble for themselves, and He told them to go back, think over it, and return after seven days. They never came back and Osho said that they must have understood the implications, and their insistence had been out of love, not out of reason.

Wherever Osho is, in strong contrast to His silence, there is a mad cyclone of energy surrounding Him. I asked Him if this was His *leela*, or was it existence creating a balance? He said that it was neither; that the world is mad, chaotic, and it is His silence that was exposing it, not creating it. He said that the perfect balance in nature will be absolute silence.

The next morning Osho began talking to a group of about ten in His sitting room. The first question was from Asheesh and he was asking that "In these times of uncertainty, the best — and the worst — seems to be coming out in those of us who are around you. Would you comment on this?"

Osho: "There are no 'times of uncertainty' because time is always uncertain. It is the difficulty with the mind: mind wants certainty — and time is always uncertain.

"So when just by coincidence mind finds a small space of certainty, it feels settled: a kind of illusory permanence surrounds it. It tends to forget the real nature of existence and life, it starts living in a kind of dream world; it starts mistaking appearance for reality. It feels good to the mind because mind is always afraid of change for the simple reason: who knows what change will bring — good or bad? One thing is certain, that change will unsettle your world of illusions, expectations, dreams..."

He went on to say that "whenever time strikes one of

your cherished illusions," then what happens is that our mask is taken away.

He mentioned how people had worked hard at Rajneeshpuram and just as we were putting the finishing touches the whole thing disappeared.

"I am not frustrated — I have not even looked back for a single moment. Those were beautiful years, we lived beautifully, and it is the nature of existence: things change. What can we do? So we are trying to make something else — that will also change. Nothing is permanent here. Except change, everything changes.

"So I don't have any complaint. I have not felt even for a single moment that something has gone wrong...because here everything has gone wrong, but to me nothing has gone wrong. It is just that we tried to make beautiful palaces out of playing cards.

"Perhaps except for me everybody is frustrated. And they feel angry at me too because I am not frustrated, I am not with them. That makes them even more angry. If I was also angry, and I was also complaining, and I was also tremendously disturbed, they would have felt a consolation. But I am not...

"Now it is going to be difficult to make another dream come true because many of those who worked to make one dream come true will be in a state of defeatism. They are defeated. They will feel that reality or existence does not care about innocent people who were not doing any harm, who were simply trying to make something beautiful. Even with them existence goes on following the same rule — it makes no exceptions....

"I can see that it is painful, but we are responsible for the pain. It feels that life is not just, nor fair, because it has taken a toy from our hands. One should not be in such a hurry to come to such great conclusions. Wait a little more. Perhaps it is always for the good — all the changes. You should just be patient enough. You should give life a little more rope....

"My whole life I have been going from one place to another place because something has failed. But I have not failed. Thousands of dreams can fail — that does not make me a failure. On the contrary, each dream disappearing makes me more victorious because it does not disturb me, does not even touch me. Its disappearance is an advantage, is an opportunity to learn to be mature. Then the best will be coming out of you. And whatever happens will not make any difference — your best will go on growing to higher peaks....

"What matters is how you come out of those broken dreams, those great expectations that have disappeared into thin air, you can't even find their footprints.

"How do you come out of it? If you come out of it unscratched, then you have known a great secret, you have found a master key. Then nothing can defeat you, then nothing can disturb you, then nothing can make you angry and nothing can pull you back. You are always marching into the unknown for new challenges. And all these challenges will go on sharpening the best in you."

The next question was from Vivek, and it shows her down-to-earth, totally female approach to life.

"Beloved Master, What is home?"

"There is no home, there are only houses.

"Man is born homeless, and man remains his whole life homeless. Yes, he will make many houses into homes and he will get frustrated. And man dies homeless.

"To accept the truth brings a tremendous transformation. Then you don't search for a home — because home is something there, far away, something other than you. And everybody is searching for a home. When you see its illusoriness, then, rather than searching for a home, you will start searching for the being that is born homeless, whose destiny is homeless." (*Light on The Path*)

Anando arrived, with Bikki Oberoi, the man who owns all the Oberoi hotels. Hasya and Anando had made friends with him in Delhi and he showed interest in helping Osho at the time. They arrived first class and the hotel staff put out the red carpet and there was much hullabaloo. My eyes bulged when I saw Anando, amongst all this fanfare, proudly walking along with my small ironing board tucked under her arm. It wasn't even disguised, everyone could see it was an ironing board, and yet she wasn't fazed at all. I had needed that ironing board so badly, and I was touched that she would carry it as hand luggage under such circumstances.

The fourth floor of the hotel was now fully occupied by *sannyasins*. A bedroom became an office, and there was always a whirlwind of activity going on in there. A few doors away Devaraj and Maneesha worked day and night transcribing Osho's discourses. Their room was always full, as people turned up to help them — Premda, who was Osho's eye doctor, handsome, conservative, German, and a bad loser at tennis. It was in this small bedroom that seemed always to be filled with breakfast trolleys, that the German Rajneesh Times came to sort out their questions with Maneesha, letters and questions from *sannyasins* and as many people who could fit in the room were welcome to help check the typed manuscripts against the tapes of the discourses.

Although Osho had rested for a few days, He did not seem as strong as He used to be. We did not know at the time, but the first diagnostic indicators of thallium poisoning were evident. Osho's eye doctor, Premda, had been called from Germany because Osho showed symptoms that included eye twitching, divergence or wandering quality of eye movements, weakness of ocular muscles and visual impairment. Premda treated the symptoms, but did not know what could possibly be the cause.

I was helping to clean Osho's rooms with the Nepali maid, Radikha. At 7.00 a.m. we would rush into His sitting room, while He was in the bath, and clean the dark, intricately carved wood furniture that obviously, no one had ever attempted to clean before. Although there was a vacuum cleaner it was more efficient to rub the red carpet with a damp rag. Rafia and Niskriya were on our heels, or rather — our backs — as they then had to set up the sitting room as a studio for discourse by 7.30 a.m.

In the evenings Osho talked in the hotel ballroom to press and visitors, at first mainly Nepali, but as the days passed the color of the audience was changing from black and grey to shades of orange. A Buddhist monk, small, with shaved head and in saffron robes began attending these discourses. He sat in the front row and asked Osho questions. Osho began by saying that, "To be a Buddha is beautiful, but to be a Buddhist is ugly." The Buddhist monk got the full treatment and I was surprised and in great admiration for the man, when he turned up the next night, and the next. In fact he came regularly for a few weeks, until one day Osho received a letter from him saying that his monastery had forbidden him to attend any more.

Each morning the very intimate talks in His sitting room continued, and after being away from Osho for the first time since I had come to Pune, seven years before, I now felt each moment was a bonus. I was living in an abundance of love, joy and the excitement of exploring The Path with the Master.

I was beginning to learn that the search for truth, the search for the "spot" inside myself that is unpolluted by personality, is a great adventure. I have no doubt that there is a "state" in which a person can be totally relaxed without any desire or need for more, a feeling so fulfilling that nothing happening outside can disturb it. I know it is so because I have glimpsed it for moments and I have seen that in Osho it is a permanent state.

Osho began to walk in the grounds of the hotel, past the tennis courts, and the swimming pool, lawns and gardens. He couldn't see much of the grounds though because His path was flanked by visitors and disciples who came to greet Him. Some of them would simply smile and wave, but others threw themselves at His feet, and that was troublesome. Watching Osho coming through the hotel lobby and out into the garden was a beautiful scene. There was always space around Osho even in a crowded place. I saw many tourists spin on their heels with amazement at the sight of Osho. Some, even Europeans, I saw *namaste* Him — though I am sure they did not know what they were doing, because after Osho passed by they had a dazed look on their face. Being totally without experience of Osho, and not expecting anything, they had been touched and were afire. Some American and Italian tourists that I watched, really saw Osho, but I don't know how their minds dealt with it afterwards.

A few disciples arrived from the West, one of them being Niskriya with his video camera. He just turned up one day, literally on the doorstep with his camera, unknown to anyone. But he had good references — he had been thrown out of Rajneeshpuram twice and had had his *mala* taken away by Sheela. Without him none of these beautiful discourses would have been recorded. Niskriya is an eccentric German film man, and when he first arrived he was experimenting with 3D film. One day he called us into his room to view these efforts at 3D, through a mirror contraption balanced between two television sets. He was so thrilled by his experiment that none of us had the heart to admit to him that actually we couldn't see anything. But Osho blew the gaff and made a good joke of it one day in discourse.

It was always risky when Osho was speaking because there was no way of knowing what He would say next. On entering Nepal, Hasya had told Osho that Nepal was, by law, a Hindu country, so please... "Don't say anything against Hinduism." In an evening discourse, in front of all the dignitaries and press men, He said that His friends had asked Him not to speak against Hinduism, but what could He do? This was the very place to speak against Hinduism, do they expect Him to speak against Christianity? No, He would save that for when He visited Italy.

At that time the film crew from Italy had got visas for Nepal and Sarjano had arrived. Applications for Osho to visit Italy were under way, and looked promising. However, it would not be good if the press announced He was visiting Italy before arrangements could be made, so we were to keep it secret. Sarjano was taking photos of Osho that night during the discourse, so was next to Osho facing the audience. I watched Sarjano, when Osho declared that He would visit Italy, and I let out a scream of laughter as Sarjano's eyes rolled up into his head and mouthing the words "Italian visa" he went through the actions of tearing up documents and throwing them over his shoulder.

We were in Nepal for three months and it was time to extend our own visas. We had not been able to find a palace, nor even a small house for Osho, and so we were still in the hotel. The situation did not look promising, even though the local people, and especially the hotel staff were loving and respectful towards Osho. The men in the laundry room were constantly requesting tickets for the nightly discourses and the maids and waiters also came. On one occasion when a waiter delivered tea to our room, and Mukti was sitting in the chair with her Walkman earphones on, the waiter exclaimed: "Is that Bhagwan you are listening to?" He then sat down and claimed the Walkman and stayed for the rest of the taped discourse.

I loved the people so much, and one day while shopping, the shopkeepers said to me, "Your guru — no good" (Osho had said in a discourse that Buddha had renounced wealth, and that is nothing — "I have renounced poverty" said Osho). And even though they had a criticism, there was no malice in it. At least they were interested in what Osho was saying.

Anyway, we went for our visa extensions and were refused.

There seemed to be no hope in Nepal anymore. The King had never had the guts to acknowledge Osho, even though a couple of cabinet ministers had come to hear Him talk. Despite endless searching, there was no land or property for sale. And on top of that, trouble with the immigration authorities only showed that the Indian government had interfered. To get a three-month extension on a visa in Nepal is routine. The country is desperate for tourists, but in our case it was different. Once again, Osho would be cut off from His foreign disciples, and nine-tenths of Osho's disciples are from Western countries.

It was in this situation and many, many others that Osho was to show us His total trust in existence, and His disciples. The idea of a World Tour was born and Osho said okay.

Ma Amrito, a Greek woman, charismatic and beautiful, who had many contacts in the Greek government and high society since her days as Miss Greece, waltzed into Kathmandu with her husband and her lover. I first saw the trio in the hotel lift and thought, "Mmm, they look interesting." They talked with Hasya, Jayesh, Vivek and Devaraj and it was decided that Greece would be the first stop on the World Tour.

Arrangements were made to visit Greece, and Rafia, Asheesh, Maneesha, Neelam and I would follow with the luggage. Osho, Vivek, Devaraj, Mukti and Anando would go first. Nirupa and Ashu were to go to Canada, their home country, as the caravan had to be made a little smaller.

The morning Osho left there were many tears. The hotel staff were crying and Radhika, our maid, was weeping uncontrollably. The private plane that had been arranged for Osho had been held up in Delhi for two days, and it was decided that Osho would fly on a commercial flight. Cliff, Osho's pilot, who had last seen Osho boarding a jet in Portland, flew into Kathmandu on Royal Nepal Airlines, and he was in the airport as Osho's car arrived. He ran across the tarmac, and was just in time to valiantly open the car door for Osho.

Cliff then came to visit us at the hotel. We ordered tea for him and Geeta, his Japanese girlfriend who was travelling with him. We were talking about Osho's flight which was to go via Bangkok and Dubai, and Cliff had already worked out a plan where he could fly back to Delhi, and take his private plane to Dubai to meet Osho. By the time room service brought tea, Cliff was gone and he arrived in Dubai in the private plane just before Osho landed. It was pouring with rain, and as Cliff saw Osho's flight coming in, he grabbed an umbrella from an Arab gentleman in the airport, and ran to the steps of Osho's plane. As Osho alighted from the craft, Cliff was there, umbrella poised, and Osho chuckled.

CHAPTER TWELVE

Crete

It was mid-February and the water of the Aegean was cold, but it felt wonderful as I swam naked in the deep, clear pool formed by the rocks with the sea gently breaking over them. The sun was shining and I looked up at the house built into the cliff, and the winding stone staircase cut into it.

The top rooms of the house were where Osho was staying, and the circular window of His sitting room overlooked the sea and cliffs. His bedroom was tucked away in the back of the house, so was dark and cave-like. This was the time He took His afternoon nap. The bathroom was between the two and Ma Amrito had done much work to modernize it for Him. Ma Amrito had rented the house for one month from a film director friend of hers, Nikos Koundouros.

The room in which I was to live and do Osho's laundry was halfway up the cliff, with a white arched balcony. Above my room were our friends from Hollywood — Kaveesha and David, who were lovers from the beginning of time, John and his girlfriend Kendra, an extremely beautiful blonde woman who had been a *sannyasin* since she was a child, and Avirbhava. Avirbhava is a Tennessee millionairess. When worried that men only loved her for her money, Osho said to her that her money was part of her. He told her that she was not only a beautiful woman, but a beautiful rich woman. He said, "Do you think that I worry that you love me only for my enlightenment?"

They had just got back from visiting an island in the Pacific which had been offered as a possible home for Osho. It was Marlon Brando's island, but proved to be unsuitable as a hurricane had recently flattened it.

Our group was growing — a beautiful Chilean family of *sannyasins*, father, mother, daughter and son had arrived from Rajneeshpuram, just by chance, not knowing Osho was coming, and had helped with the preparation of the house. Besides the domestic side of the work many *sannyasins* flew in to deal with the world press. Almost every country in the world was represented by journalists from magazines and newspapers. Television crews came from Germany, Holland, U.S.A., Italy and Australia.

Osho started giving discourses the day after He arrived and within a few days there were five hundred *sannyasins* from the U.S.A. and Europe. He sat under a carob tree in the courtyard, and musicians sat together on the stone patio and played as Osho entered and when He left. Everyone screamed with surprise and delight as He danced with Vivek playfully dancing around Him; they moved together and then apart and laughing all the time they danced up the steps together and through the large oak doors into the house.

On the days when the spring weather was stormy we sat inside the house in a huge room on the ground floor; but we filled that room to capacity and it overflowed with people sitting up the stairs and on the window sills.

Osho answered questions from disciples and the world media in discourses held twice a day. It was as though we were reliving the times when the wise man was sought after and consulted for his guidance. The press asked Osho questions about their political leaders, the pope, birth control, the death penalty, marriage problems, women's lib, money, health — both of body and mind — armaments and meditation. Yes, there were a few questions about meditation, but of course, the usual yellow journalism was there with the same old questions:

"You are also known as the sex guru......?"

Osho: "The definition which calls me a sex guru is not only false, it is absurd. To put it right: I am the only person in the world who is anti-sex. But that needs tremendous understanding. You cannot hope for that understanding from journalists.

"There are at least four hundred books in my name, and there is only one book about sex. Only that book is talked about; the three hundred and ninety-nine, nobody cares about, and those are the best. The book on sex is just preparing you so that you can understand the other books and go higher, dropping small problems, reaching to the heights of human consciousness — but nobody talks about them."

And the subject asked most by journalists:

"Do you miss the Rolls Royces?"

Osho: "I never miss anything. But it seems the whole world is missing my Rolls Royces. It is a very insane world. When the Rolls Royces were there, they were jealous; now that they are gone, they are missing them. I am simply left out! They may be there again, and people will start feeling jealous....

"Just the other day a few beautiful photographers were here. All my people tried to prevent me from being photographed by the side of a Honda, but I insisted that this picture should be taken. The Honda does not belong to me, neither did those Rolls Royces. But let people at least enjoy; they will feel good. It is very strange that people's minds should be concerned about things with which they have no concern at all."

On money:

Osho: "...I am sorry to say I don't understand anything about finance. I don't have any bank account. I have not even touched money for thirty years. I have been in America for five years — I have not seen a dollar bill.

"I live totally trusting existence. If it wants me to be here it will manage. If it does not want me to be here it will not manage.

"My trust in existence is total.

"The people who don't trust in existence trust in money, trust in god, and trust in all kinds of idiotic things."

Question: "Is the name Bhagwan written in your passport?"

Osho: "I have never seen my passport. My people take care of it. When I was in jail in America I had no phone numbers of my attorneys, or of the commune, or of my secretaries — because in my whole life I have never phoned. The U.S. Marshal was surprised and asked, 'Who should we inform that you have been arrested?' I said, 'Whomsoever you like. As far as I am concerned, I don't know anybody. You can inform your wife, she may enjoy hearing what her husband is doing — arresting innocent people without any warrant.'

"I have such a different way of life that it sometimes looks unbelievable. I don't know where my passport is right now. Somebody must be carrying it, somewhere."

Osho had just left Nepal, the land where Gautam the Buddha was born, and here we were on the first step of the world tour, in Greece — the land of Zorba.

Osho: "Zorba is the foundation of the temple.

"Buddha is the temple itself.

"For the New Man I have given the name Zorba the Buddha. I want no schizophrenia, no split between matter and spirit, between the mundane and the sacred, between this-worldly and that-worldly. I don't want any split because every split is a split in you, and a personality, a humanity divided against itself, is going to be crazy and insane. And we are living in a crazy and insane world. It can be sane only if the split can be bridged.

"Zorba has to become Buddha, and Buddha has to understand and respect its own foundation. Roots may be ugly, but without those roots there are not going to be any flowers."

On vegetarianism Osho said: "It seems to me that killing animals for eating is not very far away from killing human beings. They differ only in their bodies, in their shape, but it is the same life that you are destroying."

Osho was asked many questions about bringing up children and teenage problems. This was strange because while the world press was asking Osho's advice on young people, this was the very "crime" for which Osho was arrested in Crete — "corrupting the youth." This was also the accusation made against Socrates twenty-five centuries before.

The archbishop of Crete was reacting in a way that proved that everything Osho had said about the hypocrisy of priests was correct: "Either he stops preaching or we use violence," threatened Bishop Dimitrios. "Blood will flow should Bhagwan not leave the island voluntarily." The archbishop was quoted in the local papers as saying he would dynamite the villa and set fire to it with Bhagwan and all his followers inside.

Ma Amrito and Mukta, with her silver hair and deep brown eyes, went to visit the archbishop to see if there was some misunderstanding. As they approached the church one of the local people shouted to Amrito, "You are the devil's daughter! Get out of here!" After they had stood on his doorstep for a few minutes and tried to explain to him that before condemning Osho he should at least hear what He has to say, the bishop screamed at them in anger, "Get out of this house."

Veena and Gayan, who had been Osho's seamstresses at Rajneeshpuram, arrived and the three of us had great fun repairing the damage that had occurred to Osho's robes and hats in the buckets of snow-water in Kulu.

Many friends were arriving and the atmosphere was festive, but I felt ill-at-ease. I had a nightmare that men were climbing through my bay windows and imagined boats moored below in the cove filled with menace. I remembered that this was the island where Gurdjieff had been carried off in a coma, after he had been shot. I was accident-prone, there was a gigantic bruise on my thigh from falling down the steps; I broke things, and my washing machine did nothing but flood the floor and give me electric shocks.

A strong wind swept the island one night. The sea was wild and the trees bent as the wind thrashed and sang its whining song. Avirbhava's boyfriend Sarvesh and I thought it would be 'fun' to go for a motorbike ride and feel the wind in our hair. Ma Amrito stood in front of us and with arms outstretched said, "No, I will not let you get on this bike." It was a racing bike, 750 ccs., and Sarvesh admitted that he hadn't ridden a bike since he was in college fifteen years before. But our minds were set and we drove down the hill to the small town of Agios Nicholaos. After five minutes I sensed that Sarvesh could not handle the bike, and as we took a corner on the sea front, the wind took us. The bike slid from under us and I felt my face slide down Sarvesh's back and then I was laying face down in the middle of the road. I had the taste of blood in my mouth and I examined my teeth with my tongue — all there — good. Blood was coming from my face and nose, hands were cut, trousers torn, one shoe missing, ankle swollen, but I felt very clear. I had never had an accident before and I was amazed at the clarity and calmness I felt. Sarvesh was lying face down in a pool of blood coming from his head. I looked at his body, and in some strange way he looked okay. I then watched his breathing and it seemed normal and relaxed. I bent close to him and said his name but he was unconscious. I watched myself give instructions to the onlookers — you, ring the police, you, take care of the bike, you, ring (and I remembered a six digit number of the villa). We went to the hospital where Sarvesh remained unconscious for forty minutes. I knew absolutely that Sarvesh was going to be alright. I got in touch with such clarity within myself that night, that the experience was worth it.

The next day I got a message from Osho. He said that I was "Stupid!" to have gone on the bike.

We went to pick up Sarvesh from the hospital and his face was blue and unrecognizable. He had severe concussion, but he did recover fully in time.

I slept all the next day and night and ventured out the following morning. After just a few minutes in the sun I felt dizzy and John, who is a doctor, told me that dizziness is a symptom of concussion, so I went back to bed.

Ma Amrito telephoned that morning from Athens, where she was meeting the chief of security, to say that everything was going well and there was nothing to worry about.

About 2.00 p.m. I heard a lot of commotion. Getting out of bed I wandered over to the door and saw Anando who told me that the police had arrived, but I should go back to bed.

Go back to bed! I got dressed quickly, remembering from my last experience with the police that what you wear when the police arrive may be what you wear for the next few days in jail. I approached the house and saw it was surrounded by shouting aggressive men in plain clothes with guns and about twenty police in uniform. Anando was being dragged off to the local jail by four policemen, as was another friend who had come to help. I ran up the steps of the porch and stood in front of the door and said to the policeman there that, "There must be some mistake. Please wait, our lawyers are contacting the Chief of Police, and this will soon be sorted out." He said to me, "I am the Chief of Police!"

I insisted that there was a mistake and higher authorities would be contacted. "I am the magistrate," said another man!

I was convinced that a terrible mistake was happening and that if only we could stop the police from entering the house until help arrived, then everything would be alright. But these men were acting as though they had been sent on an emergency, dangerous mission. It reminded me of the arrest in Charlotte when the men arresting us did not know what they were doing, but thought they were arresting dangerous terrorists.

The men had split up in groups of two and three and were prowling around the house trying to find an entrance. I ran after two of them who were about to climb in a window and stood in front of them and screamed "No." They tried to push me aside but I wouldn't let them near the window.

My face was bruised and cut by the bike accident of two nights ago and I think that gave me courage that they would not touch me. If they did, I knew for sure that I would have made things very bad for them by accusing them of creating my wounds. Maybe they knew that too, but whatever went through their minds about the mess my face was in, they let me get away with harassing them a lot.

Japanese Geeta came to help and, although she is less than five feet tall, she was a strength to be reckoned with as she pursued the men trying to climb in windows.

I ran around the house and each time I saw them about to break in I stood in front of them. On one corner of the house a plain-clothes policeman stood, legs apart and in his hands held above his head was a huge rock. He looked like Goliath in the biblical story, and he was about to throw the rock through the window. I saw that behind the window were Asheesh and Rafia and our video equipment. If he threw the rock through the window then they would be hurt very badly. I stood between "Goliath" and the window and shouted at him:

"I thought the Crete police were friends of the people,

but you are just fascists!" Two more policemen in uniform came to join him and one of them, his face turning bright red, shouted back at me, "We are not fascists!" Goliath put the rock down.

Then I heard the sound of breaking glass, and running around the corner I was in time to see three policemen climbing up the four feet of wall and entering through a window into the house. I saw them crossing the floor towards the staircase, and out of the corner of my eye saw that the main door was also being opened. I clambered through the broken window after them and ran towards the spiral staircase that led to Osho's rooms. I made it up the stairs before them. I knew where I was going and they hesitated — expecting machine guns, maybe.

As I reached the top of the stairs Rafia was poised with his camera taking photos of the men as they ran up the stairs. I got to Osho's bathroom and at the same time I saw two or three of the men grab Rafia and take him forcibly into the sitting-room. I thought for a minute that they were going to beat him up, but there was nothing I could do. Kendra followed a few minutes later and went into the sitting room after the men and I saw that Rafia was lying on the floor with two men on top of him, but he managed to slip the film from his camera to Kendra.

John was standing next to me and we called to Osho through a crack in the door to let Him know what was happening. He said to tell them He would be out in a minute. "Goliath" appeared at the top of the stairs and the spiral staircase was now crowded with police all trying to get up, as was the corridor outside Osho's bathroom. I said, "Please, we are peaceful people and there is no need to use violence." Goliath said that it all depended on us whether or not they used violence. I said that we had not been violent with them.

They tried to move me away from the bathroom door, but again I think my battered, determined face stopped them being violent with me. I was saying to them, "Please, just let Him finish in the bathroom. Some of the men kicked down Osho's bedroom door and rushed in, guns at the ready.

John was also in the corridor as Osho emerged and a great lot of shoving started. I turned to the Chief of Police and said that so many men were not needed, to please send the thugs back downstairs, so he did, leaving about eight or ten of them clumsily escorting Osho into His sitting-room as He calmly walked to His armchair and sat down.

I saw Rafia as we entered. He was sitting on a chair facing the door and his face was flushed, his hair all over the place, and he looked shocked. I noticed that as Osho sat down He gave Rafia a penetrating look, and I presumed He was seeing if he was okay.

John sat on one side of Osho's chair near the window and I sat on the other side. The police surrounded the chair in a circle and commenced shouting all at once in Greek. This went on for what seemed like five minutes and Osho turned to me and said, "Get Mukta to translate." I went down the stairs accompanied by the Chief of Police and called across the downstairs room for Mukta, who came running. Now with a translator we were not much better off because the police were still shouting.

Osho calmly asked them if he could see their papers and why they had come. They waved papers that Mukta started reading, but it was very chaotic in the room. I had the feeling, then, that these men had been ordered to get Osho out by a certain time because they kept looking at their watches and their anxiety and aggressiveness would rise.

Osho said that He would leave, no problem, but to give His people time to arrange a plane and pack His things. They could stand guard over Him until it had been done, but why arrest Him? They shouted, "No!" — He had to come with them, "Now."

They seemed so insistent on taking Him away with them that I shouted at them that they could not take Him before we packed His things. I said: "You have a very sick man here, and the whole world is watching what happens to this man. If you should harm Him in any way then you will be in trouble." I said to take Him without His medicines would cause Him much harm. I remember at the time feeling a little embarrassed to be calling Osho "a very sick man" right in front of Him, knowing that He is much, much more than that!

I looked across at John. He was sitting motionless and silent, his face a blank screen on which anything could be projected. I projected that his very stillness was a warning for them to take it easy.

The confusion continued and the men argued and shouted amongst each other. The tension seemed to be mounting and subsiding in a rhythm not unlike big waves at sea.

One policeman had enough of the delay and roughly moved towards Osho and placed his hand on Osho's wrist, which was resting on the arm of His chair as always when He sat relaxed. He said, "We take you now!" and made as if to yank Osho out of the chair. Osho gently, with His free hand, placed it on top of the policeman's and patted it. He said, "There is no need to use violence." The policeman dropped His hand and took a respectful step back.

The Chief of Police was saying that he had to arrest Osho and there was nothing he could do about it. It was his orders.

It was decided. Osho stood up and as they started to lead Him away, I rushed to Osho's medicine cabinet and stuffed my pockets with everything I could lay my hands on and was in time to walk down the spiral staircase with Osho, holding His hand.

Osho turned to me as we walked down the stairs and in a gentle and concerned voice asked me, "And you,

Chetana, how are you?" I couldn't believe it! We could have been going on a quiet afternoon's walk without a care in the world and He was asking after my health. I said, "Oh, Bhagwan, I'm fine."

We walked across the downstairs room, surrounded by police, where we had enjoyed such beautiful discourses only a day before. They had got their prey and were not going to let him escape. We walked through the huge wooden doors out on to the porch and there were a few stunned *sannyasins* looking shocked and helpless. Mukta was having a screaming match with two of the policemen in Greek and Osho turned to her and said, "Don't bother to talk to them, Mukta, they are idiots."

We reached the car and Osho turned to me and said that I was to stay behind and pack the trunks and suitcases. I nodded my head and He got in the car, followed by a policeman. It was a small car and Osho had a policeman on either side of Him. Devaraj and Maneesha were on the scene and I shoved all the medicines I had into Devaraj's pockets.

It looked as though they were going to drive off with Osho to god knows where, without any one of us with Him. I stood in front of the car and leaned over the bonnet and shouted to the Chief of Police, who I was beginning to feel I knew quite well by now, very slowly and very loudly, "The-doctor-goes-in-the-car!   The-doctor-goes-in-the-car!" Devaraj was standing at the ready and although the car door was just being closed, one of the policemen got out of his seat and Maneesha pushed Devaraj in, followed by the policeman. They looked very crowded in that back seat, with Devaraj balancing his doctor's bag on his knees and Osho pushed up in the corner.

As the car sped down the dusty driveway out of sight, it registered in my mind that Osho was wearing *that dress* — the one I had dreamt about in Rajneeshpuram.

We did not know where the police were taking Osho, and one story was that they intended to send Him to Egypt on a boat. That story was true and it took twenty-five thousand dollars to bribe the police in order to allow Osho to leave the country safely.

I found Mukti and Neelam, thinking that if Osho was to be deported then they should arrive with Him in India. The idea of Osho arriving in India alone was terrifying — you heard what He said about money and His passport.

I packed about a dozen giant-sized metal trunks. Osho's chair was put in a wooden crate; there were suitcases and smaller trunks — altogether about thirty pieces of luggage.

I then went to Heraklion Airport where Osho was waiting for a flight to Athens. His treatment from the police had improved tremendously since they had received twenty-five thousand dollars.

Osho was sitting in a small room surrounded by armed police and giving an interview to a reporter who was from Penthouse magazine, of all places.

It was raining, but that did not stop the hundreds of *sannyasins* from celebrating outside the building. We were singing and turning the disaster into a festival! Planes were coming in to land from all over Europe and the U.S.A., and *sannyasins* were pouring off them having just arrived to see Osho. I hugged one friend after another that I hadn't seen since the destruction of Rajneeshpuram, and with everyone in tears the news spread quickly that Osho was already leaving the country. They had arrived just in time to wave good-bye to Him.

The airport was filled with thousands of *sannyasins* and all the local people from the village, Agios Nicholaos. As the time drew closer for Osho's departure I went into the airport lounge, and it was an incredible sight — thousands of people in red and orange. A voice would call out, "There He is," and everyone would rush to one area of the airport, and then another voice would call out "No, there He is," and the thousands of people would move as one body. I was reminded of a huge ship on a rough sea, where everyone is tossed from one side to the other by the waves.

We were expecting Osho to walk through the airport, so the air was tense with expectation, excitement and songs.

I was standing with Anando, having rushed up the stairs to the terrace to watch the planes. We saw Vivek, Rafia, Mukti, Neelam and a few other *sannyasins* board and naturally thought that Osho was to get on that plane. Our hearts fell to our stomachs when the plane took off without Him and our fear was that some trick was being played. But then we saw a car pull up alongside a small plane on the runway and that was it — yes, it was Devaraj and Osho. They were getting in the smaller plane going to Athens and Anando said, "I have a ticket for that plane," and with that she disappeared into the crowd, calling over her shoulder for me to please send her clothes after her.

I watched as the plane took off surrounded by thousands of friends in various stages of confusion and sadness, and then I went back to the empty villa to wait and see what was to happen next.

Osho's last words to the press before leaving Greece were:

"If a single person on a four-week tourist visa can destroy your two-thousand-year-old morality, your religion, then it is not worth preserving. It should be destroyed."

CHAPTER THIRTEEN

Silently Waiting

March 6th, 1986, 1.20 a.m.
Aboard the small jet with Osho were Vivek,
Devaraj, Anando, Mukti and John.

The plane took off from Athens, destination unknown —
even to the pilots. In the air they asked John, "Where to?"
John didn't know.

Hasya and Jayesh were in Spain working for a visa for
Osho, and John was in touch by telephone. "Spain is not
ready yet," said Hasya. Spain was never ready! It took two
months of negotiating for them to say no.

The plane gained altitude and was moving fast —
nowhere!

At the villa in Crete I stood poised, ready to follow,
with the thirty pieces of luggage.

I looked around at the villa — broken windows, doors
hanging on their hinges, battered in by the police — signs
of brutality and injustice.

Kaveesha and David, Avirbhava and Sarvesh — who
was too concussed to travel but too hyped-up to stay in
Greece — Ma Amrito and her five-year-old son, Sindhu,
Maneesha, Kendra and I were to travel as a group and wait
in London for news.

I received a message from the plane that Osho was
asking how I was, and had said, "Take care of Chetana."

Before arriving in London we heard that Osho had been

refused entry into Switzerland, France, Spain, Sweden and England. Canada and Antigua were to follow. Not only was Osho refused entry into these countries, but his plane was met with armed soldiers and police. *Sannyasins* were contacted in each country in advance and lawyers were working to help, but nothing could be done.

In Osho's words from the book *Beyond Psychology*:

"...from Greece we moved to Geneva, just for an overnight rest, and the moment they came to know my name they said, 'No way! We cannot allow him into our country.' I was not even allowed to get out of the plane.

"We moved to Sweden, thinking that people go on saying that Sweden is far more progressive than any country in Europe or in the world, that Sweden has been giving refuge to many terrorists, revolutionaries, expelled politicians, that it is very generous.

"We reached Sweden. We wanted to stay overnight because the pilots were running out of time. They could not go on anymore; otherwise it would become illegal. And we were happy because the man at the airport...we had asked only for an overnight stay, but he gave seven-day visas to everybody. Either he was drunk or just sleepy; it was midnight, past midnight.

"The person who had gone for the visas came back very happy that we had been given seven-day visas, but immediately the police came, canceled the visas and told us to move immediately: 'This man we cannot allow in our country.'

"They can allow terrorists, they can allow murderers, they can allow mafia people and they can give them refuge — but they cannot allow me. And I was not asking for refuge or permanent residence, just an overnight stay.

"We turned to London, because it was simply a question of our basic right. And we made it twice legal — we purchased first-class tickets for the next day. Our own jet was there but still we purchased them in case they started saying, 'You don't have tickets for tomorrow, so we won't allow you to stay in the first-class lounge.'

"We purchased tickets for everybody just so that we could stay in the lounge, and we told them, 'We have our own jet — and we also have tickets.' But they came upon a by-law of the airport that the government or anybody cannot interfere with. 'It is our discretion — and this man we won't allow in the lounge'.

"In the lounge, I thought, how can I destroy their morality, their religion? In the first place I will be sleeping, and by the morning we will be gone.

"But no, these so-called civilized countries are as primitive and barbarous as you can conceive. They said, 'All that we can do is, we can put you in jail for the night.'

"And just by chance one of our friends looked into their file. They had all the instructions from the government already about how they were to treat me: I should not be allowed in any way to enter into the country, even for an overnight stay in a hotel or in the lounge; the only way was that I should be kept in jail.

"In the morning we moved to Ireland. Perhaps the man did not take note of my name amongst the passengers. We had asked just to stay for two or three days — 'at the most seven, if you can give us.' We wanted time because some other decision was being made, and they were delaying it, and our movement was dependent on that decision.

"The man was really generous...must have taken too much beer; he gave everybody twenty-one days. We moved to the hotel and immediately the police arrived at the hotel to cancel them saying, 'That man is mad — he does not know anything.'

"They canceled the visas, but they were in a difficult situation — what to do with us? We were already in the land, we were in the hotel; we had passed a few hours in the hotel. They had given us twenty-one days on the passports, and now they had canceled them. We were not ready to go; we had to wait still a few days.

"You can see how bureaucracy covers its own errors. They said, 'You can stay here, but nobody should come to know about it — no press, nobody should come to know that Bhagwan is here because then we will be in trouble.' This whole journey has been an exposure of the bureaucracies.

"And just now I have received the information that all the countries of Europe, jointly, are deciding that I cannot land my plane at any airport. How will that affect their morality — refueling the plane?"

I set foot on English soil, after eleven years' absence, like a samurai in fighting mood. Kendra had been in touch with John on the telephone from Osho's plane and had heard the story that England had not only refused to allow Osho in the country, but they had kept Him in prison overnight.

Our two tons of luggage was put on a trolley the size of a truck and the porter kept muttering to me, "Oh! luv, they're gonna take you apart for this. Oh! luv, they'll never let you in the country with all this."

Maneesha, Kendra and I were walking alongside the trolley while Avirbhava took care of Sarvesh, whose blue, swollen face looked quite frightening. David waited outside, while Kaveesha knew the art of traveling — at every opportunity she sat silently.

We didn't want to say we were arriving from Greece, so when the two customs officers asked where we were coming from Kendra, with a flip of her blonde waves of hair that had fallen seductively over one side of her face, said, "Somewhere else!"

"Somewhere else? Mm," echoed the official.

"And where are you going?" he continued. "Somewhere else, I suppose," conveniently answering his own question.

"Yes," said Kendra.

"Okay," he said.

We were such a colorful group of people, and our amount of luggage so out of the ordinary, that in a few airports the officials volunteered that we must be a theater group, to which we agreed, of course.

We settled in a flat in Kensington where we were to spend the next two weeks silently waiting.

Sannyasins all over the world were silently waiting throughout the whole world tour. Osho's people, wherever they are in the world, and whatever their outward circumstances, are all moving together on an inner journey. I think we were all experiencing the same inner difficulties and challenges while Osho was literally living in an airplane, looking for a place to land.

Our connection with Osho, and with each other through Osho, is so deep that, as far as I understand, we are moving together as one body, and time and space do not enter into it. Whether a disciple is sitting next to Osho physically or ten thousand miles away, the distance depends on that person's meditativeness.

In Pune when Osho was speaking every day, it was very clear that there existed a collective consciousness. We were all connected, often experiencing similar emotions and changes, and even having the same thoughts. It was a common occurrence that Osho would answer someone's question in discourse that was éxactly the question you had wanted to ask, word for word; and many times Osho would speak on subjects that a few friends had been discussing just the night before. I heard from many people that this was their experience. It was uncanny — almost as though He had been eavesdropping.

Now in London, there was nothing we could do — we did not know Osho's whereabouts or when we would meet again, and it was a great opportunity to be in the moment. To think of the past or to worry about the future was dangerous. Dangerous for both mental and physical health. We were in a situation that was fertile for mind-fucking, and the only way out — was in. I was to ask Osho:

"Beloved Master,

When things become difficult for me I take refuge in the here-and-now. In the moment all is still, and it is the only way for me to stand on the razor's edge. And yet a doubt comes in that I am escaping what is really happening: I may simply be wearing blinkers. Beloved, please help me understand which is true."

Osho: "Never listen to the mind. Mind is the great deceiver. If you are feeling silent and still in the present moment, that experience is so valuable that mind has no authority to judge it. Mind is far below it.

"Mind is always of the past or about the future. Either memory or imagination, it knows nothing of the present. And all that is, is in the present.

"...Life consists only of moments; there is no past life, there is no future life. Whenever life is, it is always in the present. And this is the dichotomy: life is herenow, and mind is never herenow. This is one of the most important discoveries of the East: that mind is absolutely impotent as far as your subjectivity is concerned, as far as your being is concerned....

"...Whenever you experience something that is beyond mind, mind will create doubt, will argue against it, will make you look embarrassed about it. These are its old techniques. It cannot produce anything of the quality that the present moment creates. In fact mind is not creative at all. All creation in any dimension of life comes from the no-mind — the greatest paintings, the great music, the great poetry — all that is beautiful, all that makes man different from animals, comes from that small moment.

"If knowingly you enter into it, it can lead you to enlightenment. If unknowingly, accidentally, it happens, then it still leads to a tremendous silence, relaxation, peace, intelligence. If it is just an accident...you had reached the temple but missed by just one more step. That's where I think all creative artists, dancers, musicians, scientists, are...just one step more.

"The mystic enters to the very core of the present moment and finds the golden key; his whole life becomes a divine rejoicing. Whatever happens, his rejoicing is not going to be affected.

"But until you have entered the shrine, even at the very last moment, mind will still try to pull you back: 'Where are you going? This is sheer madness! You are escaping from life.'

"And mind has never given you any life. It has never given you any taste so that you can see what life is. It has never revealed any mystery. But it is constantly pulling you back, because once you enter the shrine it will be left outside, just where you leave your shoes. It cannot enter into the shrine. It is not in its capacity, its potential.

"So be watchful. When the mind says to you that you are escaping from life, say to the mind, 'Where is life? What life are you talking about? I am escaping into life, not from life.' Be very alert about the mind because that is your enemy inside you, and if you are not alert, that enemy can sabotage every possibility of growth. Just a little alertness, and mind cannot do any harm." (*The Path of the Mystic*)

After two weeks the news came that Osho was on His way to Uruguay. Uruguay! Where is that? we asked each other. South America! But isn't that where there are military coups every couple of years, and secret police that take people for interrogation, never to be seen again? It was an unknown and potentially dangerous country to us.

I remembered when in Nepal we looked at an atlas of the world and wondered where to go. The whole world was available, and now the world had become very very small. There was nowhere to go. Hasya and Jayesh had been making enquiries all over the world and there wasn't a country in which we were welcome. The message that governments were receiving was that we were terrorists. America was informing countries that were indebted to them that they had to put pressure on Osho.

I have not been able to understand why the American politicians went so berserk over Osho. I know that what He says is against their culture, society, beliefs, but that He should be so persecuted for speaking the truth is hard for me to understand.

I asked Rafia, who was born and brought up in America — although I would not call him an American — what he thought it was that made the Americans behave in such an insane way. Speaking with a throaty drawl and twinkle in his eyes he said, "Well, Osho laid waste to all the gods of America — the first being the money god." He said that the materialism of America is such that everyone aspires to have a great car, and Osho had not one but ninety-six Rolls Royces.

He said that the idea that the American has of being a great frontiersman was also upstaged. In just five years a piece of Oregon desert had been transformed into a model city and farmland where thousands of people were living and dancing. Rafia remembered when he first arrived in Oregon from California and saw the bumper stickers on the cars that read "Better dead than red," and the posters with Osho's face with a cross through it indicating "wipe him out."

Then, of course, there is the Christian god. Reagan and his government were fanatical Christians and Osho was saying:

"In the past two thousand years Christianity has done more harm to humanity than any other religion. It has slaughtered people, burned people alive. In the name of God, truth, religion, it has been killing and slaughtering people — for their own sake, for their own good.

"And when the murderer is murdering you for your own

good, then he has no feeling of guilt at all. On the contrary, he feels he has done a good job. He has done some service to humanity, to God, to all the great values of love, truth, freedom." (*Jesus Crucified Again, This Time in Ronald Reagan's America*)

Where there is god there is also the devil, and America's devil is communism. In the commune we created a higher form of communism and it worked. "For the first time in the history of the world, five thousand people have lived as a family. Nobody asked any body's country or religion or caste or race. Every year twenty thousand people around the world used to come to see this miracle. The American politicians became disturbed by the success of the commune…"

"What is it about Osho that drives public officials to attempted murder? What makes the U.S. attorney general, the U.S. attorney for Oregon, a federal magistrate, and federal judge and justice department officials join in an assassination conspiracy? The answer was perhaps best stated by best-selling author Tom Robbins, when he said:

"…the authorities intuitively sense something dangerous in Bhagwan's message. Why else would they have singled him out for the kind of malicious persecution they never have directed at a Filippino dictator or a Mafia don? If Ronald Reagan had had his way, this gentle vegetarian would have been crucified on the White House lawn.

"The danger they intuit is that in Bhagwan's words…there is information that, if properly assimilated, can help to set men and women loose from their control. Nothing frightens the state, or its partner in crime, organized religion, so much as the prospect of a population thinking for itself and living free." (*Jesus Crucified Again, This Time in Ronald Reagan's America*)

I would sometimes wish that Osho did not have to expose politicians and priests. I would think why can't He just talk to us of magic, quietly somewhere where no one in the world cares. But Osho cared, and it becomes more evident each day how the unconsciousness of man is destroying the planet. He had to speak the truth because He could do nothing else.

"There is no need to be angry, there is no need to carry any complaint. Whatever they have done, they will have to reap the crop also. They have exposed themselves. And this is the way all these vested interests have been behaving with people who stand for truth, so it is not new... But one thing that makes me glad is that a single man without any power can frighten the greatest power in the world, can shake it from its very roots... I will manage to expose them. There is no need to be angry with them — just expose them. Bring their true face before the world. That's enough..." (*Jesus Crucified Again, This Time in Ronald Reagan's America*)

Each country that refused Osho entry was showing its true face. It was an insightful lesson to see that all the so-called democratic countries are mere puppets belonging to America.

We were aliens, wherever we went.

CHAPTER FOURTEEN

Uruguay

Enlightenment Day, March 21st. I left London airport for Uruguay with four bodyguards. Hasya and Jayesh hired the security men who were specialists in counter-insurgency, counter-terrorist work, and trained in communication, demolition and firearms; each one with his own particular skill. They were to guard Osho while He was in Uruguay, as we had no idea what we were walking into. They stood around me like soldiers and looked threatening, and I felt well taken care of.

Osho was staying in a hotel in Montevideo when I arrived and that same day I went to tidy His room for Him. He was sitting in a chair next to the window and He looked tired. Devaraj told me that Osho had been very weak in Ireland, and could not even walk the distance of the corridor outside His room. I touched His feet and sat beaming at Him. I asked Him how He was and He nodded that He was okay. He wanted to know if I was fully recovered from the accident, and I told him that although I knew I had been stupid to go on the motorbike in the first place, I had found it a valuable experience. He didn't say anything, and I gave Him a drink of water and then tidied His room while He sat silently.

We did not celebrate His Enlightenment Day that year, and I remembered that in Kathmandu He had already said that He did not want special celebration days, but we were to celebrate every day of the year.

At the hotel were Anando, Vivek, Devaraj, John, Mukti and Rafia and they were soon telling me of their days spent in Ireland, penned up in the hotel, not allowed to even leave the second floor where their rooms were. It was like a voluntary house arrest situation. They saw only the four walls of their rooms, or someone else's — which was identical anyway — all day. The local police said they had received threats from the IRA regarding Osho, so security men guarded Him twenty-four hours a day, and the hotel was filled with whispered Motorola conversations and mattress barricades. When Osho left the hotel after three weeks the hotel staff were there to say good-bye to Him, and Osho told the manager that He had been very comfortable in the hotel, it had been a home to Him. Now, in Uruguay, Osho was asking us to please telephone the hotel in Ireland and ask them for the recipe of the chutney they gave Him; and to tell them that it was the best *chutney* He had ever had.

Hasya and Jayesh had arrived in Montevideo and found a house for Osho in Punta del Este. It was said to be the riviera of South America, and proved to be so beautiful that we were in wonder that the rest of the world did not know about it.

The next day, Jayesh, Anando and I drove for three hours through the flat, green countryside, to Punta del Este. The house was three minutes' walk from sand dunes that led to a long flat beach and the sea! The sea air in that area was reputed for its healing powers and it smelt clean and sweet.

The house was magnificent, and as it was built originally as two houses, then joined into one, it was huge. Outside, framed by tall eucalyptus trees with their multi-colored peeling trunks, was a lawn garden, swimming pool and tennis court. The neighborhood excelled Beverly Hills, said Hasya and John, who had been living in Hollywood before moving to Rajneeshpuram.

Osho's rooms were at the top of a winding staircase. On a small landing we put His dining table, opposite a thirty-foot-high narrow window, through which trees could be seen. There was a small corridor and at one end was a large modern bathroom, almost as good as Osho's bathroom at Rajneeshpuram, and at the other, a bedroom. The bedroom was not the greatest, but it was the only room in the house with an air conditioner and complete privacy. It was dark and one third of the room was partitioned off by a sliding oak paneled door. This small room had a strange feeling to it and always had a weird smell. We used to joke that there was a ghost there. But the house was spotlessly clean, and Osho was pleased.

When He arrived He walked around with His hand on His hip admiring the house and gardens. After a couple of days He came to sit in the garden every day. It was such a joy to see Him walking down the steps, holding Vivek's hand, past the pool and to His chair that was placed ready for Him. One day He came out wearing what I call His nightie — a long white robe, and no hat, but with His Cazal sunglasses on, the ones we used to call His mafia glasses. The scene had an intimate and eccentric touch. Sometimes He would do work with Hasya and Jayesh and sometimes with Anando, or He would just sit, in perfect stillness, for maybe two or three hours, until Vivek would come to collect Him to tell Him that His lunch was ready. He never read anything, He never even shifted His body in the chair, just sat motionless.

While He sat by the pool we would all stay discreetly out of sight. Osho, without asking, always creates a feeling in people to respect His privacy. When He is with us in discourse, He gives so much, that if He walks around the garden, or when He eats, He is left entirely to Himself. Should He meet anyone just by chance then it is quite something to see with what totality He will greet that person; His look will penetrate, and I have been left shaken from accidental meetings with Him — but still, it feels much better to give Him His privacy. So although we were living in the same house as Osho He sat silently alone when He was not talking to us in discourse.

Anando told me about one day when she was sitting with Osho in the garden reading Him newspaper clippings and letters that had arrived from disciples. A strong wind from the sea blew up and the tall fir trees towering over the house started to sway and shake their pine cones down like a shower of small rocks. The cones were landing around her and Osho, thud! thud! and she urged Osho to move under the shelter of the roof. He said in a voice, totally matter-of-fact, "No, no, they won't hit me," and He calmly sat there, while Anando jumped as cones rained down on either side of them. She was to remember just how relaxed He was and how ordinary was His certainty that He would not be hit.

After about two weeks, the police put us under surveillance, and they watched the house twenty-four hours a day from their car, slowly circling the house. This meant the end of Osho's walks in the garden. He was now confined to His room, with the blinds drawn for safety. We were always in fear that some harm would come to Osho, and it often meant that His life was restricted to His room. But He always said that anyway He just sits silently with His eyes closed, so it makes no difference. He said that if one is happy with oneself, centered, there is no need to go anywhere because you cannot find any place better than your own inner being. "...I am always myself wherever I am. And because I am blissful wherever I am the place becomes blissful for me." ...Osho

The neighborhood was quiet as the tourist season was just finishing and winter was approaching. This quiet secluded place was to become a diamond mine for me; an exploration and discovery of treasures within myself, as Osho gave one key after another that opened new doors of mystery.

For the next few weeks I forgot the world completely; it felt quiet and peaceful. The private security men went home, and we even made friends with the police. Our fear and disillusion with the world because of its treatment of Osho were answered by Him:

"Trust simply means that whatever happens we are with it, joyously, not reluctantly, not unwillingly — then you miss the whole point — but dancingly, with a song, with laughter, with love, whatever happens is for the good.

"Existence cannot go wrong.

"If it does not fulfill our desires that simply means our desires were wrong." (*The Path of the Mystic*)

Hasya and Jayesh were constantly visiting different countries trying to find a home for Osho, in case Uruguay should not work out. They made a forty hour flight to Mauritius, at the invitation of the prime minister, only to discover that he wanted six billion dollars for Osho to enter his country. France asked for ten million dollars for what was virtually a five year lease. Twenty-one countries had now denied Osho entry, some countries that we had not even thought about! Such fear that Osho would destroy the morality of their country, just by landing in the airport.

Osho started giving discourses twice a day. He would come down the winding staircase, cross the shining red-tiled floor, hands in *namaste*, and enter the beautiful open sitting room where there was room for about forty people to sit. His talks were much different here, as it was a very intimate situation and He spoke quietly and slowly. He no longer spoke with the fire with which He had delivered his talks at Rajneeshpuram and in Pune. Finding questions to ask was a great "cleansing of the unconscious," as Osho said; sometimes He would answer five or six questions in one sitting and He did not always accept the questions we asked. Maneesha had quite a job collecting questions from us, because it is not always easy to find a question when the last one you asked maybe got you a zen stick for an answer.

"...Remember one thing, when you ask a question be ready for any answer. Don't expect a certain answer that you would like; otherwise there is not going to be any learning, there is not going to be any growth. If I say you are not right at a certain point, try to look at it. I will not be saying it just to hurt you. If I am saying it, I mean it.

"And if you start feeling hurt by small things, then it will become impossible for me to work. Then I have to see what you would like. Then I will not be a help, then I will not be a master to you." ...Osho

Osho would also speak about the beautiful space that a disciple arrives at when there are no more questions:

"...That is the real work of a master, a mystic, that sooner or later the people who are with him start feeling questionless.

"To be questionless is the answer."

"Beloved Master,

"This morning, as you spoke of the 'questionless answer,' I watched my questions dissolving into silence, which I shared for a moment with you. But one question survived, and that is: If we don't ask you questions, how are we going to play with you?"

Osho: "That's really a question!

"It will be difficult, so whether you have the questions or not, still you can go on asking just the same. Your question need not be yours, but it must be somebody else's, somewhere. And my answer may help somebody somewhere, sometime. So let us continue the game.

"I cannot say anything on my own. Unless there is a question, I am silent. Because of the question it is possible for me to respond. So it does not matter whether the question is yours; what matters is that the question is bound to be somebody's, somewhere.

"And I am not only answering you. I am answering, through you, the whole of humanity...not only the contemporary humanity, but also the humanity that will be coming when I will not be here to answer.

"So find out all the possible angles and questions, so that anybody, even in the future when I am not here, who has a question can find an answer in my words.

"To us it is a play. To somebody it may become really a question of life and death."

With a sickening thud, the realization hit me that Osho knew He would not be recognized or understood in His lifetime. This was for posterity. My hopes, my dreams, that somewhere in the world His work would flourish and hundreds of thousands of people would come to see Him, had no reality. That He would be giving discourses on satellite television to millions and that He would be able to see hundreds of his disciples attain enlightenment was not to be.

While answering a question from Maneesha, He said:

"It may take time, but there is no scarcity of time. And there is no need that the revolution should happen before our eyes. It is contentment enough that you were part of a movement that changed the world, that you played your role in favor of truth, that you will be part of the victory that is going to happen ultimately." (*Beyond Psychology*)

I would be spun, delirious, while He spoke on techniques for leaving the body, hypnosis as a technique for remembering past lives, ancient Tibetan, Sufi and Tantric techniques — but He always brought us back to witnessing. He said that techniques for leaving the body are good to give an experience that shows that you are not the body, but that is all. To understand past lives and to know that you have been here before, it is good to see that you are moving in a circle, to know that the same mistakes have been made before, but meditation and witnessing are needed to jump out of the wheel. He gave us techniques to experiment with that showed the power of mind over body, and experiments in telepathy to see how in tune and interconnected we were with each other.

It was the birth of the Mystery School.

In the garden was a thatched roof games room, and it was here that Kaveesha would hypnotize a group of us at a time. We experimented with telepathy, and as the group became harmonious and close, the daily routine of cleaning the house and cooking was so smooth it felt as though no one was really working. The whole day revolved around Osho's talks and our experiments with different techniques. We used to report to Him how things were working, or not working, for us, and He would give further guidance — each time taking us one step further into unknown territory.

Osho, while taking us on great flights of mystery, continued to tell us that the greatest mystery is silence and meditation.

"Spirituality is a very innocent state of consciousness where nothing happens, just time comes to a standstill, all desires are gone, there is no longing, no ambition. This very moment becomes all...

"You are separate, totally separate. You are only a witness and nothing else." ...Osho

He said that witnessing has to be done in a very relaxed state. It is not concentration: it is an awareness of everything you do, breathing, eating, taking a walk. He told us to start with simple things — watching the body, as though we are separate from it — watching the thoughts that cross the screen of the mind, as though watching a movie, and watch when emotions come and know that they are not us. The final step is when we are absolutely silent and there is nothing to watch: then the witness turns upon itself.

To one person he said that she was not yet ready for witnessing, because she would feel a split within herself. He told her that first she had to express negative emotions (but only in privacy — never throw it on other people) because to witness you have to be without repression. I think if a person feels comfortable with witnessing, if a feeling of peacefulness and joy is there, then it is a good criterion that you are ready for it. Like any method for meditation, if you feel good, then it is suiting you.

He spoke on the seven levels of consciousness, and the limitations of psychology and psychiatry in the West — which is far, far behind the East in this field. I listened to these discourses with my antennae quivering, I was listening with such a sense of urgency and fascination that my head tingled.

During these weeks I was going through a process of trying to distinguish reality from imagination. I asked Osho four or five questions about reality and imagination and was starting to think that nothing in my life was real. I spent many hours alone walking up and down the beach trying to get it. I finally understood when Osho said that He never did tell us to discriminate between one and the other: that reality is that which never changes, and imagination, if watched, disappears. The two can never be present at the same time so there is no question of discrimination.

Looking back, I can't relate to the questions that were burning me up then. Maybe because Osho has helped me to understand them. I think that without a master I would have gone crazy with the existential angst and I would have become stuck on one question, maybe for life.

I used to walk alone through the beautiful streets lined with fir trees and eucalyptus, the mansions empty of life because of the season, trying to understand who I was. All my thoughts amounted to nothing. I couldn't work it out.

Was I simply the energy that surged through me when I closed my eyes?

Was I the expression of that energy?

Or was I the awareness of that energy?

Osho said that energy, as awareness, is the closest to

the very center of existence. He said that it is all one energy, but in thinking, or expressing, then the energy is moving towards the periphery... "Drop backwards step by step," He said. "It is a journey to the source, and the source is all that you need to experience...because it is not only your source, it is the source of the stars and the moon and the sun. It is the source of all."

While I was doing the laundry and while cleaning Osho's rooms, I was thinking of questions and at the same time still trying to digest the discourse that had happened just a few hours before.

"Where is the definition between my inner world and the outer world? When each event outside is seen through my eyes, my perception, it seems to become my world, so is therefore inner. And on the other side, if the witness is my inner reality, and yet the witness is universal, then I seem to have flipped inside out once again," I asked.

"Chetana, you are getting crazy!" said Osho.

I was. As I walked around the sand dunes and the beach, the dialogue with the inner master would continue:

"Maybe I exist only because I think I do!"

"Maybe without thoughts I wouldn't exist at all!!"

Osho has said that the mind will never understand truth because it is far above and beyond the mind, but I had to try somehow, if only to fall exhausted and realize that my mind was useless in the world of the mystic. I had heard Him say that the mind could not grasp the inner world, but it was not my understanding, I had not experienced this for myself. So day by day I was driving myself crazy, trying to work it all out.

Osho told a beautiful story:

"A mystic king built a great city and within that city he made a temple with red stones outside, and inside it is made of small mirrors...millions of mirrors inside. So when you go inside you see yourself reflected in millions of mirrors. You are one, but your reflections are millions.

"It is said that once a dog entered and killed himself in the night. Nobody was there: the guard had left the temple, locked it and the dog remained inside. He would bark at the dogs — millions of dogs. And he jumped from this side to that side and hit himself against the walls. And all those dogs were barking... You can see what would have happened to the poor dog: the whole night he barked and he fought, and he killed himself by hitting himself against the walls.

"In the morning when the door was opened the dog was found dead and his blood was all over the place — on the walls — and the neighbors said, 'The whole night we were puzzled about what was the matter. This dog continued barking.'

"That dog must have been an intellectual. Naturally he thought, 'So many dogs, my god! I am alone and it is nighttime and the doors are closed, and surrounded by all these dogs...they are going to kill me!' And he killed himself; there was no other dog at all.

"This is one of the basic and essential understandings of mysticism; the people we are seeing all around are only our reflections.

"We are unnecessarily fighting with each other, unnecessarily afraid of each other. There is so much fear that we are gathering nuclear weapons against each other — and it is just one dog, and all others are just reflections.

"So Chetana, don't be intellectual. Don't think about these problems; otherwise you will get more and more puzzled. Rather become aware and you will see the problems disappearing.

"I am not here to solve your problems but to dissolve your problems — and the difference is great." (*The Path of the Mystic*)

Without asking Osho questions, He would not speak, and when He did, He was telling us of great mysteries and secrets and I heard Him say that although He knew that much of what he was saying was going above our heads, it had to be said. I had the feeling that He had to say everything He could to us because time was running short.

Osho told no jokes during these talks, but that does not mean that they were without laughter. One night we were laughing so much that we couldn't stop. I remember looking at everyone — Hasya was there that night — and I remember looking at her and we made each other laugh even more. Our laughter continued uncontrollably long after Osho had left the joke behind and was talking on something "serious." Japanese Geeta had a shrill and startling laugh which used to make Osho laugh whenever He heard her. He would stop speaking and they would simply be laughing together, apparently at nothing, while the rest of us would catch the infectious laughter and eventually everyone would be laughing. He said that laughter is the greatest spiritual phenomenon:

"The master's laughter and the disciple's laughter have exactly the same quality, the same value. There is no difference at all.

"In every other thing there are differences: the disciple is a disciple, he is learning, groping in the dark. The master is full of light, all groping has ceased, so every act is going to be different. But whether you are in darkness or in full light, laughter can join you.

"To me, laughter is the highest spiritual quality, where the ignorant and the enlightened meet." (*The Transmission of the Lamp*)

But the reality of the political situation regarding Osho's visa was serious. Although it had been decided to give a permanent resident's visa to Osho and even a press statement prepared to that effect, the very next day it was canceled. Sanguinetti, the President of Uruguay received a message from Washington. He was told that if Osho became a resident of Uruguay then the loans that America were about to give Uruguay would be canceled. Simple!

Hasya and Jayesh were traveling most of the time. The idea of living on an ocean liner was in the air, and Hasya and Jayesh had traveled to England to check out the situation with buying redundant aircraft carriers, and they had then gone to Hong Kong to look at a ship. Osho felt dizzy even if He saw someone else sitting on a swing, so it seemed impossible that He would be able to be on a ship. But despite this, He went totally into making intricate plans for living on a ship. I have never heard Osho say no to anything. When Hasya said that we thought living on a ship would be bad for His health, He said: "Well, if I have got used to being on this planet, my body will get used to being on a boat. This way you people will have freedom." When not flying all over the world Hasya and Jayesh were in Montevideo with Marcos. Marcos was a Uruguayan businessman who had contacts in the government. He was a big-hearted, innocent man, and he was working very hard to enable Osho to stay in his country.

One night Osho called Vivek and Devaraj to His room and said to them that He no longer felt safe in Uruguay. He wanted to go back to India.

Uruguay lost its charm at this point and I felt we were surrounded once again by menace. Two days later the police, who had been diligently watching the house for the last ten weeks, stopped. This felt weird to us: maybe someone was going to harm Osho, and the police did not want to be involved? We got in touch with the police, and this time, even paid them to stay outside the house.

The atmosphere was getting tense, as Hasya and Jayesh were away and John and a Chilean *sannyasin* called Isabel, who had just arrived, were now continuing the liaison work with the government, but with a different contact. They did not feel to work with Marcos, and instead they worked with their own contact and friend in the government, called

Alvarez. He too was a beautiful man, and he became a *sannyasin*, but I never quite trusted him. He was just too charming, too handsome.

When we first arrived in Uruguay the government had received telex messages from NATO sources, marked "diplomatic secret information," the source of which was the U.S.A. The information in these telexes was that we (Osho's disciples) were drug traffickers, smugglers and prostitutes!

One day during the last few weeks of our stay the police turned up on our doorstep wanting to search the house. We had heard that this was dangerous because it was a common thing that drugs were "planted" on people if they were undesirable in any way and no crime had been committed. Keeping them on the doorstep, because they had no warrant, I raced up the stairs to Osho's room, where He was talking to Hasya and Jayesh. I entered, and said that the police were here. Osho continued talking to Hasya as calmly as you like, as though nothing was happening. I left the room and five minutes later Hasya appeared and said that she had to finally stand up and say to Osho that she was sorry, but she was unable to listen to what He was saying, her attention was downstairs with the police, and she had to go and see what was happening.

The police went away, but already the situation was complicated and undesirable, and now that Osho said He wanted to leave it was finished.

But it was not quite finished, because we refused to see the reality of the situation. In the second week of June, John and Isabel were given a promise by Alvarez that it was okay for Osho to stay for at least another six weeks, and after that it was almost certain that he would get a resident's visa. This was good news to us, something that we wanted to hear.

I went to Montevideo on June 16th to the dentist, and as usual called in to see Marcos and his family. He was frightened as he told me that he had heard that if Osho was not out of the country by the 18th June, then He would be arrested. President Sanguinetti was in Washington meeting Reagan, negotiating the new loans for Uruguay, his first visit in many years.

I went straight back to our house, told Vivek, who told Osho, and immediately plans were made to arrange a private plane, and a new country to land in.

Jamaica was to be our new hope. By the end of the day I was packed, and early the next morning I left on a flight to Jamaica with Rafia. Osho was to follow in a private plane with Vivek, Devaraj, Anando and Mukti.

The day Osho left Uruguay telephone calls from Washington were received in the Uruguay Home Office, every hour, on the hour, asking whether Osho had left the country.

In the afternoon of the 18th at 5.00 p.m. Alvarez telephoned saying that he had received a telegram from the Immigration Department saying that Osho had to report to the immigration department before 5.30 p.m., or else he would be arrested.

I heard that at about 6.30 p.m. Osho left the house that had become our mystery school, just as three police cars were arriving. The police followed Osho's car to the airport, and while all the *sannyasins* from the house, with Marcos, celebrated with songs and danced with Osho, they watched with stunned faces. The tense atmosphere at the airport was diffused in the celebration as Osho made His way to the waiting jet.

More police cars screeched into the airport as the jet climbed high and only two flickering tail-lights could be seen, disappearing into the night sky.

The United States of America announced on 19th June that Uruguay would receive a new loan of 150 million dollars.

CHAPTER FIFTEEN

You Can't Hide Me

R afia and I arrived in Montego Bay, Jamaica after Osho's plane, because we had stopped in Miami. I was feeling faint from the heat and the root canal I had had done at the dentist's the day before was throbbing to such an extent I could have screamed.

We were met at the airport and taken to a house that Arup had found for Osho. Arup, steadfast and loyal, had survived working with both of Osho's female tyrants — Laxmi and Sheela — and had come through smiling. And now, having remained in contact with Hasya and Jayesh, who were in Portugal, she heard how dangerous it had become in Uruguay for Osho and so flew immediately to Jamaica and found a place of refuge. The house belonged to a tennis celebrity and was a sprawling bungalow in its own grounds, with a swimming pool, and a beautiful view of the island.

Most of our group had stayed behind in Uruguay to settle up the house and wait to see what happened next. The people of Uruguay that we had met were starting a court case against the government, because not only was their refusal of Osho's resident's visa illegal, but it destroyed the Uruguayans' illusion that they were a free country. It hurt to see that they were owned by "the people in the North" as they referred to the Americans.

As soon as we arrived we received the good news that

Osho had been given a tourist visa at the airport in Kingston, Jamaica, without any difficulty, but then the bad news that ten minutes after Osho's plane had landed, an American Navy Jet had flown in. It was suspicious. Anando had seen it land, and as two civilians alighted and crossed the tarmac to the terminus she had quickly moved Osho and the others out of the lounge and into taxis. We knew that our telephones were tapped in Uruguay and in fact Anando had asked Osho a question about it: "Why do people always tap our telephones? Are they trying to get spiritual guidance on the cheap?"

After five minutes of gossip I retreated to the room that I was to share with Anando. It was small, but air-conditioned and cool, and I looked in the cupboards wondering whether it was worth unpacking or not. Then I took some pain killers for my tooth and slept for fourteen hours.

The next morning, while I was taking my breakfast, there was loud knocking at the front door. I looked through the window and saw six very tall black men, dressed in khaki shorts and holding large sticks. They said they were the police. Anando went out to speak to them and they sounded angry and asked that everyone who had arrived in Jamaica the day before should come outside with their passports! She assured them that we all had legal entry visas, and asked what their problem was. They said that we had to leave the island — now!

When they left Anando rang Arup, who was staying at a nearby hotel, and Arup got in touch with our tennis star, who knew people in the government, hoping to be able to sort things out.

It seemed, even to us, that a mistake must have been made. During the next couple of hours we made many phone calls to people who were friends of the tennis star and could help, we hoped. "Very strange," said our friend, "whenever I mention who is calling I am told that so-and-so is not in his office today. Nobody seems to be in their office today, or at home. I can't get hold of anyone who will help."

Two hours later the police came back. This time my heart sank, as they took our passports and canceled our visas. Mercifully, we managed to keep Osho out of sight, so He was not subjected to standing on the porch in the scorching heat. The men were very aggressive, and the all too familiar stink of fear was there. Did they also think they were confronting dangerous terrorists, as had all the police we had met in America, India and Crete?

When Anando asked them why we were being ordered out of the country they simply said, "Orders." When she persisted in asking for more information they told her that the orders were under the National Security Act. Osho had to be out of the country by sunset.

We did not have a plane, or even a country to which we could go! Certainly we could not stay in Jamaica, because we were frightened for Osho's safety.

Cliff, who was Osho's pilot and had met Him in Dubai with the open umbrella, was there and started phoning all over America to find a charter plane company that would take Osho somewhere. Most charter companies refused when they knew who their passenger was, and it was not easy to disguise the fact. Not knowing where you are flying to is also a disadvantage when trying to hire a jet. Flight plans have to be made in advance of any journey, and agreed on between the pilots and the country to be approached.

Hasya and Jayesh were in Portugal trying to arrange a resident's visa for Osho to visit there, but they said that the permission had not been given yet. The rest of Europe was out of the question, and Devaraj even had the idea of Cuba. But Osho had said to Hasya a few weeks before: "No, Castro is a Marxist."

What with the narrow escape in Uruguay, and now

this — Vivek was finished. She said that she wanted nothing more to do with anything! She was angry and said she wanted to leave the group. This made me nervous. I was always nervous when she fell into one of these dark moods.

I heard that Osho had been up earlier that morning in the brilliant Jamaican sunshine and looked all over the house. He walked in the garden and around the swimming pool and was seen by Leroy the gardener, who was so overwhelmed by the sight of Osho that he went home for the day and said, "That man is really something. I ain't never seen a man like that before." Osho made plans for air-conditioners to be installed in the sitting room, where He could resume discourses, but now He sat silently in His room and I took Him messages about the plans that we were making.

I was scared. I thought that at any moment the police ("Were they really police?" I asked. "I don't even know what a Jamaican policeman looks like"; they looked like very strong thugs to me) would be back, and we would all end up dead, looking like a typical photograph in *Newsweek* or *Time* magazine. And who in the world would care?

By early afternoon Cliff had managed to arrange for a plane to fly from Colorado to collect us, and now all we had to do was wait! The plane was due to arrive at 7.00 p.m. and so at about 6.00 p.m. Cliff, Devaraj and Rafia left with the luggage for the airport. They would ring us as soon as they had loaded the plane and we could drive straight to the airport.

That left just Anando, Vivek, Maneesha and me with Osho, and the house was isolated, in the countryside. After 7.00 p.m. passed, each minute seemed like an eternity and then...all the lights went out. The electricity had been cut off and it was pitch dark. I thought, "This is it!"

I found a candle and put it in a glass and stumbled through the dark to Osho's room. He was sitting in a chair next to the air conditioner, which of course had ceased working, and the room was getting very hot. He was perfectly relaxed but concerned about the air conditioner, because usually we had a generator so that the air conditioner never stopped, but He didn't know that. I left the candle with Him and went back to the sitting room where we were all searching for candles and waiting for the phone to ring.

Eight o'clock came and still no phone call from the airport. I went to Osho's room to see how He was, and He wasn't in His chair. The room was in darkness and although I called out His name He did not answer. I stood there for several minutes and was just about to scream in panic when the door of the bathroom opened and He walked towards me carefully carrying the makeshift candle holder so it didn't burn His fingers. I was so happy and relieved to see Him, and I can only describe the look on His face as delight. Absolute delight. He was smiling like a child playing a game. I showed Him I had brought a better candle holder and He said, "No, this one is good." I said that it would burn His fingers, but He liked it, and carried it over to His chair and sat down. So I put the candlestick down and left Him sitting there with two candles glowing while I went to join the others.

A knock at the door almost finished me off completely, but it was our tennis star. He had come to see if we were alright because of the blackout and he also brought his wife and child. I reasoned to myself that nothing awful was going to happen if the man even brings his family here to meet Osho.

The telephone rang! The plane was here and we quickly got the last few things together, and as Osho walked out to the car He smiled and *namasted* everyone.

I drove with Osho and Arup to the airport. It had been decided to fly to Portugal. Arup's mother, Geeta, also a *sannyasin*, had a house in Portugal, and although it was too small for Osho, at least we knew a "house owner" there.

Portugal loomed up as the end of the road, and the end of all our hopes of finding a country for Osho to live in. Our fears all along had been that Osho would have to go back to India and because of our last experiences in India it seemed to be the worst thing that could happen. We thought that Western disciples would not be allowed to visit Him.

We took off for Portugal — and landed in Spain!

There had been a misunderstanding with the flight plans. But no harm done, just a little confusion, and a wait of one hour in Madrid while we refueled. Actually it was probably for the best, because when Osho landed at Lisbon airport, met by Hasya and Jayesh, He just sailed through immigration and got a visa without any problem. If our flight plans were being watched, then we were not the only ones who got confused. Osho disappeared "out of sight" for six weeks.

In Lisbon we went straight to the Ritz Hotel. We smuggled Osho up in the back elevator and did not sign Him in the register because we wanted to be low profile. He had a suite which adjoined a bedroom and bathroom that Vivek and I moved into.

The flight had been a difficult one for me because of the tension and Vivek changing her mind about whether she wanted to stay with the group or not. Osho as usual bedded down in the plane and only awoke for food and the toilet. He asked me for a Diet Coke, and when Vivek overheard, she said to me, "Don't give Him a Diet Coke, they are not good for Him. Tell Him they are finished!" Now I have never tried to stop Osho doing anything, but with Vivek watching me I bravely said to Osho, "You have had your last Diet Coke."

"What!" He said, sitting up, His eyes large.

I felt like I had just walked into a lion's den — Jamaican policemen had nothing on this!

"No more Diet Coke?!"

"Eh!" I muttered, wishing He wouldn't look at me with those eyes while I was trying to tell a lie. "They are finished." Fortunately, this turned out to be the truth, but He insisted that we get more for Him as soon as we landed. Now the funny thing is He drank nothing but Diet Coke for three years after this. Whether or not it was just coincidence, I don't know.

Our first morning in Lisbon, I was woken up by the sound of Osho's voice: "Chetana, Chetana." ....I will never forget that. Drifting out of sleep and hearing His voice calling my name. He had walked through the connecting room into our room, and was hungry. He eagerly walked towards the empty dishes that I had been too tired to put outside the door. "No, Osho, that's last night's food," I said and I went to find Mukti to see if she could come up with something from one of her Igloo carrying bags that accompanied her everywhere. While traveling on private jets Osho enjoyed experimenting with different foods that were packed in the kitchenette and fridge. He discovered biscuits that He liked very much and then it was up to us to enjoy the task of finding the same ones again. While in Mecklenberg County Jail Osho was given a yogurt — Yoplait — and He liked it so much that for years after we had an arrangement whereby it was sent from America to wherever Osho was.

On each flight He spent a lot of time in the bathroom, experimenting with different soaps and creams. He found an aerosol spray, "Evian" — spring water that felt cool when sprayed on the face, and for years He continued to use it. He had an uncanny knack for taking a liking to things that had just gone out of stock, or the company had gone bankrupt.

When He liked something He really liked it. A hair conditioner called 'Cool Mint' had been found in a small town in Oregon one day on a shopping trip and He liked it very much because it made His head feel cool, and continued to use it for years. He would use a bottle every few days, but when we tried to get more we found that the company that made it was in Canada and had no customers outside Bend, Oregon. We made special arrangements with them whereby they sent crates of Cool Mint to Germany and sannyasins in Germany forwarded them to whatever part of the world Osho was in.

He also liked a green minty cream called Mila Mourssi, and again He was using a jar every few days. This cream came from a small shop in Los Angeles which was going out of business. Osho was the owner's best customer so we were negotiating with her to sell us the complete stock, plus the recipe so we could continue making the cream ourselves.

This was always a great challenge for the *sannyasins* who did His global shopping for Him. We wouldn't tell Him how difficult it was, of course, until after we had received it. We knew He would say that He didn't want to trouble anyone. He was shaking the whole planet, but that was different.

It was such a joy to be able to give Him a shampoo or soap that He liked, and to hear Him say, "I like that very much," with such a quiet enthusiasm, and His eyes shining. He is a very simple man, and He does not ask for much.

After a few days in the Ritz, it was decided that if anyone was looking for Osho in Lisbon, The Ritz would be the obvious place. Anando found a beautiful and deserted hotel (once again we were off-season), in a nearby town called Estoril. Plans were made to leave The Ritz at night and to smuggle Osho down to the garage without having to walk through the main reception area. Anando, Hasya, Mukti and I were to wait outside Osho's room and then smuggle Him into a waiting lift so no guests or hotel staff would see Him. When He emerged in the corridor before we expected Him, wearing His white nightie, and with his long flowing beard, Anando jokingly tried to persuade Him to wear a trench coat with the collar turned up, and a hat on His head with the brim turned down.

"You can't disguise me!" He said.

Then Vivek tried to persuade Him, but He said,

"No, no, they won't recognize me without my hat!"

I left in the first car and Osho was to follow in a Mercedes that was waiting in the hotel garage. We had the idea that American agents or journalists may be looking for Osho and so we sped through the narrow winding streets, pirouetting our way up and down blind alleys and inventively shaking off any would-be pursuers.

I was to hear later from Anando that in contrast to our fears and worries Osho was totally relaxed. He didn't have the burden of a mind that projected into the future all the possible calamities that *could* happen. As He entered the garage He smiled at the garage attendants and *namasted* them as they stared back at Him with their mouths hanging open.

Hasya and Anando were trying to usher Osho into the car with haste when He stopped. Looking at Hasya He started telling her how nice the mat in His bathroom in the hotel had been. It was so comfortable when He stood on it in bare feet.

"Please, Bhagwan, get in the car!" Hasya urged.

He walked a few more paces. Yes, that particular bath mat had been great. He would like one like that in the next place.

After a two-hour drive we arrived at the hotel and quietly moved up the large staircase to where our rooms were. Immediately I started unpacking, which was a mistake because the room that Osho was in had a smell of musty perfume, which we had not noticed, and He began to get an asthma attack.

Devaraj gave Osho some medicine, but the only cure was to leave the hotel and go back to The Ritz. It was now about

2.00 a.m. and Vivek telephoned Hasya and Jayesh to come and pick Osho up. We tiptoed down the staircase, past the proprietors, who were asleep in front of a dead television set. Their door opened out into the hall, and we crept past the backs of their heads and out into the awaiting car. I stayed the night just to settle things up in the morning and make up a suitable story to explain our strange behavior.

After a few more days at The Ritz, a house was found for Osho. It was situated on a mountain-side, the only landmark on the horizon being a castle with a golden dome-shaped top, and below that, a forest. A pine forest! The house was in the middle of a pine forest, and so at last we were able to give Osho the pine forest that we had been promising Him for four years at Rajneeshpuram.

Not only was the pine forest at the end of the road in Rajneeshpuram, but this pine forest was to be at the end of the road for the world tour.

We bought new furniture for Osho's rooms, and stored the existing antique furniture in another part of the house. We cleaned His rooms and made them as zen-like as possible, with a Ritz bath mat in the bathroom. His bedroom opened out onto a balcony that was literally part of the forest. He used to have lunch and dinner on the balcony, and do work with Anando. He walked around the house and made plans for improving it, waving His arm towards the pool and suggesting we get some swans. Then the rest of the group arrived from Jamaica, so on the surface we were all ready to start again; but it never happened.

I no longer had any hopes, even though we visited mansions and palaces that were for sale, and the visa situation was always almost finalized, but...I felt weary.

We prepared a room where Osho could resume discourses, but He only sat on His balcony facing the pine forest. After about ten days the weather changed and mists crept up the mountainside and swallowed up the forest. Osho called Anando to His room and said:

"Look, a cloud has come into my room."

The mist was very bad for His health, and He was becoming asthmatic, so He could no longer sit on the balcony, but was confined to His room. He never left His room after this for the rest of the time we were in Portugal.

I heard that He said much later to Neelam that He had been very disappointed to see that Portugal had very strange vibes, that it had no possibility of meditation at all.

We lived in the forest with Osho for more than a month, but we were in hiding, to enable the necessary immigration papers to be filed before the newspapers announced the arrival of the "Sex Guru," and freaked everyone out.

It didn't feel right to be hiding Osho from the world. A diamond should reflect its rainbow colors for everyone to wonder at. This was the reason why He had left India. We had taken Osho around the world to find a place where He could talk to His people. He wasn't asking much — just to be able to share His wisdom.

I spent all these weeks in bed with a mysteriously swollen foot. The cause was never discovered, but everything was suspected from the bite of a poisonous spider to osteomyelytis. I lay in bed all day watching the flowering chestnut tree shining like gold outside my window, and listening to the constant, sharp, crack, crack, crack, of the pine cones as the heat of the sun made them burst and send their seeds showering to the ground.

If the undercurrent for me was one of sadness, it doesn't mean I lived in it all the time. As a group we were very happy and delved deeply into the delights of the first body — food! We had great feasts together, sitting at the long wooden table on the balcony that looked down the mountain to the plains on one side and on the other, up to the castle. Or, we sat inside in the great dining room around a huge oak circular table. I explored the forest, and swam in the pool when there was no one around to order me back to bed, and it was like this that we lived for four weeks.

Then one day the police came.

Two cars with about eight policemen drove down the winding path to the house and at first said they were lost. This was obviously a lie, and five minutes later they said they wanted to look around the house and that they were suspicious of us because we never left the house, and we didn't go sightseeing like other tourists. They said that Portugal was having a lot of problems with drug smugglers and terrorists.

I went to my room to dress in suitable clothes for jail and although my mind felt clear, my legs turned to jelly. This was a shock to me, because it had never happened before. I had never felt any nervousness in my body and would have thought that I was used to this kind of drama by now. It was at this moment that I realized that I was close to breaking down in some way, and the strain of the last ten months had stretched me to my limits.

I went to the front door where Anando was talking to the police. They left, but they came back the next day, and posted two men in a car in the driveway to watch us twenty-four hours a day.

Osho said He wanted to go back to India. We called Neelam, who was in Italy, to come so that she could travel with Osho and make arrangements for Him in India. He was to say to her, "I cannot use my body very long now; it is very painful to be in the body. But I can't leave you all like that — my work is not finished."

The date for Osho's departure arrived — 28th July. That day we stood in the small hallway of the house as He came down the stairs, and, with Milarepa playing the guitar, we sang our hearts out. If this was the last time we were to be seeing Him then let it be beautiful. I didn't want Him to see me with a miserable face, I wanted Him to see that one of the many gifts I had received from Him, was that of celebration. My sadness turned into a deep acceptance, and a true alchemical change happened and I danced like never before. Moments like this are like dying, and how many times had I faced this moment over the last year? How many deaths had I gone through, each time we were all separated and left standing alone in the unknown?

Osho was to say to Neelam:

"Look at the trees. When a strong wind comes, it seems to be destructive. But it is not. It is like a challenge for the trees, for the plants, to see if they are longing to grow or not. After the strong winds, their roots go much deeper into the earth.

"You might think, 'This plant is too small; the strong wind will uproot it.' But no, if the plant accepts that when the strong wind comes, it will go with it, it will be saved...and not only saved but will be more certain than ever that, 'Yes. I want to live!' Then it will grow very rapidly because the challenge of the winds has given it so much strength.

"If the tree or the plant doesn't go with the wind and is destroyed, don't feel sad for it: it would have been destroyed, if not by this wind then by another, because it does not have a deeper urge to live. And it does not know the law of existence — that if you go with existence, it protects you. It is your fight which destroys you."

Osho spent a long time dancing with each one of us, through the house, onto the porch and then by the car, where even Rafia, who was taking photographs, was tickled by the master to dance with his cameras flying. Only Vivek couldn't dance, she fell into Osho's arms crying — her own unique dance.

We followed Osho's car to the airport, where we stood on the roof of the terminus staring at the plane that was to take Him away.

The plane turned down the runway and revved up for its final charge across the earth, and we watched together, as one solid block of silence. I could see Osho's hand waving in the window as it sped past, and then He was in the sky. Two words fell out of my mouth...empty boat....

I was in a vast ocean, in an empty boat.

CHAPTER SIXTEEN

Relationships

I waited for one month in London after Osho's departure to India. It then seemed safe to try and enter the country again. Vivek had left two weeks before and she told me that when the date came for my arrival in India, she told Osho that nothing had been heard from me, so she was worried whether I had arrived or not. Osho just chuckled.

Osho was staying as a guest in a friend's house in Bombay and for the first few weeks I lived with Milarepa in a room which was to double as my laundry room.

Osho was giving discourses in the evenings to a group of about a hundred people, but this was to grow as *sannyasins* from the West arrived, most of them having not seen Osho since He left America. The discourses were titled "Beyond Enlightenment." As I hadn't yet understood what enlightenment was, it was mind blowing to conceive of anything beyond it! I was still at the beginning of my journey, or so it felt. My relationship with Milarepa was more on my mind than enlightenment at this time, and so I will wander off 'The Path' and gaze into the valley of relationships, to show how Osho has helped me understand what it is that drives men and women crazy over each other.

Osho talked to us in hundreds of *darshans* and discourses about our relationship problems. It seems to be the main stumbling block for Western disciples and the area where our energy gets diverted and we go around and around in the same circle. In the early Pune years in *darshan* every night couples sat in front of Osho and told Him of problems they had. He listened with infinite patience and tried in so many ways to explain to us to not take things too seriously, and to grow in love and understanding. He sometimes gave meditation techniques for couples to do together.

I was having my first affair with meditation in these early years and I did not understand how it was possible that people could be so easily diverted. In meditation I felt so fulfilled and content with myself that I had no need for "the other." There is a fine balance to find though, because I had also heard Osho say that He did not want us to live like nuns and celibate priests. And then of course there is the natural pull of biology and that cannot be fought with a mind concept such as "I am a meditator — I do not need to be with anyone." If a period of celibacy and aloneness comes naturally, then that is something else. Whatever comes naturally has to be allowed. Periods of aloneness that have lasted a year or two have come to me naturally and then I have swung into relationships again.

My definition of a relationship is when two people are together after the flower of love has withered and they stay together out of neediness, attachment and hope that the love will become aflame again, so meanwhile they struggle with each other. This becomes a power game, a continual swing between who is the most domineering of the two. It takes incredible awareness and courage to see when the love affair is becoming a relationship and to part from each other as friends.

The most important thing for me is to live fully, to explore my own inner depths and express myself creatively. If being with someone in a love affair enhances me in these ways then I go with it. I do not want to even try to give solutions for how two people can stay together. I give no value at all to a marriage that is "made in heaven" and lasts for ever, because I think it is an impossibility. There may be exceptions in the world, but I have not met these people.

The monks and seekers of truth in the past, and even today in monasteries, have renounced love and sex. They have cut themselves off from the opposite sex and I can understand why — when I fall in love with somebody it can cause a great disturbance. All the emotions, like anger, jealousy and desires that I had thought were finished, rear their ugly heads.

To be with Osho and allow all the colors of life is a great challenge. Nothing is denied, only one thing is added — awareness. Osho shares His wisdom with us and then He stands back and gives us total freedom to understand, or not. He trusts that if we do not understand now then through our own experience, our intelligence will sharpen and one day we will get it. He does nothing to interfere in this process at all.

At the heights from where Osho was looking it must have seemed simply ridiculous that we were caught again and again in the misery-go-round of relationships. The way I heard Him speaking to us it seemed so easy. Why can't we live our love lives simply, why do we always have to suffer? My understanding is that one reason is dependency, and dependency comes when I am using the other as a means to avoid looking at my aloneness. It has always been difficult for me to swallow what Osho says about relationships because it goes against my deepest conditioning. All the songs I ever heard sung were about "MY man," "MY woman," and to think that two people are absolutely free and no one belongs to anyone has taken me a few years to digest.

"Freedom is such a joyful experience. Your lover is enjoying freedom, you are enjoying freedom. In freedom you meet; in freedom you depart. And perhaps life may bring you together again. And most probably.... All the researches about love relationships indicate a certain phenomenon which has not been accepted by any society up to now. And even today, when I say these things, I'm condemned all over the world. When your man becomes interested in another woman, it does not mean that he no longer loves you; it simply means just a change of taste.

"In the new world, to which I have dedicated my whole life, there should be no marriage — only lovers. And as long as they are pleased to be together, they can be together; and the moment they feel that they have been together too long, a little change will be good. There is no question of sadness, no question of anger — just a deep acceptance of nature..." (*The Golden Future*)

In the East arranged marriages are common, although they are now going out of fashion. It was one way to manage the uncertainty of love — by creating the institution of marriage. I have heard Osho say:

"The old marriage failed. The new marriage is failing because the new marriage is simply a reaction to the old marriage. It is not out of understanding, but out of reaction, revolt — 'love marriage'.

"You don't know what love is. You simply see some beautiful face, you see some beautiful body, and you think 'My god, I am in love!' This love is not going to last, because after two days, seeing the same face for twenty-four hours a day, you will get bored. The same body...you have explored the whole topography; now there is nothing to explore. Exploring the same geography again and again, you feel like an idiot. What is the point?

"This love affair, this love marriage is failing, it has already failed. The reason is that you don't know how to wait so that love can happen.

"You have to learn a meditative state of waiting. Then love is not a passion, it is not a desire. Then love is not sexual; then love is a feeling of two hearts beating in the same rhythm. It is not a question of beautiful faces or beautiful bodies. It is something very deep, a question of harmony.

"If love arises out of harmony, then only will we know a successful life, a life of fulfillment in which love goes on deepening because it does not depend on anything outer; it depends on something inner. It does not depend on the nose and the length of the nose; it depends on an inner feeling of two hearts beating in the same rhythm. That rhythm can go on growing, can have new depths, newer spaces. Sex can be a part of it, but it is not sexual. Sex may come into it, may disappear in it. It is far greater than sex.

"So whether the person you love is young or old does not matter." (*Beyond Enlightenment*)

In a *darshan* I had in 1978 I asked Osho what my chief characteristic was. I had heard Osho say that according to Gurdjieff the journey to self-discovery could only begin once the chief characteristic of a person was known to them, and being unable to discover it on my own I asked for help. Osho's answer was:

"You have a good characteristic: it is love, mm? So remember it, because love can create great trouble and can create great joy also. One has to be very very alert, because love is our basic chemistry. If one is alert about one's love energy, then everything goes right. The characteristic is very good, but one has to be very alert about love. Always love something higher than yourself and you will never be in trouble; always love something bigger than yourself. People tend to love something lower than themselves, something smaller than themselves. You can control the smaller, you can dominate the smaller and you can feel very good with the inferior because you look superior — then the ego is fulfilled. And once you start creating ego out of your love, then you are bound for hell.

"Love something higher, something bigger, something in which you will be lost and which you cannot control; you can only be possessed by it but you cannot possess it. Then the ego disappears, and when love is without the ego, it is prayer."

I found this answer very mysterious and understood it to mean that I should cast my awareness towards love itself, the energy that is without the pull of biology. To love love itself because the energy is much vaster than I am, and I could not touch love, could not manipulate or control it — it had to possess me. It was an answer that was for me at that time, above my head, I had yet to grow into it.

I have spent many years with Osho very happily without a boyfriend and thinking that it all seemed to be finished. These were peaceful easy years but layer upon layer has continued to fall away exposing the depth to which the roots of desire go.

The first week we arrived in Rajneeshpuram I was standing by the old barn when a pick-up truck pulled up and about a dozen men jumped off the back and made their way to our eating area. They were all dressed in cowboy hats, jeans and boots, and yet one of them stood out. I could only see his back, but the way he walked...I fell in love. His name was Milarepa, and that day, after we had had lunch we went for a walk through the hills and I didn't get back to my laundry room until way after tea time. It was the beginning of seven years of impossible dreams.

Milarepa had a sense of freedom that I longed for in myself. But, clouded by my own biology, I didn't look within. I was forever trying to capture and contain what was outside of me, and he led me a merry dance! He had a great love for women — many women — and I found myself totally focused and lost in him. I knew I was caught in obsession, but there was nothing I could do about it. Sometimes while walking through the old mountains to his house, climbing up the muddy and snowy slopes to where he lived I would say to myself, "Don't do this, don't go to visit him," but I moved as if in a trance, towards one disastrous situation after another.

Osho learned of my affair through Vivek and one day in discourse He said:

"...Chetana has a boyfriend, Milarepa — Milarepa the Great. Milarepa is just a lady-killer, continually killing ladies here, there, and everywhere. And I can't even recognize him!"

He went on to joke about how He was always looking for Milarepa during drive-by — such a lady-killer — Osho wanted to see how He looked, but He kept missing him.

"Who is this Milarepa?" He asked. "He is certainly a personality like Lord Byron in that even though he goes with so many ladies, no lady feels offended. They all accept that he is such a person that you cannot possess him."

The result of this playfulness on the commune was to make my greatest fear (of losing Milarepa to another woman) magnified. All the women in the commune were now interested in who this man was! Even years later women would approach Milarepa and say "Aah! So you are Milarepa, I always wanted to meet you."

Each time I saw Osho privately to take Him tea or to accompany Him on the car ride He would ask me how Milarepa was. He would chuckle at me as I told Him of Milarepa's new affairs and my distress. Many times I asked Osho: "Should I finish with him?" but He would always say no. Once when I asked and He said no, because I would miss him, I answered that I wouldn't miss him for long. But then Osho said: "But he will miss you...." What could I do?

In my own stubborn way I wanted to "go through" everything with one man. I didn't see the point in changing partners, having a honeymoon and then facing the same problems again. I had heard Osho say that the problem has to be tackled from within. That by changing the lover the problems will not change.

"It is just like changing the screen when the projector and the film are the same. So you can change the screen — maybe a better screen, a bigger screen, a wider screen, but it is not going to make any substantial difference, because the projector is the same and the film is the same.

"You are the projector and you are the film, so again you will project the same things on a different screen. The screen is almost irrelevant. Once you understand this then you can see the whole life as *maya*, as a magic show. Then everything is inside; the problem is not outside. Nothing has to be done there. So first one has to realize that it is oneself; then the whole problem shifts and comes to the right place from where it can be tackled and solved. Otherwise you can go on looking in wrong directions, there is no possibility for any change."

I do not think that this means a person should drag himself around in an unhappy relationship though. My stubbornness made me unhappy and now I see that there is no time to be miserable. My life is moving so fast into the unknown and anything can happen. This is so obvious and yet difficult to remember each moment. If I don't remember it moment to moment life slips out of my hands, I look back and say, "If only I had remembered that 'this too shall pass'...."

Vivek was very upset on one occasion about a broken love affair and I said to Osho, "She will get over it in time." He said: "Time is not needed — time is needed only when you are living in the past. If you are living in the present, then you can drop your miseries right now."

One evening Milarepa and I were walking through the mountains together, the moon was full, snow was gathering in the clouds, the ground was frosty; it was the most perfect time and I had never felt so relaxed and close to him —

and then he said that he wanted to be alone that night. I was always torn between admiring the courage he had to go for what he really wanted and at the same time furious with him that it wasn't what I wanted.

We had been together for six months and decided to go on holiday. We spent a beautiful month together in California, where my parents came over from England and spent some days with us. During this visit I saw just how far I had moved away from the "norms" of society, and how there were no connecting bridges. Except love of course, but that can only be expressed silently. My father asked me about having children and I told him that there would be no children. He said, "But one's whole life is for having children, the whole joy in life is the children." I said, "No, I have first to give birth to myself. I do not have the time to devote to bringing up a child." I told him that the world is overpopulated already and at least you will see among Osho's *sannyasins* that a few thousand people in the world are not adding to the overpopulation, and instead are trying to improve the quality of life and not increase the quantity. It is very rare to meet a *sannyasin* with a child. You will see that all religions in the world try to increase their numbers by making birth control a sin. They are not interested in the quality of life, they only want to increase the numbers of their flock.

Nobody could have been more surprised than myself at the change my maternal instincts took when I began meditating. When I was twenty I had a child, but being unmarried and not capable of taking care of the baby financially at the standard I would have liked — I thought he was a King — I gave the child up for adoption. I was disturbed and depressed for a long time after the adoption and I had received "help" from a Christian unmarried mothers counselor, such as, "Well I hope this will teach you a lesson!"

My maternal instincts were so strong (Sun in Cancer on the mid-heaven for those of you who understand astrology!)

I decided that as soon as I was financially able then I would have five children — with or without a husband. Being pregnant and giving birth had been the most beautiful experience I had ever had. I had felt one with the earth and totally at ease. I thought abortion was murder and the right of a child to live should come before the mother's. After doing Dynamic Meditation for a few weeks my maternal instinct disappeared so completely that it left no trace, no afterthought, nothing. Since that day I have been focused on giving birth to my own being and found that meditation brings that same feeling of at-oneness as pregnancy does.

Being in a love affair in a commune is more challenging and more alive than being in a relationship within the boundaries of society and family. For one thing the circle of friends is bigger and more varied so two people are not forced to be together all the time just out of necessity. Surrounded by so many friends who are all seeking to be more loving and understanding it is easier to drop misery and have a good laugh with each other as we discover we are all suffering the same jealousies and possessiveness. If a love affair ends, then in a few weeks at the most the healing process is over, whereas in a city or society where you feel a stranger, years of suffering can happen. Also, the function of the commune is to make a person aware of his absolute aloneness. I know this sounds contradictory, but it is not. Living in a commune, I feel I have space to be myself, I don't have to conform to social etiquette. I feel that I am supported in every way to express my spontaneity and uniqueness. If I feel like being in silence and ignoring everyone, then that is also perfectly acceptable.

When Rajneeshpuram was destroyed, Milarepa and I were separated and we missed each other. He joined us in Uruguay and we traveled together to Portugal, England and then to India. Osho got a lot of mileage out of our relationship.

When Milarepa arrived in Uruguay Osho said:

"When Milarepa came I asked Vivek, 'Has he brought his guitar? And what else does he do?'

"She said 'He does nothing else — just plays on his guitar and chases women.'

"I said, 'Enquire if he has got his guitar. Then he should start playing guitar; otherwise chasing women the whole time will not be good for his health. So once in a while, just to get some rest, he can play guitar.'

"But he has not brought his guitar. I think you should provide him with a guitar, because he has lost everything. Now he has nothing to be worried about losing; he can go on chasing...." (*Beyond Psychology*)

And he did chase — Milarepa was attracted to Vivek and they wanted to spend a night together. When Osho asked me why I looked upset and I told Him, He said to me that if we can't allow our lovers freedom to enjoy other people even around Him, then we were behaving exactly like the rest of the people in the world. "If it can't happen here, then where can it happen?" He asked. The truth of this simple statement hit me and I turned around and understood, or rather I saw things in their proper perspective. When Osho can be so loving and patient with us then surely I can at least relax and not create a fuss if my two friends want to spend some time together.

I have reminded myself many times that I am not with Osho to get married, or create a perfect relationship with someone. If I had wanted that then I could have stayed at home in Cornwall and settled down with a nice farmer or fisherman.

During our six months in Bombay I noticed that Milarepa and Vivek were both starting to get "edgy." They hadn't shown any interest in each other since being in Uruguay and Vivek was happy with Rafia. But Rafia was away and I noticed that something was being repressed between the two of them and the atmosphere was tense.

They were unhappy and so one night I just took off, went to stay in a friend's flat and didn't come home. They were both so happy the next day and it changed the whole atmosphere among everyone. I never told them that I had gone away to get out of the way, and they didn't say anything to me either, but just to see two good friends happy over such a small thing was a breakthrough for me.

I have heard Osho say that His people are related to each other through Him. It is my lover's love of Osho that inspires me and enhances our love. We are, after all, two seekers on the path. That we meet along the way is a bonus, a little show of extravagance on the part of existence. When two people share a love for a man like Osho, who is overflowing with love, then their relationship already takes on new dimensions. Whenever Osho answered a poem or question from Milarepa I would be touched far deeper than had I written it myself.

Although Milarepa and I had been together almost seven years we had not lived together continuously. We had always had our own places and because of that our love affair had lasted, but when we arrived back in India we were living together and it was more difficult. We were both in the position of not wanting to separate and yet not really happy together.

I think no couple should live together for more than a few days' holiday. The more space is felt between two people the more alive the love is. It is good that each have their own place to live and there is no certainty that you will meet each day. There is an ancient story I like very much:

Two lovers were very much in love and the woman wanted to marry. The man said he would marry her on one condition — that they live in separate houses, one on each side of a large lake. "If we meet by chance — maybe we will meet out boating on the lake, or maybe we will meet while taking a walk one day — then that will be beautiful."

Osho has told this story many times and whenever I heard it, it always gave me the horrors. Now I understand it — though it takes time.

I heard that one day in Rajneeshpuram Osho had said with exasperation, "None of you have understood what I have been trying to tell you about love."

The first year we were back in Pune Osho was once again answering our relationship questions in discourses:

"...As far as I am concerned, I am not interested in your personal relationships; that is absolutely your own nightmare. You have chosen to suffer — suffer. But when you bring a question to me, then remember that I am simply going to say the truth of someone who can observe without being a party to anybody. This is not ordinarily the case in the world. Whenever you go to someone with a question about your personal relationship and the suffering it brings, the worldly way is to console you.

"Although men and women have suffered together, creating all kinds of troubles for each other, there has not been in ten thousand years any revolution, any change in their relationships.

"I want to help you to see clearly how you are creating your own world. To me, you are your own world, and you are your world's creator... Be strong; have some stamina, and make an effort to change.

"I would like you to be more individual, more free, more alert, more conscious, more meditative. And these situations can be great opportunities for meditation. But if you get angry, freak out, start defending yourself, then please don't ask such questions. I have no interest at all. Your relationship is your business.

"My simple concern here is meditation. And this is very strange: rarely do you ask questions about meditation. That does not seem to be your main concern, and to you it seems not a priority — it is not the first item on your mind. Perhaps it may be the last thing on your laundry list, but certainly it is not the first; the first things are stupid things, trivia. You waste your time, you waste my time." (*The Hidden Splendor*)

"Without meditation every love affair is doomed to failure." ...Osho

On hearing Osho say one night in discourse that couples fought because they were repressing their sexuality, I thought I had a revelation. I thought I was sexually repressed, so with my heart in my writing hand, I wrote a question to Osho saying just this. He answered my "very serious" question with joke after joke about English ladies and women approaching middle age, and finally joked that my misunderstanding was all because Milarepa was playing around again!

"You have been with me so many years — how can you say you are sexually repressed? You will ruin my reputation!" Osho said as He tried to make light of my situation.

I was furious. The next morning, while answering someone else's question Osho said:

"All the tangles of life, of love, of relationship are created by our unconsciousness. We don't know what we are doing, and by the time we become aware it is too late. What has been done cannot be undone...

"Just last night I answered Chetana's question very lightly and very lovingly and very joyously. I joked about it, but she was pissed off — I could see her face. Milarepa was angry.

"You don't know what you are doing. What you are doing is almost beyond your hands; you are reacting. If Chetana had heard what I was saying...I was simply saying, 'Don't take it seriously!' I was laughing about it, but she could not laugh. You all laughed because it was not your problem. The more you laughed the more you made her serious....

"In each person's life the time of change comes. And one of the greatest things to remember is that when you change a certain pattern of life, you have to change naturally. It is not in your hands. Biology makes you capable of sex at the age of thirteen or fourteen; it is not your doing.

"At a certain age, as you are coming closer to forty or forty-two, the biology's purpose is finished. All those hormones that have been propelling you are disappearing. To accept this change is very difficult. You suddenly start thinking as if you are no longer beautiful, that you need a face lift.

"The West is continuously imposing on nature, demanding how things should be. Nobody wants to become old, so when the time of transition from one stage of life comes, a very strange phenomenon happens — and that is what is happening to Chetana. It is going to happen whether I say anything about it or not, just as a candle comes to the very end, has only a few seconds more, and before it will be gone, at the last moment the candle suddenly becomes bigger with all the power. Nobody wants to go."

He then explained how a dying person can suddenly become completely healthy, as though the disease has disappeared. The family and friends are happy, but really it only signifies death. It is the last spurt of life. The same happens with sex — a last effort — and so my mind was becoming overwhelmed with sex.

"...When you are no longer young and the hormones in you are going to disappear, and the interest in sex is going to die — before dying it will explode with its full force.

"If you go to a psychoanalyst, he will say that you are sexually repressed. I cannot say that, because I know that this sudden overwhelming sexuality will be gone by itself, you don't have to do anything. It is the signal that life is passing through a change. Now, life will be more calm and more quiet. You are really entering into a better state.

"Sex is a little childish. As you become more and more mature, sex loses the grip over you — and it is a good sign. It is something to be happy about; it is not a problem to be solved. It is something to celebrate.

"In the East no woman ever feels the trouble of the transition from youth to old age. In fact, she feels immensely happy that now that old demon is gone and life can be more peaceful. But the West has been living under many illusions. One is the illusion that there is only one life. That creates immense trouble. If there is only one life and sex is disappearing, so you are finished. Now, there is no more opportunity; there will not be any more excitement in life. Nobody is going to say, 'You are beautiful and I love you and will love you forever.'

"So first, the illusion of one life creates a problem. Second, the psychoanalysts and other therapists have created another illusion that sex is almost synonymous to life. The more sexual you are, the more alive you are. So when sex starts disappearing one starts feeling like a used cartridge; now there is no point in living; life ends with sex ending. Then people try all kinds of bizarre things: face lift, plastic surgery, false breasts. It is stupid, simply stupid.

"It is a great need of man, and particularly women, to have attention — attention is nourishment, a woman suffers immensely when nobody pays attention to her. She has nothing else to attract people by: she has only her body. Man has not allowed her to have other dimensions where she can become a famous painter, dancer, or a singer, a learned professor. Man has cut all other dimensions from the woman's life where she can be attractive and people will pay respect even while she becomes old. Woman is left only the body by man, so she is so much concerned with the body that it creates clinging, possessiveness, fear that the person who loves her, if he leaves, perhaps will find another person. And without attention she starts feeling almost dead: What is the use of life if nobody is paying attention to you? She does not have an intrinsic life of her own.

"But here with me you have to learn something. The first thing is a deep acceptability of all the changes that nature brings to you. Youth has its own beauty; old age has its own beauty too. It may not be sexual, but if a man has lived silently, peacefully, meditatively, then old age will have a grandeur of its own.

"Love happens only when you are beyond biological slavery; then love has a beauty. Not only is it to be accepted when life is going through a biological change, but it has to be rejoiced that you have passed over all that stupidity, that now you are free from biological bondage. It is only a question of conditioning. One has to accept life. But your unconsciousness does not allow you to accept life as it is. You wanted something else.

"It is perfectly good when sex disappears. You will be more capable of being alone. You will be more capable of being blissful, without any misery, because the whole game of sex is nothing but a long misery — fighting, hate, jealousy, envy. It is not a peaceful life.

"It is peace, silence, blissfulness, aloneness, freedom, which give you the real taste of what life is.

"Life is for the first time self-oriented; you don't have to beg from others for anything. Nobody can give you blissfulness; nobody can give you ecstasy. Nobody can give you the sense of immortality and the dance that comes with it. Nobody can give you the silence which becomes a song in your heart." (*The Invitation*)

This discourse had a tremendous impact on all the women in the *ashram*, both young and old. There was not a woman who could not identify with the problems Osho was talking about. It seemed He answered all women and not just me, as is always the case when He speaks.

I had not seen what had been happening to me over the four or five months that Milarepa and I had been living together. He was attracted to very young people and I lost my own integrity, my own worth, by comparing myself and feeling, of course, that I fell short. I did not have the bubbling personality of a teenager, and so I was feeling lacking. I became confused about whether I had any personality at all. I became unaware of myself and focused my attention on everyone around me.

I began to use self-hypnosis on myself to discover the roots of the pattern that my mind had regarding relationships. With a few exceptions I had always fallen in love with men who were basically not interested in having a girlfriend. Men who above all else valued their freedom and the way I related to them threatened that. For an hour every day for more than a week I lay down on my bed and hypnotized myself. I went into my unconscious with the question, from where comes this pattern? It slowly entered my consciousness and I understood that the pattern was in fact my mother's. Her lover deserted her when I was in her womb, and while a child is in the womb it not only inherits the physiology but also the psychology. Even while in the womb, the mother's moods and emotions affect the child. I was born and brought up for my first few years with the idea that a man whom one loves is someone who leaves you. When I was a small child and then later in adolescence, I was continually having crushes on boys who did not want to be with me. It came naturally to me to want the man I couldn't be with.

Discovering that the source of my mind's patterns were not even mine but my mother's, gave me a great freedom. I no longer had to be a slave to thoughts that, after all, were not mine. Sure, this did not instantly mean that no thoughts came, but I had some distance from them now. I still loved Milarepa, but I began to value my own freedom now and not try to take his. I saw that without my own freedom I was a beggar, and would always be looking to someone else for help.

The thing I had dreaded most, happened — Milarepa and I became very good friends. The madness and the desire fell away in our relationship and what I had feared was in fact the most beautiful thing that could have happened. Now I look at him and I feel great love. He is still as intriguing as ever, but I don't want anything from him. And from his eyes I see love without fear, love that melts me.

"Everything changes — and love is not an exception.

"Now perhaps I am the first person who wants to make it understood by everyone that love changes: it begins, it comes of age, it becomes old, it dies. And I think it is good the way it is. It gives you many more chances of loving other people, to make life richer — because each person has something special to contribute to you. The more you love, the more rich you are, the more loving you become.

"And if the false idea of permanence is dropped, jealousy will drop automatically; then jealousy is meaningless. Just as you fall in love and you cannot do anything about it, one day you fall out of love and you cannot do anything about it. A breeze came into your life and passed. It was good and beautiful and fragrant and cool, and you would have liked it to remain always there. You tried hard to close all the windows and all the doors, to keep the breeze fragrant, fresh. But by closing the windows and the doors, you killed the breeze, its freshness, its fragrance; it became stale." (*Beyond Psychology*)

When my relationship with Milarepa ended, before it started anew as friendship it was a painful but fertile time for looking at myself. To find myself without someone, my aloneness showed stark white against a blackboard. This is one of the great things about being on the spiritual path — everything is used as an inner exploration. The more painful the experience is, the more incentive there is to look in and not relax in daydreams. Thinking becomes dangerous in these situations and I found myself on the razor's edge of awareness.

A year of aloneness passed and when I was once again feeling settled in my life, the great mystery that I call love happened again. Only this time it is different. I have broken my pattern of the one-way ticket love, and I find my love affair a great sharpening in awareness. Each moment we are together feels like the only moment we have. I no longer have the illusion of time stretching into eternity with this person, because my life has taught me that things change all the time. This creates both a lightness and depth.

I still feel jealous sometimes, but I no longer torture myself with it — I don't chew it around in my mind like a piece of cud. A jealous thought comes, and I can say, "Hello, this is jealousy." I ask myself if I want to be miserable, or do I want to drop it? How can I be miserable when I only have This moment to spend with my lover? He will be gone tomorrow — and so I decide to enjoy today. It is a matter of choice — choice above habit. And the only way is to be in the moment.

I have my own idea that the spiritual path moves in an upward spiral, rather like a high mountain path. Because of this I experience the same "trips", emotions, etc., repeating themselves and yet...each time a little different, a little higher, with a little more consciousness. Before becoming a *sannyasin* I avoided jealous situations by never committing myself to one man. The only exception was Lawrence and he loved me in a way that I felt secure in his love. We were living together and yet, he was moving with other women. The occasional one, that he liked very much, he would bring home for me to meet. My friends said to me that I couldn't possibly love him because I wasn't jealous. I was puzzled!

I have recently understood Osho to say that if there is jealousy there is no love — that jealousy is connected with sex not love.

I have needed to explore all dimensions of relationships possible, and live out all passions and unconscious desires.

This may not be true for all seekers on the path. I don't know.

Over the years I have seen my dragons and demons unfurl and rear their ugly heads. Once I am aware of them, then with a conscious effort I can see them as habit patterns that are interfering in my freedom.

I am more able to watch my woman's neediness now and it is amazing, but when I become aware of it a distance is created and it doesn't color me — it just passes. For instance, saying good-bye to my lover, He might be saying: "See ya later," and without me even speaking — there's still a smile on my face, and everything's fine — but my eyes feel like empty begging bowls and the voice inside says:

"Later? See me later? but where? when? what time?" But I catch it. It's just a glimmer, but I've caught it. I see it for a moment — this "Where, what time, will we ever meet again?" It is there. And then I realize that this is it, and it goes back to prehistoric times, when women were wholly dependent on the man to bring back meat to their cave for them and the children. But it's out of date! I mean, hell, I don't even eat meat!

To be with a person in a light and playful way, and for the friendship to be simply a day-to-day communion with each other, is, I think, what Osho has been moving us all towards.

But the last thing Osho said to me about love affairs was: "Every love affair is a disaster!!!"

It is important for me to emphasize that in using Osho's words and quotes from His discourses, I use them in my context and with my understanding. It is possible to apply Osho's words to suit any situation. Osho cannot be said in words, but I use His words as I understand them, because my understanding is all I have to offer.

The love I feel for Osho has always been spiritual, my relationship with Him has been that of meditation.

It is the same for both male disciples and female, there is no question of biological attraction. If I can experience this love with Osho then one day I hope I can experience it with everybody and every living thing on the planet.

Osho: "The Master is an absence. Whenever you become an absence two zeros dissolve into each other. Two zeros cannot remain separate. Two zeros are not two zeros: two zeros become one zero.

"Just a few days ago I said that from my side there is no relationship, the relationship between a master and a disciple is a one-way traffic. Chetana wrote me a beautiful letter saying, 'You told it very nicely, it was a sugar-coated pill, but it has stuck in my throat.'

"Chetana, drink a little more of me, so that it can go down the throat. Drink a little more of one who is not. I can understand, it hurts. It is a bitter pill, even though sugar-coated. It hurts to feel that the relationship is only from your side and not from the master's side. You would like it that the master also needs you. You would like me to tell you, 'I need you, I love you very much.'

"I can understand your need, but that will not be true. I can only say 'I don't need you, I love you.'

"Need exists only with the ego. I cannot relate with you, because I am not. You can relate with me because you are still there. Because you are there you can go on relating with me, but that relationship will remain only so-so, lukewarm.

"If you also disappear the way I have disappeared, then there will be a meeting — no relationship, but a merging. And relationship cannot satisfy. You have known so many relationships; what has happened through them? You have loved, you have been friendly, you have loved your mother and father, your brother and sister, you have loved your woman, your husband, your wife. You have loved so many times, you have created relationships so many times. And you know, each relationship leaves a bitter taste in the mouth. It does not make you contented. It may satisfy for a moment, but again there is dissatisfaction. It may console you, but again you are left in the coldness of loneliness.

"Relationship is not the true thing. The true thing is communion, the true thing is merger. When you relate you are separate, and in separation there is bound to remain the ugly, mischievous and agony-creating ego. It disappears only in the merger.

"So Chetana, drink a little more of my absence, drink a little more of my love which does not need you. And then the pill will go down the throat and you will be able to digest it. And one day will arise, the great day, when you will also love me and will not need me.

"When two persons love and both have no need for each other, love takes wings. It is no more ordinary, it is no more of this world, it belongs to the beyond. It is transcendental."

(*Unio Mystica, Volume I*)

CHAPTER SEVENTEEN

Pune Two Diagnosis: Thallium Poisoning

Heraclitus says, "You can't step in the same river twice," and Osho says, "You can't step in the same river even once."

So there is no such thing as Pune Two.

When I arrived in Pune in the beginning of January, 1987, I felt I had aged a hundred years, if not more. I had lived many lifetimes, many deaths; I had been in gardens overflowing with flowers and I had seen them destroyed.

And yet Osho was still going for it...He was still trying to lead us along the path towards what He calls every human being's birthright — enlightenment.

It was during this three-year period between 1987 and 1990 that Osho spoke forty-eight books, and considering He was sick for about a third of the time, this is stupendous!

Osho had spent four months in Bombay, and the first night He arrived in Pune, at about 4.00 a.m. 4th January, the driveway of the *ashram* was lined with *sannyasins* to greet Him as He lay on the back seat of the car, asleep. He woke up and waved to people without getting up from His blanket, and looked very much to me like a small child that had been woken in the middle of the night.

Three hours later the police arrived, with a writ to stop Osho from entering Pune. The writ had been issued to be served on Osho as He entered Pune. Had the writ been served on the road, then Osho would have been breaking the law by entering Pune. However, Osho had left Bombay in the night to avoid the heat and heavy traffic on the road, and the police had missed Him by just a few hours. They pushed their way into the *ashram*, into Lao Tzu House and into Osho's bedroom, where He was still asleep. No one had ever gone into Osho's room while He slept, and it felt like the greatest intrusion and insult. I was standing at the top of the stairs with Vivek, Rafia and Milarepa. Being foreigners we had stayed out of the way and Laxmi and Neelam were talking to the police. From the top of the stairs we could hear shouts coming from Osho's room — Osho's voice. Shouts continued for about ten minutes and then Vivek went down the stairs and entering Osho's room she asked the policemen if they would like a cup of tea! She said they looked relieved, as though they had taken on more than they realized and were glad to get out of it.

On January 10th, in discourse Osho told us what had happened:

"I was in Bombay. One leader, a president of some powerful political group, wrote a letter to the chief minister and sent a copy to me. The letter was to tell the chief minister that my presence in Bombay would pollute the atmosphere.

"I said 'My god, can anyone pollute Bombay? The worst city in the whole world...' For four months I was there; I never went out even one time, I never even looked out of my window. I remained in a completely closed room — still, you can smell...as if you are sitting in a toilet! This is Bombay.

"...And then pressure was brought on one of my *sannyasins* in whose home I was a guest for four months: if I'm not removed from his house, he, his family and his house, with me, will be burned.

"One sometimes wonders whether to cry or to laugh.

"...I left Bombay on Saturday night and the next morning my host's house was surrounded by fifteen policemen with guns.

"...I reached here at four o'clock in the night, and within three hours the police were here. I was asleep. As I opened my eyes, I saw two policemen in my bedroom.

"I said 'I never see dreams, particularly nightmares. How have these dodos managed to come inside?' I asked, 'Do you have any search warrant?' — they didn't have — 'Then how have you entered my private bedroom?'

"They said, 'We have to serve a notice on you.' Sometimes one wonders whether we use words in our sleep. Is this the way to serve a notice? Is this the way to be a servant of the people? All these are servants of the people; we pay them. They should behave like servants...but they behave like masters.

"I said 'I have not committed any crime. I have just slept for three hours, is it a crime?'

"One of them said, 'You are a controversial person and the police commissioner feels your presence may provoke violence in the city.'

"...And on the notice...I said, 'Read it. What is my crime?' My crime is that I am controversial. But can you tell me — has there ever been a man of any intelligence who was not controversial? To be controversial is not a crime. In fact, the whole evolution of human consciousness depends on controversial people: Socrates, Jesus, Gautam Buddha, Mahavira, Bodhidharma, Zarathustra. They were fortunate that none of them entered Pune.

"The police officer misbehaved. I was lying down on my bed and he throws the notice over my face! I cannot tolerate such subhuman behavior. I immediately tore up the notice and threw it away, and I told those police officers, 'Go and tell your commissioner.'

"I know that a notice from the government should

not be thrown away, but there are limits! First, the law has to show humanity and respect for human beings. Only then can it expect respect from others." (*The Messiah, Volume I*)

The police commissioner refused to cancel the order, but wanted to leave it suspended, with certain conditions he stipulated for the *ashram*, as "norms" of behavior. There were fourteen conditions and some were dictating the content and length of Osho's discourses. He was not allowed to speak against religions, or speak in a provocative way. Only one hundred foreigners should be allowed to stay in the *ashram*; and only one thousand visitors could be allowed in the gate, and each foreign name should be taken by the police. The conditions stipulated how many meditations a day we should do, and how long each one should be; that the police had the right to visit the *ashram* any time and that they should attend discourses.

Osho responded to these conditions with a lion's roar. He was afire in discourse as He responded with:

"Is this the freedom for which thousands of people died?

"This is a temple of God. Nobody can say to us that we cannot meditate for more than one hour....

"I will speak against all religions because they are pseudo — they are not true religions. And if he (the police commissioner) has any intelligence to prove otherwise, he's welcome...."

"We don't believe in countries and we don't believe in nations. For us, nobody is a foreigner."

And in response to the police entering, "No. This is a temple of God, and you will have to act according to our directions." (*The Messiah*)

Osho said that if the police commissioner and the two policemen who broke into His bedroom were not removed from office, then He was going to take them to court.

In the third week of January Vivek went to Thailand for three months, so I stayed in her room, and did her work. We were once again in a paranoid and dangerous situation. Vilas Tupe, who had tried in 1980 to kill Osho by throwing a knife at Him, announced to the press, "We will not let Osho live here in peace." He demanded the arrest of Osho under the National Security Act and threatened that two hundred karate and judo trained members of his organization (*The Hindu Ekta Andolan*) would storm the *ashram* and take Osho away forcibly. We were also threatened by the government, who went as far as having bulldozers waiting outside the *ashram* gates, to come and flatten the *ashram*.

I had the additional worry that any day the police would come, cancel my visa and deport me. There were many nights when I could not sleep because there were threats that the police were going to invade the *ashram*. We had an alarm bell to alert everyone and in the house we each had a door or window to guard. I was locked behind the glass doors that led to Osho's room because if the police came again it would be over our dead bodies that they took Him away. The police came twice in the night and many times in the day, but they did not enter Osho's house again.

After months of fighting in the courts by our *sannyasin* lawyers and one courageous Indian lawyer, Ram Jethmalani, the harassment from the police gradually ceased, and Vilas Tupe was ordered not to enter Koregaon Park. The mayor of Pune apologized to Osho and helped prevent action from the government's demolition team.

Throughout the next two years Indian consulates around the world were harassing *sannyasins* and would not give a visa if it was suspected that they were coming to India to see Osho. Many *sannyasins* were stopped at Bombay airport and put on a plane straight back to where they had come from, with no explanation at all. But despite this the wave of visiting *sannyasins* was to become tidal.

It seemed like the war was over. We could begin living once again, silently with our Master.

And then Osho started dancing with us as He entered Chuang Tzu Auditorium for the discourses, and when He left. The music was wild and I used to feel energy raining down on me and then shooting up like the flames of a fire as I screamed at Osho in gibberish, not knowing what I was saying. I just had to shout something, because it was too much to contain. Then the stop exercise began, when Osho, while working us all up into a frenzy with the dance, would suddenly stop, His arms in mid-air, and we all froze. He used to look into someone's eyes during this freeze and it was a powerful thing to be on the receiving end, looking into the mirror-like quality of emptiness.

This period reminded me very much of our energy *darshans* from Pune One and I felt Osho was having to do a lot of 'work' to rebuild the force of energy that was present then. Arriving back in Pune, it had been dismal to see how the *ashram* had become run down. The buildings and gardens had not been kept well by the skeleton crew of people who had been living here. The people in the *ashram* in these first few months were a motley crew and there was not the usual alive and vibrant feeling that is around *sannyasins*. We consisted of a few Goa freaks — Westerners traveling around India who had visited the *ashram* out of curiosity — a few brand new *sannyasins*, and a few worn out old *sannyasins*. I watched Osho dancing with us in the auditorium those few weeks with a totality and strength that was beyond anything we could respond with. He was charging the very atmosphere with electricity and talking fire in His discourses and I saw that He was starting again. He was beginning from scratch with us all.

Whatever magic it is He creates, it was working. *Sannyasins* started arriving — gingerly at first. The last few years had been hard lessons for everyone, and many *sannyasins* had created lives for themselves in the world — houses, cars, jobs — that they were reluctant to abandon. However, hundreds of people did simply "drop the lot" and arrived vulnerable and wide-eyed. By the end of February the commune was simmering — the pot was on the boil! Side by side with celebration, Osho began to tell us how He felt about the situation of the world:

"...And as I went around the world, my discovery has become absolutely clear: this humanity has come to a dead end. To hope for anything from this humanity is sheer nonsense. Perhaps a few people may be saved — and for them I go on creating the Noah's Ark, (of consciousness), knowing perfectly well that perhaps when the Noah's Ark is ready, there may not be anybody left to be saved. They may have all gone their own ways." (*The Hidden Splendor*)

He said that two hundred enlightened persons are needed in the world. "But from where to bring those two hundred people? They have to be born amongst you — you have to become those two hundred people. And your growth is so slow, there is every fear that before you become enlightened the world will be gone.

"You are not putting your total energy into meditation, into awareness. It is one of the things that you are doing, amongst many; and it is not even the first priority of your life.

"I want it to become your first priority. The only way is that I should emphasize, deeply into your consciousness, that the world is going to end soon.

"...Immense responsibility rests on you because nowhere else in the whole world are people trying, even in small groups, to achieve enlightenment, to be meditative, to be loving, to be rejoicing. We are a very small island in the ocean of the world, but it does not matter. If a few people can be saved, the whole heritage of humanity, the heritage of all the mystics, of all awakened people, can be saved through you." (*The Razor's Edge*)

In addition to these shattering discourses on the state of the world, Osho told jokes and played jokes. We were never allowed to take life seriously with Osho — sincerely, but not seriously. He played games with Anando during the discourses, teasing her about ghosts and as He walked through her room to reach the auditorium, this was always a good time for the two of them to play jokes on each other. Osho would walk out of the auditorium, having stunned people with His discourse, then He would take a turn left, with a mischievous grin on His face, into Anando's bathroom, where He knew she was sleeping in the bathtub. (Discourse in Chuang Tzu became so full there was a rota system, and so Anando used to listen from her bathtub, complete with pillows and blankets.) Osho liked to knock on her door and hear her scream, and once she hid in the bathroom cupboard, which had a false back. She waved an arm at Him around the bathroom door as He walked through her room, and when He followed, the bathroom was empty. He opened the cupboard door and He immediately started pushing hard on the back of the cupboard and there were screams of laughter as the wall started to fall down, exposing Anando and a small crowd of very surprised people standing in the corridor outside. I used to enjoy these games so much because they reminded me of the many stories Osho told of tricks He used to play on people when He was young. He obviously enjoyed having tricks played back on Him, and Anando was the right person to do it.

Anando had been 'haunted' by a knocking sound in her room that used to wake her each night and Osho teased her about this. Once, in the middle of the night, Osho called me and told me to go and play a joke on Anando. He said I was to go and knock on her door and then slowly open the door and push into the room a dummy in a wheelchair, dressed as a man. We had the dummy because Anando had made it and sat it in the corridor, legs crossed and reading a newspaper for Osho to encounter on His way to morning discourse. I have never seen anything faze Osho, and this occasion was no exception. Twice a day for years He had walked down the corridor towards Chuang Tzu and great care had always been taken that no one or no thing should be in His way. And yet on the morning when He came across a complete stranger sitting and reading a newspaper as though in his own sitting room, Osho did not even do a double-take. He simply chuckled and walked over to the figure to have a closer look. But...I had great success when I wheeled the apparition into Anando's room because my knocking on the door had disturbed her and as she looked up, still half asleep, she saw "it" lit only by the reflected light from outside. She did not recognize her own creation in the shadows and screamed.

"So playful, so childlike, so non-serious, so alive is the approach of Zen."

On the occasions when I was Osho's caretaker I was always very quiet with Him, in awe. "Silent," said Osho. I very rarely had any news or gossip to tell Him, and when He asked me: "What is happening in the world?" I would not have much to say because my world consisted of which trees had new leaves and whether or not the paradise flycatcher was visiting the garden.

Anando was down to earth and playful with Him. She told Him of all the news happening inside and outside the *ashram*. I listened to her one day talking to Osho about politics; her understanding of Indian politics was impressive; and she knew all the names, all the parties. She and Osho chatted away like two old friends with a mutual knowledge of friends and foes. I think Anando and I made a good balance between us.

Vivek was both; she seemed to encompass both our personalities, and her relationship with Osho was always a mystery to me, because it felt so ancient. She went away many times during these three years, but each time she returned Osho welcomed her back and immediately gave her the choice of whether she wanted to be His caretaker, or whether she wanted to just relax and do nothing. There was never a question about her freedom to do anything whatsoever she liked in the *ashram*. It was an exception He made for her that applied to no one else. There are no rules without exceptions, and no two people are ever treated the same by Osho. The same question asked by two people will likely get two totally opposite answers.

During this time we took care of Osho as a team. It was no longer a job for one person, because of His weakness and ill health. Amrito, Osho's doctor, although British and male, fitted perfectly with Anando and I, as he was becoming increasingly feminine, but with a clear and unemotional approach. I have never seen any hesitation or "no" in him regarding Osho, and Osho said of him many times that he is a very humble man.

Osho started having trouble with His teeth, so over a period of about three weeks He was having a lot of dental sessions. Geet, assisted by Nityamo, who is a dental nurse, Amrito, Anando and I attended the sessions.

I was sitting on the floor next to Osho's chair at one session and He said to me, "Stop chattering, be silent." I didn't know what He meant, I was sitting as silently as I could possibly sit. I thought I was meditating. But meditation was new to me and I could never be sure if what I felt was really meditation, or my imagination. At the slightest indication that what I thought was meditation, was not, I would say, "Oh, to hell with this," and stop even trying. I would instead think on purpose: that is, I would consciously plan a painting I wanted to do or something. My experience in meditation shows it to be a very vulnerable and fragile state, and so easily a thought would come that, "It is all rubbish." At the beginning, that is, and I was at the beginning for many many years.

So although I thought I was meditating, when Osho

would say to me, "Be quiet, Chetana, stop chattering," I became very confused, and angry. He would tell me that my mind was chattering non-stop and was disturbing Him, and I didn't know what He meant.

For more than seven days this continued, and each day I was closing my eyes and trying to go deeper inside myself in an effort to reach a point where what Osho said did not disturb me. During the rest of the day I would feel relaxed, but then the session would start again and I became tense. I was angry and upset and one day He said to the other people there:

"You see how angry Chetana is with me?"

I would think to myself, "Why is He picking on me? Has everyone else transcended their mind? Is everyone else in silence?"

That is what made me angry in fact, that I was the only one there who was not able to meditate. Me, who had experienced such magic.

Two weeks passed and I was always in trouble for chattering, for making too much noise. Finally, one day Osho said for me to sit on the other side of His chair. During this session He turned towards the empty space where I had been sitting and said, "Be quiet, stop chattering." After the session was over He said to me that it wasn't me that had been disturbing Him, but there was a ghost in that spot. He said that sometimes a spirit, or ghost, can use someone's body and that I was a receptive vehicle. It had been using me to chatter. And He said, "But don't tell the cooks," (the kitchen is right next door). "Don't tell the cooks, or they will be frightened and won't want to work." He said that one day He would talk about ghosts. Then I remembered that this was the same room and the exact same spot where, years ago in Pune One, I used to be possessed.

I think ghosts, like dreams, are not to be taken seriously. They are just another color in the rainbow, another dimension that we sometimes become aware of.

Pune Two Diagnosis : Thallium Poisoning — **247**

When I realize that my inner world is, as yet, unexplored territory, and meditation is a full time "job" so to speak, then I understand why Osho does not put any emphasis on the world of esoterica and ghosts. I could become lost in that world, and still, mysterious as it might be, it is outside of me. It will not help me to grow in awareness.

That there exist other dimensions that are rarely seen and cannot be explained, is a certainty. Thoughts, for instance. What are they made of? How is it possible that people's thoughts can be read, if a thought is not a thing of substance?

Osho was awoken from His sleep one day when I became locked in Anando's bathroom, and was calling for help. He could not possibly have heard my actual voice, but He asked me later what had happened at a certain time, and why I had been calling.

He has even said that there are thoughts in our minds without our knowing.

For the first time since I had been with Osho He began missing discourses. Some days He would be too weak to come and speak to us. He developed pains in His joints that made it impossible for Him to do anything but lie in bed all day. I had seen Osho in situations that proved He could be completely detached from pain, for instance, having a tooth extracted, and that same day coming to give a two-hour discourse. On another occasion He was having an injection into the shoulder joint, after a massage with Anubuddha, one of the body workers in the *ashram*. Anubuddha and I were sitting on the floor talking to Osho while the doctor prepared and then began the difficult injection. The doctor could not find the right spot between the bones where the joint was and so tried many times. Each time the needle went in Anubuddha and I winced but Osho continued talking to us relaxed and without so much as His breathing changing or any change on His face. Osho was to say to Anubuddha that the enlightened man is in fact more sensitive to pain, and yet He can experience that He is separate from it. I have never seen Him worried or showing fear and I know with myself it is always the psychological fear of pain — not knowing what it is — that weakens me.

In November 1987 Osho contracted what normally would be a simple ear infection, but which took nearly two and a half months to resolve, with repeated troublesome injections of antibiotics and local surgery by a Pune ear surgeon. It was at this time that His doctors were alerted to the possibility that He had been poisoned.

Samples of Osho's blood, hair and urine, together with X-rays and His medical history, were sent to London for examination by pathologists and experts. After detailed and exhaustive tests, it was their opinion that the symptoms from which Osho had been suffering since being incarcerated by the US Government were consistent only with poisoning by a heavy metal such as thallium.

CHAPTER EIGHTEEN

"Can We Celebrate the Ten Thousand Buddhas?"

O sho said to me on more than one occasion that going to America had destroyed His work. I could not understand what He meant by this and used to say to Him, "No, at least you are known all over the world now. You have exposed the politicians in every country, and your *sannyasins* have matured and grown so beautifully." But I didn't understand. I didn't know He was dying of poisoning.

Looking back at the last three years I realize just how much "work" Osho had to do to create the same high energy that we had attained as a group in Pune One.

I remember once when He was resting all day, He got up for lunch, then on returning to bed He said that He had no work. I said, "For someone who is doing no work, you are doing so much. No work! — there are thousands of people out there who feel that you are 'working' on them."

He said, "That's true."

In a discourse in Uruguay I heard Him say:

"I have seen thousands of my people changing without their knowing; they have changed so drastically, but the change has happened almost underground. Their mind has not been even allowed to take part in it — just from heart to heart." (*Beyond Psychology*)

I know this is true because I have seen so many people totally transformed around Osho. Sometimes we do not realize just how much we have changed, because we are living so close to each other — just like a parent seeing the child everyday doesn't see how he is growing. But it happens sometimes that a distance is created — not a physical distance, but a distance created within myself when I have been in meditation. And in this space I feel to touch the feet of all my fellow travelers.

My diamond days did not only consist of the cutting of the diamond, there were many days that were just sparkling light. The days being close to Osho, doing small things for Him, like taking Him food, seeing to His laundry, just being near Him and watching Him in the simple way He lived. The way He lived so totally, silently and gently. To see Him do a small thing like fold the hand towel that He kept by His bedside was enough, but these small things elude description and so it is that the most precious diamonds will remain unsaid.

Osho's sewing room was unique — Gayan, Arpita, Asheesh, Sandhya and Veena were kept busy constantly, because Osho was not fussy and yet very fussy. Opposites met here when He would be so easy about what He wore that He never even knew in advance what His robes would be, not even the fancy celebration robes. The robe would be put out for Him to put on with the matching hat and socks. With the "winged" style, sometimes we would have a disaster, when the fabric would be too stiff to make a wing and it would look extremely weird. There was one dress that stuck out like armor and looked so funny. Osho called Gayan down to His room for her to see what the mistake had been. It was about five minutes to discourse time and I said that I would give Him another robe for discourse. "No, no," He said, chuckling, "Let me wear this one, just to see people's reactions." I had to put my foot down on this occasion and insist that He not wear it. I knew people would only laugh, but He didn't care. On the other hand He enjoyed choosing materials and sometimes would reject a dress after He had chosen the fabric. I said to Him, "But you chose the fabric!" He said, "Yes, but I don't always know..."

He said to me, "Bring out my festival dresses...every day is a celebration." And then a week later: "Why do you give me these gaudy gold dresses? I like plain dresses." When He liked a robe it was so beautiful the way He would touch it, and looking pleased would say, "I really like this one, this is simple and yet rich" — and He would do it every time He wore it, as though seeing it for the first time. Most of all He liked to wear black.

When Vivek returned from Thailand she changed her name to Nirvano — for a fresh start — and brought Osho a tray filled with imitation gold and diamond watches. He liked these very much and for the next year He continued to receive and then give away watches. We asked everyone going to Bangkok to bring back a watch for Osho, so that He could give it away. Osho loves to give gifts and no matter what He gave, whether it was something very expensive or something small, it was given with the same love. There was no difference in what or to whom He gave. We made a cupboard for Him, filled with gifts, and He chose things for people with such care. He used to open the cupboard door to see what He had to give away and many times He would call me into His bathroom, and there He would be, squatting Indian style, looking into His bathroom cupboard, and one by one He would pick out a shampoo, a cream, and with each one He would say, give this to...and give this to.... Sometimes it would be a few minutes to seven and time to go to Buddha Hall and He would give me twelve or more gifts to give to people. On our way back from Buddha Hall He would ask me if I had given the gifts yet!! With Osho everything is done NOW. There is no other time for Him.

Anando and Nirvano decided to build a "walk-way" in the garden for Osho, so that He could take some exercise and see the garden on the days He was not well enough to come to discourse. He agreed, although I suspect He knew He would not use it more than a couple of times. They also had the idea to build an art room for Osho. He used to paint so beautifully years before, but then had become allergic to the smell of the felt pens and inks. An art room was designed, adjoining His bedroom, where He could paint with air brush, inks, pens — everything we could find that did not smell. The room was made of green and white marble and He liked it so much that although it was very very small, He slept in it for nine months, and called it His little hut — but only painted in it once.

One day He called me into His "little hut." It was monsoon and the rain was falling hard.

He said: "This is how Haikus are written:
Meditation
Raindrops falling on the roof.

They are not poems; they are pictorial" ...and then He lay down and went back to sleep.

Plans were made for a swimming pool to be built for Osho, and an exercise room with the latest exercise machines. Everyone was busy exploring every possible method that would help keep Osho anchored in His body while He fought the poisoning for nine years. That was the length of time given that the damage would last. From Japan we tried potions that were supposed to draw out toxins, and special baths and even a radiation belt that with the right amount of radiation was proved in Japan to cure many illnesses.

Friends from all over the world, from an alchemist in the remote hills in Italy to a famous Japanese scientist, sent medicines and herbs for Osho to try.

But Osho was getting increasingly weak. He stopped discourses in the morning and instead had massage sessions with Anubuddha and Japanese Ananda. He still came to speak to us in the evenings though.

He began to suffer from syncopal episodes, "drop attacks," suddenly falling to the ground, which raised the possibility of damage to His blood vessels, particularly in the heart. We were constantly worried (it actually terrified me!) that He would fall when no one was there, and would break a bone. And yet we didn't want to hover around Him all the time and intrude on His space.

In March when we celebrated Osho's thirty-fifth year of enlightenment in the new Buddha Hall that looked like a space ship with its new roof, the series "The Mystic Rose" began. This was the series that gave birth to a new meditation, a new group, and a new salute — each revealing the magic of Osho's spontaneity. The salute was "Yaa Hoo!" and we greeted Osho when He entered and left the Hall by raising both our arms and shouting in unison "Yaa Hoo!" This really tickled Him. Each night when Osho went to sleep I would pull the blankets over Him before turning out the lights and creeping out of the room. As I pulled up the blankets He would look at me with laughing eyes and say, "Yaa Hoo! Chetana."

The whole commune had a Zen stick during this series, and the echoes of its force can still be heard. For a few days there had been some giggling and small disturbance in the audience, and one night it happened while Osho was answering a question about silence and let go. The atmosphere was such that it felt as though we were moving higher and higher with Him, together as one. It was a discourse in which one almost forgot to breathe, and just as the silence and Osho's voice were stretched almost beyond the skies — there was an outbreak of hysterical laughter. Osho continued talking, but the laughter increased and then a few more people started to laugh with the mad laughter. Osho paused and said, "This has gone beyond the joke"...but still the laughter continued. With everyone stopped in mid-flight, the minutes ticked by... Osho looked out into the audience and with great majesty and serenity, He put the clipboard down, stood up, *namasted* everyone and walked out of Buddha Hall. He said, "Don't wait for me tomorrow night."

As He stood up I ran to the door to accompany Him in the car back to His room. I felt sick with shock and when we reached the room, I bent down to change His shoes for Him. I wanted to apologize, for surely my unconsciousness is no different than anyone else's — but I couldn't speak. He said for me to call Neelam, Anando, and His doctor, Amrito. By the time they came Osho was already lying in bed, and He talked to them from His bed for nearly two hours. He said that because we were not able to listen to Him, then why should He come to Buddha Hall each night? He was in a lot of pain and He was only living for us; it was just for us that he came to speak each night, and if we couldn't even listen....

It was freezing cold and dark, except for a small bedside light, and Osho was speaking in a whisper, so that Neelam, Anando and Amrito had to put their heads very close to Osho, in order to hear. I was standing at the foot of the bed watching in such shock that I didn't even know what I was feeling. I would say to myself, "What are you feeling?" and I didn't know. I was a blank, I could not register what was happening for me. Osho was saying that He would leave the body, and Neelam was crying. Anando tried joking with Osho, but His sense of humor did not seem to be functioning — a very dangerous sign. Finally, my emotions came like a tidal wave and I began sobbing, "No, you can't leave. We are not ready. If you leave now, then I'm going with you." He paused and lifted His head off the pillow to look at me...and I cried, and yet also felt a sense of being in a drama. We were all shivering with cold and crying, when finally Neelam said: "Let us leave Osho to sleep."

Osho used to take a night snack. It changed with how He was feeling, but during these few months He would take a snack two or three times in the night. It used to help Him to sleep if His stomach was full and He told us once that it was something that had started when His grandmother was looking after Him and she used to give Him sweets. His snack was due at about midnight, and so when He called me I took it in, and while He sat up in the bed, I sat on the floor. I waited...but He did not say anything more about leaving His body. In fact He talked of other things, as though nothing had happened, and so I kept very very quiet, and was not going to remind Him.

He came to talk to us the next night and ever since that night the audience was no more an audience, but a gathering of meditators. The quality of our listening changed, and even now, with new people arriving, they slip into that quality like a silk glove.

A few weeks later at the end of each discourse Osho began to take us into a meditation that started with gibberish. Everyone in the hall would let fly the nonsensical garbage of their minds. Osho would then tell us to "Stop — as though totally frozen," and we sat as still as statues. Then, "Let go" and we collapsed onto the floor. While we lay on the floor Osho gently urged us into the silent spaces that were to become our home. He gave us a taste of our inner world where we would one day reside permanently. And then He would bring us back and ask: "Can we celebrate the ten thousand buddhas?"

The diamond is the hardest substance in the world and I have had some of my hardest days with Osho while He has been trying to hammer my unconscious woman's conditioning. A conditioning centuries-old; that is so deep that it is difficult to disassociate myself from it and see that it is not me.

You have to understand that by "centuries-old

conditioning" I mean that my woman's mind was programmed by my mother, and hers by her mother, etc. Also you need to, if not accept, then at least play with the idea that our minds are not "new." Our minds are a collection of thought patterns that have been passed down through the ages.

Nobody has ever given women so many opportunities to evolve as individuals and be free from slavery as Osho has. It has always been a matriarchal society around Osho.

I have enjoyed hearing all the praise going to women in Osho's discourses over the years and have heard men *sannyasins* moaning that they were born the wrong sex in this life. But it was in the early part of 1988 that Osho gave women a different kind of attention. It seemed that we had received so much compassion because we needed it. Women's conditioning is harder to break through as we have allowed ourselves to be treated as slaves and deep down women still have a slave mentality. In response to a question from Maneesha when she asked about disciples receiving special treatment, He said:

"...it is not a question, Maneesha, that special treatment means 'moving into Lao Tzu (Osho's house) and having private, daily chats with the Master.' If you are aware of what you are asking...do you see your jealousy? Do you see your woman?"

He went on to explain that people come to see Him only for their work. That not everybody in the commune could do the same work. Somebody had to take His food, somebody had to take notes and do His secretarial work. He explained why Anando was suited to her work, and Maneesha had her work. He went on to say:

"The first commune was destroyed because of women's jealousies. They were fighting continuously. The second commune was destroyed because of women's jealousies. And this is the third commune — and the last, because I am getting tired. Once in a while I think perhaps Buddha was right not to allow any woman in his commune for twenty years. I am not in favor of him: I am the first who has allowed men and women the same, equal opportunity for enlightenment. But I have burnt my fingers twice, and it has always been the jealousy of the women.

"Still, I am a stubborn person. After two communes, immense effort wasted, I have started a third commune, but I have not created any difference — women are still running it. I want women here in this commune not to behave like women. But small jealousies...." (*Hyakujo: The Everest of Zen*)

I was also to get a shock one evening sitting in discourse, when Osho said:

"...This very morning, Devageet was working on my teeth. For the first time in years, when I left his dentist's chair, I asked him, 'Are you satisfied?' ...Because I could see his dissatisfaction — that he has not been able to do the work he wanted to do on my teeth.

"In the evening I told him to finish it, because who knows about tomorrow? I may not be here, then fixing my teeth will be absolutely absurd. He did try his best but I am a master who is teaching everybody to be present at every moment. And even people who are close to me go on asking me, 'Do you love me Bhagwan?'

"I cannot do otherwise. It is not a question of your qualities, my love is unconditional. But I can see the poverty of the human heart. It goes on asking, 'Am I needed?' And unless you are free from the desire to be needed, you will never know freedom, you will never know love and you will never know truth.

"Because of this anecdote, I have to report to you: Chetana works hard continuously, taking every care for my well-being, but she still goes on asking, 'Do you love me?' I am on the dentist's chair under maximum gas and she is asking, 'Do you love me?' And because I had promised my dentist that 'I will not talk...' but it is impossible.

"Because I did not say 'I love you' she must have become so disturbed that she forgot to put the towel in my bathroom. I had to take a bath without a towel. Later on, when I asked her, she said, 'I am sorry.'

"But it is not only her situation. It is almost everybody's situation. And my whole teaching is that you have to be respectful to yourself. It is falling from dignity to ask this — and particularly from a master whose love is already being given to you. Why be a beggar? My effort here is to make emperors of you.

"The day, the moment you will understand the tremendous glory of being present, nothing is needed. You are enough. Out of that arises the great joy, 'Aha! My god! I have been here and was looking everywhere else.'"

I had not consciously demanded "Do you love me?" but the Master works on the unconscious. He brings unconscious desires to the surface because once seen and understood then they have no influence on the person any more.

This incident had evolved out of a series of dental sessions in which Osho had been working on my unconsciousness, while Devageet had been working on His teeth.

While Devageet would be hovering over Osho's mouth, dental tools poised, Osho would be talking the hind leg off a donkey. At a typical session would be Amrito, Devageet, Nitty, Anando sitting on a stool on Osho's right, where she would be taking notes, and me sitting on His left, next to Nitty. Osho would occasionally bring out His hands from under the blanket with which we covered Him, and take a swipe at Nitty, or Ashu, who sometimes assisted Devageet. Or He would hold one of their hands, making it very difficult for them to work. Anando would have the buttons on her dress pulled, or her throat and heart *chakras* tapped. It was a lot of fun, except I was usually without my sense of humor during these sessions. The monologue would go like this:

Osho: "I can hear your thoughts.... Chetana, this is not it.... Chetana, be a witness.... Where is my Anando? (takes hold of Anando's hand).... Chetana has to be in her place. This is not her hand.... I don't want to interfere with anybody's freedom.... Chetana you are forcing me to speak. I know you more than you know yourself. Drop the need to be wanted. I can see the difference in your hand (He is holding my hand).... Chetana be silent, be a watcher.... Leave my hand! (He drops it abruptly and puts it back under the blanket.) ...Be there Chetana. Just be there. Yes, with your tears. I am hard, but what I can do? I have to be hard on myself. Just be without jealousy...Devageet! (Yes Osho) Chetana is too much harassing.... Can't you just be — that's my whole teaching — just BE. (wagging His finger at me!) ...Chetana, your function is just to be.... Where is Chetana? Just hold my hand otherwise you will be lost. I say sometimes hard things which I would not normally say. Don't take offense, just meditate over it.... Chetana, you can go and do your work if you want. Any excuse is good for the unconscious.... I can hear a sob and also the door open and close.... I want you to be here once and for all. But don't ask it again and again. Be silent and be here.... I am cruel, I don't care about consequences.... If you ask again Chetana... No! Chetana is weeping, but weeping is not to help. Do you see my tears for Chetana? Asking to be wanted, that is what she has to drop.... What a drama on a small stage, where except me, nobody is aware.... Laughter in an empty theater.... Women are difficult as far as understanding is concerned.... What a difficult task to be a master.... Take note, Anando, that Chetana is still wanting, and she has everything that I can give.... (Then He would start searching for the button on Anando's dress), saying: Searching for the button... What happened to your button? Take note that I tried to find the button but I could not. It has to be there. You are hiding.... Chetana, I can hear your mind. The eternal need to be needed. I want everybody to be here out of love not out of need...."

Sessions like this would last for hours and while His teeth were undergoing a series of treatments, maybe it would take weeks. I was not sleeping well during this period because part of Osho's program was having a snack about every two hours through the night. He would call me, I would take Him the snack, be there while He ate it, and then I took the dishes back to the kitchen. By the time I went back to bed, and slept for about an hour, it was time for the next snack. For about ten weeks I didn't sleep more than two hours at a time. I guess, what is known as R.E.M. sleep was disturbed. The necessity to dream seemed to be so strong that dreaming was happening to me even before I was asleep. I have heard Osho say that if a man sleeps eight hours, then six hours will be dream sleep.

I was amazed to see what a mess my unconscious was in. Days, months, can go by and life seems easy and everything is fine, and then suddenly I had the opportunity to see what was going on at night and I realized that my mind is totally mad! Normally a person is not aware of all the dreams, but if they are continually woken up in the middle of a dream, then they can see it, and it's just an amazing mess of release and unburdening of the unconscious.

As this whole process got disturbed, then I began to get a bit delicate. I was "touchy" to say the least. Looking back it seems impossible that I should have been hooked so easily, but Osho knows exactly where our buttons are and when to press them. It also seems impossible that, sadly, I could not understand what He was trying to do. My ego, my mind and its workings, was so transparent, so out there — how come I couldn't see through it?

I was angry, crying and disturbed and asked Osho why He had been shouting at me. He said that He had been telling me to sit silently and be a witness to myself and what is happening around me — and it was not enough for me. It was not enough for me to just sit silently. He said He was not shouting at me, but shouting at my unconscious. Couldn't I see that it is my conditioning, my mind that is ruling me? He said I was comparing myself with Anando thinking that she was in a better position than me. He said that Anando was just doing her work — and I should do mine. But my conditioning was saying that she is getting more. "Can't you see?" He said.

He went on to say that He thought that this was why Buddha never allowed women to be initiated. That women had been treated as commodities and they supported it. Women want to be needed and think that if they are not needed then someone else will be used in their place and they will be useless. He said that the conditioning of wanting to be needed is so great, so deep, that it was not possible to see it for yourself. Someone had to show it to you. To be needy is to be without dignity. "It is humiliating. Stand alone." He said, "Be enough unto yourself."

Osho had just finished His dinner while this conversation was happening. Anando and I were sitting on the floor and Osho was at His dining room table. I looked at Him and saw how tired He was, what a hopeless and thankless task He seemed to be doing. He was trying to help me to wake up and I was getting angry with Him. I looked at Him, slightly bent at the shoulders with weariness, what did He gain from trying to help me? Nothing! He looked ancient — an ancient seer with an impossible mission. His compassion is endless, His patience and love is as vast as the sky. I cried and touched His feet.

A month passed and Osho's health took another turn for the worse. So many times He was to say to me that He could not believe that the United States government could be so cruel.

"Why they didn't just kill me?" He said.

The pain was increasing in His joints, especially the

right shoulder and both arms. "My arms feel crippled." He was very wobbly when He walked and He began to spend more time in bed. His days were becoming shorter and shorter. One day He got up at 5.00 a.m., had taken a bath and then breakfast, and while walking back to the bedroom from His dining room He looked at the clock on my table and said "Oh! 7.00 a.m. My day is finished. Another day!" It was seven in the morning, and for Him it was the end of another day. He used to laugh that we called His meals, breakfast, lunch, supper, because in fact they were only snacks and He did not know what time of day it was unless we gave the snack a name.

He began to sleep in the daytime more often, so He did not do secretarial work with Neelam and Anando as before. Anando, and sometimes Neelam, would come and talk to Him while He was eating lunch or supper. He dictated a book to Anando during His meal times. A book that covers His whole philosophy, *The Philosia of Existence: The World of Osho.* It was an intimate scene, Osho sitting at the small table, under which He always crossed His feet, resting on the table leg or a cushion, and Anando and Neelam sitting on the floor with their notepads and letters. One wall of the dining room was entirely glass, and it looked out onto a rose garden that was illuminated at night.

It was on one of these occasions that Osho said, "Chetana can write a book," and He gave me the title, *My Diamond Days with Bhagwan,* subtitled, "The New Diamond Sutra." I told Him that when I had first become a *sannyasin* I wrote to Him saying that I would give Him a diamond, and at the time I was puzzled why I made such a promise, because I knew I would never have the money to give Him a diamond. I didn't realize when He gave me the book to write what a gift He was giving me, and so I was never able to thank Him.

He didn't give me any guidelines for the book, nor, as time went by, did He even enquire if I had started writing.

He mentioned Diamond Days only once to me and that was a mysterious happening. It was in August 1988 and Osho called me on the beeper system. It was the middle of the night, and I hurried down the corridor with the worrying thought that He may be having an asthma attack. I unlocked the door, and saw that He was sitting up in the bed wide awake, the room in darkness except for a small bedside light. The cold air and minty fragrance of the room woke me up. "Bring a notepad," He said, "I have something for your book." I returned with a notepad and pen and sat on the side of His bed where He could observe what I was writing. He dictated the following page to me, and said for me to write the names in a circle. He made sure I had got it right and then lay down and went back to sleep. I never queried it with Him, or even mentioned the list to Him. I simply put it in my file and that was that. I never told anyone about it, and have always considered it to be 'for the book.' It is interesting to see that although He spoke of twelve people, He gave me thirteen names. But then, Nirvano's name was to be dropped although that was not known at the time.

In the center of the circle is 'Bhagwan' and going around the circle clockwise the names are: Jayesh, Avirbhava, Nitty (Nityamo), Nirvano, Kavisha, Maneesha, Devageet, Neelam, David, Chetana, Hasya, Anando, Amrito.

He said: "Twelve can be named. The thirteenth remains unnamed. This has been my secret group. The secret group of thirteen. In the middle the unknown Bhagwan."

It was eight months later that Osho formed the Inner Circle of which there are twenty-one members. The above "secret group" was never given a function to perform by Osho, they simply remain what they are — a secret group.

After each time Osho was sick, when He came back to give discourses He looked very frail, and as though He had moved light years away from us. But as He started talking He gradually became stronger. It was noticeable how His voice became more powerful and after a couple of days He looked quite different. He always said that talking to us keeps Him in the body, and the day He stops talking, then He will not live much after that. He looked so strong when He was talking that it was difficult to believe that He was sick, but that was the only time in the day when He had any strength. He was saving all His strength to come and talk to us.

I had never heard Osho mention anything He said in discourse after it was over, as though the things He said came out of the blue, and were not retained in His memory. But there was one evening after a talk when He said to me that didn't I think He had put a certain point over very clearly? The way He emphasized it made me take a second look, and it was:

"On the stage it is all acting.
"On the stage it is all simply drama.
"Behind the stage it is pure silence.
"Nothingness, rest, relaxation.
"Everything has moved to total tranquillity."

He began talking on Zen but it was more as though He was preparing an atmosphere of silence than talking. He would pause and say "...This Silence..." almost pointing to it, or pause and draw our attention to the sounds around us — the creaking of the tall bamboos; the sound of rain, the whine of the wind amongst falling leaves: "Listen..." He would say, and a blanket of silence would descend on Buddha Hall.

I could never know whether Osho was joking, or using a situation as a device, or whether things really were as they appeared. For instance, ghosts: Osho had said many times in discourses that there are no such thing as ghosts, they are only man's fear. He also knew that I was intrigued by the idea of ghosts and I even told Him once that I had met only friendly ghosts and was not afraid of them. In any situation around Osho the only way I could be with it was to take it absolutely sincerely because that is how He was. On the subject of spirits and ghosts, He said that He doesn't mind these spirits as long as they don't disturb His sleep. He called me on several occasions and asked if someone had been into His room.

On one occasion, He called Anando in and told her that He saw a figure walk through the door, cross the room in front of His bed and go and stand behind His chair, before coming back across the room and try to touch His feet, and then walked through the door again. He said He had been sleeping peacefully, and this spirit had disturbed His sleep. He wasn't sure if it was a dead spirit or someone with a deep longing to be with Him. He thought it might have been me, as she walked like me and her body was like mine. I had actually been sleeping while this spirit was walking through doors. It had been a particularly nourishing sleep, one of those times when one is half asleep and half awake, but totally rested. So when Anando told me, I thought well, who knows, maybe I did. Maybe my longing was satisfied during my body's rest and that's why the sleep had been so nourishing.

Osho's room is behind a small corridor and the access to that corridor is a double glass door, which is usually kept locked, and His room is always locked. One end of the small corridor is Osho's room and the other end is a room where I would sometimes stay when I was helping to take care of Him. A few times He has called me into His room and said that He has heard someone knocking on the door. This did not seem possible, because the doors had been locked and no one could get into the corridor. It has been happening for a couple of years, though not often, except lately. It first happened when Nirvano was here and He told her someone had been knocking on His door and to find out who it was. This was at 2.00 a.m. She went around to everyone's room in the house to ask if we had been up and knocking on Osho's door. Nobody had, and the guards at the gate were not aware that anyone else had entered the house. It happened many times since but the mystery was never solved.

Four days before Osho's birthday celebration on December 11th 1988, He became very sick. Nirvano and Amrito were taking care of Him and I was doing the laundry in a room just opposite His room. The house felt deathly quiet and dark. I knew He was very sick, but I did not know why, or what was wrong. Then came a week when I received no laundry from Him at all and I knew that He must not be moving from the bed, not taking a bath, and not changing His clothes. Osho never wanted people to know when He was very sick, because then people worry and get depressed and the whole energy in the commune goes down and it does not help anybody. He almost died during these few weeks.

CHAPTER NINETEEN

The Last Touch

I n the book, "The Sound of Running Water" there is a statement made by Osho in 1978, in response to a question, "Why do you call yourself Bhagwan?" Osho said:

"When I see that my people have reached a certain level in their consciousness, then I will drop the name Bhagwan."

On January 7th 1989, the name Bhagwan dropped and He became simply Shree Rajneesh.

It was later that year in September that He dropped the name Rajneesh. He was now without a name. We asked that we might call Him Osho. Osho is not a name, it is a common form of address used in Japan for a Zen master.

Osho had given instructions to Anando a couple of months before that He wanted Chuang Tzu Auditorium to be made into a new bedroom for Him. She found people to do the work, the materials were ordered from all over the world and the work was progressing. Osho specified in detail everything He wanted and it seemed as though for the first time He was to get a bedroom exactly how He wanted. He visited the site on a few occasions and took care with Anando over each small detail. He had never had a say in how His room would be and it was a great joy to know that at last it was going to happen. Also His present room was damp and because He was in bed most of the time, it was in darkness. It was like a cave.

As the white Italian marble went in place and the dark blue glass panels reflected the twenty-foot diameter crystal chandelier, it became clear to many people that this was not a bedroom — it was a temple, a *samadhi*. But although we knew it, we brushed it aside. We could not allow ourselves to see the obvious — Osho was building His own *samadhi*.

When He came back to talk to us in January 1989 His talks were sometimes as long as four hours. This had never happened before and I think now of what Osho said about the flame of a candle: "Just as a candle comes to the very end, has only a few seconds more, and before it will be gone, at the last moment the candle suddenly becomes bigger with all its power." He was then sick for a few weeks and came back to talk to us in March. I was to ask Him my last question and for the first time we sent our questions in unsigned. Although I didn't ask about reincarnation Osho answered:

"...The very idea of reincarnation, which has arisen in all the Eastern religions, is that the self goes on moving from one body to another body, from one life to another life. This idea does not exist in all the religions that have arisen out of Judaism — Christianity and Mohammedanism. Now even psychiatrists are finding that it seems to be true that people can remember their past lives. The idea of reincarnation is gaining ground.

"But I want to say to you one thing: the whole idea of reincarnation is a misconception. It is true that when a person dies his being becomes part of the whole. Whether he was a sinner or a saint does not matter, but he had also something called the mind, the memory. In the past the information was not available to explain memory as a bundle of thoughts and thought waves, but now it is easier.

"And that's where, on many points, I find Gautam Buddha far ahead of his time. He is the only man who would have agreed with my explanation. He has given hints but he could not provide any evidence for it; there was nothing available to say. He has said that when a person dies his memory travels into a new womb — not the self. And we now can understand it, that when you are dying you will leave memories all around in the air. And if you have been miserable, all your miseries will find some location; they will enter into some other memory system. Either they will enter totally into a single womb — that's how somebody remembers their past. It is not your past; it was somebody else's mind that you have inherited.

"Most people don't remember because they have not got the whole lump, the whole heritage of a single individual's memory system. They may have got fragments from here and there, and those fragments create your misery system. All those people who have died on the Earth have died in misery. Very few people have died in joy. Very few people have died with the realization of no-mind. They don't leave a trace behind: they don't burden anybody else with their memory, they simply disperse into the universe. They don't have any mind and they don't have any memory system, they have already dissolved it in their meditations. That's why the enlightened person is never born.

"But unenlightened people go on throwing, with every death, all kinds of misery patterns. Just as riches attract more riches, misery attracts more misery. If you are miserable, then from miles away misery will travel to you — you are the right vehicle. And this is a very invisible phenomenon, like radio waves. They are traveling around you; you don't hear them. Once you have the right instrument to receive them, immediately they become available. Even before the radio was there, they were traveling by your side.

"There is no incarnation, but misery incarnates. Wounds of millions of people are moving around you, just in search of somebody who is willing to be miserable. Of course, the blissful does not leave any trace. The man of awakening dies the way a bird moves into the sky, without making a track or a path. The sky remains empty. Blissfulness moves without making any trace. That's why you don't get any inheritance from the buddhas; they simply disappear. And all kinds of idiots and retarded people go on reincarnating in their memories and it becomes every day thicker and thicker.

"Be very conscious about your desires and your longings because they are creating the seed for your new form already — without your knowing." (*The Zen Manifesto*)

The Zen Manifesto is Osho's last book. April 10th, as the discourse finished Osho said His last public words:

"The last word of Buddha was *sammasati*.

Remember that you are a buddha — *sammasati*."

As He said these words a strange look came over Him, as though a part of Him had flown away. It looked as though He had become disconnected from His body. Standing up looked like such an effort for Him and He was having difficulty walking. As He came outside to the car I looked at His face and it had a strange expression as though He didn't know where He was. This is only my interpretation, and it is because of my lack of understanding that I have to use these words. I never did understand what happened to Osho that night. In the car on the way back to the house Osho said to me that something strange had happened to Him. I said, yes, that I had noticed something. He later repeated it, and He seemed as mystified as me, but He never explained to me what had happened. Several days later He said that He didn't think He would be able to speak again.

For a few months Osho was too weak to come to Buddha Hall, and He rested in His room. People were becoming less dependent on His presence to help them with meditation and whereas a few years before we would have been disturbed and worried, we now began accepting life without seeing Osho each day.

Artistic creativity exploded in the *ashram* for the first time. Dance, mime, theater, music in the streets and so many people painting who had never painted before. We had never had the space to explore our creativity in the last two communes. When we had arrived the gardens were run down, but now...when I walk into the *ashram* I pause: my senses go "hush...." I have walked into another world to the sound of the waterfall, the coolness of the canopy of hundreds of tall, flowering trees, a feeling of peace and relaxation. This feeling of silence is not the silence of the graveyard — there are hundreds of people, laughing, playing, and I walk through the *ashram* thinking, "Why is everyone smiling at me?" Then I realize that they are not smiling at me — they are just smiling!

When Osho became too weak to talk with Neelam each day on commune affairs, He did the 'work' while eating lunch and supper with Anando, whom He called His "daily newspaper," and Jayesh. Every day He asked if the commune was running well without Him, and it was. It seemed that for the first time we were beginning to "get it". There were no more power trips, no hierarchy, people were now working because they enjoyed working, and not because of reward. He also wanted to know if the new people arriving were taken care of and did the new and old people mix together.

He asked that all the *ashram* buildings be painted black, with blue glass windows, and that we build black pyramids on new properties. He chose luminous green pillar shaped lights to line the white marble roads, and light up the gardens at night. He always noticed if even one light was not working, and He insisted that the swans should have a light in their pond "so that they don't feel left out." He never missed the smallest detail in making the ashram beautiful for us. And He noticed the people who were standing outside Buddha Hall guarding — He was concerned that everyone should be able to go inside Buddha Hall, so when He noticed the same person outside too often He said they should have a turn going inside.

Osho gave me all the paints and airbrushes that He had received, and although I did not know how to use the brush, He gave me a lot of encouragement to paint and told me to learn with Meera (a wild and beautiful Japanese artist). When He passed through my room to His dining room, He would walk over to my table looking for a painting, saying "Anything...?" And if there was something left on the table for Him to see He would pick it up and look very carefully, sometimes taking it over to the light for a better view. It was hard for me to accept this appreciation though, because I thought I couldn't paint.

Towards the end of monsoon in August it was a time of great celebration in the *ashram* when Osho came to sit with us in silence. It seemed as though we were entering a new phase with Osho and the joy of seeing Him again was not dampened by the message He sent with Anando for everyone. His message was, "Few have understood my words."

As He entered He encouraged everyone to dance by waving His arms and the hall exploded with music and screams of delight. Then for ten minutes we sat with Him, and in those ten minutes I reached the same heights in meditation that before would take me one hour to settle into. On the way back to the house in the car Osho would turn to me and ask, "Was it alright?" Alright? It was sensational! Fantastic! Every night He would ask this question with such innocence, as though He hadn't been the one who created the explosion. He was concerned that no one was missing Him speaking. I told Him that we were all so happy to see Him at all, that nobody ever mentioned missing the discourses.

Later in that month, what started as a suspected earache turned into a wisdom tooth extraction for Osho and there were complications in the healing. There were many dental sessions, and in each session Osho was stressing that He was fragile and His "roots in the earth are almost broken".

In a session on August 20th He said, "It is really strange. The symbol *Om* appears before me. The symbol of *Om* appears only at the time of death."

When the session was finished, He sat up and drew the symbol on Anando's notepad for us to see.

29th August — "The figure of *Om* has been standing constantly before my eyes in blue colors."

I remember this session well, and I remember at the time thinking that it was too fantastic, too outrageous. How could I accept that Osho was talking of His death being close. "No," I thought, "it is just a ploy to get us enlightened."

Osho came to Buddha Hall to sit with us and music played, interspersed with silence. Osho was very pleased with the "meeting" as He called it. He said many times that He felt that at last he had found His people, and that the people here now are very good people.

"The meeting was so good, people are responding so well. No one has tried to work with so many people at this level and the music has come to my liking — just where I want it. I only want a few more days — not even weeks, and you all have to help me to be in the body." He said this in a dental session.

After a year of tremendous effort — and Osho instilling a sense of urgency in Anando, saying that, "If my room is not ready soon, it will be my grave!" — Chuang Tzu was ready for Osho to move into, and on August 31st, we were very happy to see Him going to sleep for the first time in the cool crystal and marble chamber.

Osho was in so much pain with His teeth that His dentist, Geet, asked if Dr. Mody, a local dental surgeon, could help. Although Osho had always said that He only wanted His own people to take care of His medical needs because their love was so much it was a healing force in itself, still He agreed that Dr. Mody could give a second opinion. When Dr. Mody came to see Osho it was very beautiful because Osho told him, with a chuckle, "You think you have come here to work on me. But I am working on you."

Osho used every opportunity to try and wake us up. For many days there were dental sessions, but although He was in tremendous pain, His main concern was us. He was telling me that my unconsciousness was harassing Him and I was a danger to Him because of my neediness.

He said many beautiful loving things, but at the time I only absorbed what He said about my neediness. He said: "You all mean so much to me. You will not understand unless I am gone." This is true because for me it was too much at the time, beyond my capacity to understand. He said: "Chetana you are such a loving being. Wherever you are you will be with me." But then He would order me out of the dental room.

One day He told me to leave as it was a matter of life and death. I sat in my room and tried to understand what He meant; whether He meant life and death for me — or for Him! Maybe He was saying that if I didn't get it, if I couldn't have enough awareness to see my unconscious conditioning, then it was really a huge barrier for me, and in that respect, maybe He meant life or death; because I just couldn't imagine that He meant life or death for Him.

When the session was finished I was told that still He had been saying that He could continually hear me asking. I was puzzled because I thought I had been sitting silently.

Avirbhava, who we first met in Crete on the world tour, attended a few of the dental sessions, and she used to sit holding Osho's feet. He said of her that her love for Him was pure and innocent. Sometimes Nirvano attended; Anando sat at Osho's side and kept notes while He tapped on her heart chakra and said He was writing notes on her heart. Amrito was always present and Osho often asked

Him to stand up and then sit down again. Then there was Geet; Ashu and Nityamo, the dental nurses — Nityamo, a Manchester lass, whose quiet manner veiled her inner strength.

For most of the time Osho was in His new room He was very sick. It was always a difficulty when anything went wrong with Osho's health because just the medicine to cure one ailment would start off a chain reaction of problems, each one worse than the other. His body was so delicately balanced and His diet and medicines were perfectly tuned to go with it. The smallest change — and how small was always beyond our imagination — would create trouble. Osho always knew what was best for His body though and it was always a case of the doctor listening to *Him*. He didn't eat a proper meal for many weeks, and for several days only drank water.

Then the great day came when He felt to eat something. A new set of lacquer bowls had arrived from His Japanese *sannyasins* who had had them made specially in a small village in Japan. They were black and embossed with silver swans in flight, on a matching tray. I served His food and sat at His feet with Avirbhava while He ate. This was one of my diamond moments. I thought that it meant everything would be well, that He was going to be better, that He would be with us forever. It symbolized so much for me and I wept with a joy that was not to last.

Non-*sannyasin* doctors were consulted and shown X-rays of Osho's jaw, and they agreed that the rate of deterioration in Osho's bone and teeth could only be caused by exposure to radiation. This happened while Osho was in jail in America.

I received a message from Osho that I was no longer to be taking care of Him. "He would like you to do His laundry," said Amrito. I was immensely touched by this because Osho had never actually said He would like me to do something before. I would always be asked if *I* would like, but never that *He* would like me to do something. I no longer attended the dental sessions, but Osho said to Anando, "Now Chetana has left, you have started." She was also harassing Him unconsciously.

As I write now it is inconceivable to me that I didn't understand what Osho was doing with me during this time. I remember how I reacted, as though in a dream, and I am amazed that I couldn't get the point. He was urging me to look IN and in and in; to see my unconscious conditioning and rise above it. I have heard Him say that many times we reach to the brink of self-realization, but then turn back. During this period I see myself as a blind person walking back and forth past the open door, sometimes even brushing my sleeve against the door frame.

It was not enough that I no longer attend the dental sessions, Osho wanted me to leave the *ashram* while the sessions were happening. Anando was to join me. The first morning we were asked to leave the *ashram* until the dental session was finished, Anando and I went to a friend's house near the river. I thought I would make the best of it, so I took my sun tan lotion and lay on the roof in the sunshine. On the walk back to the *ashram* I was saying, "What a wonderful way to spend the morning, Anando, I think I will do this every day. This is great!"

I was asked to leave more frequently, and sometimes I had nowhere to go. One day I sat for five hours on a stone wall in the street lined with banyan trees at the back of the *ashram*. The whole joy of having a morning in the sun was gone. The idea to escape to the Himalayas kept entering my mind. I felt helpless in my exploration to find the unconscious voice that was continually asking, asking like a beggar. I couldn't probe any deeper, I couldn't understand and yet I knew that Osho never did anything without good reason. He never uttered one word that was not coming from His understanding and His effort to awaken us.

Being in Osho's house and knowing that at any time I could be disturbing Him without knowing it became a strong incentive to be in the moment. If I could be conscious and in the moment, then surely my unconsciousness could not make noise.

While in the laundry room I was very careful not to daydream, because I knew that those are the moments when unconsciousness is at work. I was continually trying to watch for those moments when the unconscious could be doing its thing without my knowing it.

One day, on returning from lunch, Amrito was waiting for me at Lao Tzu gate and he said that Osho had sent a message that Anando and I were to move out of the house immediately.

I thought I took this well. I was feeling gratitude for the last few days for being pushed, in a way, into going inside. When I spend most of the day aware of treading the path to discovering my inner self, the result is that I feel very good. I expressed my gratitude, and went to pack. Strange though, I felt nauseous.

Friends came to help me pack. As the nausea got worse, I reeled about between the mess of packed boxes, saying how good I felt, if only I hadn't eaten such a greasy Indian lunch.

"Of course," I said, "it's not emotional, it's the greasy food."

My belongings were removed and already a *swami* was getting ready to move into my room.

As I walked from Lao Tzu Gate to my room along the marble road I looked at the tree called "Flame of the Forest" that stretches across the road. Each night as Osho drives to Buddha Hall, this tree showers the road with orange flowers. The road is hosed down and scrubbed before seven o'clock, and there is not a stray leaf in sight. But, then, just before Osho comes, the tree covers the road with flowers and it looks like an offering to the gods when Osho's car drives through those orange flowers.

I was walking past the "Flame of the Forest" and I felt very sad to be leaving the Master's house like this — because how does one know that this is not the beginning of a total change in the *ashram?* Maybe men will do everything. Maybe other women will even have to leave. Osho had been the first mystic to give women a chance, but perhaps the women's conditioning is too deep. Who knows, this may be the end for women. I went to my room and vomited.

Anando and I moved to our new rooms in Mirdad House, just across the road from the *ashram.* I had just got everything moved in when Amrito telephoned me. He said that he had just told Osho that Anando and I had moved out of His house, and Osho said:

"Tell them they can move back in again."

I sat on the doorstep and cried.

On the same day, Osho moved out of His new room. He had been there for just two weeks and had called it "magical", "unique", and, "It is really California." He asked Amrito if His old room was still there. (Osho had asked that the room be remodeled as a guest room.) While Amrito was still nodding his head, Osho got out of bed and walked out of "California" and straight back into the old room. He never said why, and nobody asked.

Osho had had ten teeth taken out, but after resting for a week He said that He would come to Buddha Hall to sit with us in silence. He said that I could accompany Him to the meeting. When I saw Him I was stunned by how much He had changed. He moved differently — slower, and yet like a child. He seemed lighter and totally vulnerable and defenseless. The strangest thing was — He looked more enlightened! More enlightened does not make any sense, and I told Him what I saw and He just smiled.

Although all these weeks I had been intensely searching

to get in touch with my unconscious conditioning, I hadn't actually seen it. I had spent a lot of time just being very quiet, a lot of time feeling that the mountain path I was on was very narrow and precarious. But I hadn't seen any sign of the conditioning, until one day in Osho's presence it was suddenly there. I was aware of my woman's neediness in the way I spoke to Him, every move I made, I felt it coming out of my eyes. Each gesture I made was saying, "Do you love me, do you need me?" My whole body was putting out this question. I was very shocked, I felt ashamed that after all this time, and after all He has given, it is still there. Then I realized it has always been there and this is the first time I have been aware of it.

I then asked myself "Why, why is this need there?"

It seems it's there because I haven't yet been in touch with my being. I am not aware that my being is enough. I still relate to the world through "the woman"; I don't relate with my being, I don't know that I am enough, because I am still "the woman." The woman is not needed. Being is enough.

Amrito was looking after Osho full time now and I used to wake Him up at 6.00 p.m. It always felt strange to me, asking Osho to "wake up" when it was Him trying to wake me up. He took a shower, came to Buddha Hall, and then by 7.45 p.m. He was back in bed. The only energy He had was saved to meet His people each night. He moved on the podium so slowly, and could no longer dance with us. He used to ask: "Do people miss my dancing?" and once I answered Him: "We can't always be dependent on you to help us celebrate. We have to find our own source of celebration." When I said it, I felt weird because it sounded cold, but it was true. He enjoys to see us celebrating and happy so much, and He noticed everyone. He said that Neelam was looking so peaceful and happy.

He was very pleased with the silence that was growing in our meditation and said many times people were really beginning to understand. "The silence is becoming so solid, you can almost touch it."

He rarely did work or talked to anyone, except Anando when she had work that was very important; then He would talk for ten minutes. When He asked me if Jayesh had asked to see Him, and I said no, Osho said, "How beautiful that people are so loving and sensitive, that they ask nothing from me."

I was happy during this time and I thought that Osho would be with us for many years to come. The last time I saw Him privately He asked me how He was looking:

"I don't look weak, do I?"

"Oh, no, Osho," I replied. "You always look great. In fact you look so good it is difficult for people to believe you are sick."

The next day I was sick. It always happened to me that I would get a cold about every three or four months. I suspected there was something psychological in it but I never understood why. Answering me in a discourse many years before Osho had said:

"Sometimes you will come very close to me and you will be full of light — that's what is happening to Chetana. I see her coming very close to me sometimes; then she will be full of light. But soon she will start hankering for the darkness; then she will have to go away from me.

"And that is what is happening to everybody here. You go on swinging towards me and away from me. You are like a pendulum: sometimes you come close, sometimes you go away. But this is a need. You cannot absorb me totally right now. You have to learn, you have to learn to absorb something so tremendous, which looks almost like death. So many times you will need to go away from me."
(*The Wisdom of the Sands*)

I saw Osho only in Buddha Hall for the last three months before He left His body, and Anando would go to wake Him for our Buddha Hall celebration, while Amrito stayed close to Osho day and night.

Nirvano had been working with Jayesh and Chitten for about eighteen months and traveling to Bombay each week for a couple of days. She told me that she enjoyed the work a lot, that it was intense and exciting. Sometimes she would come to the evening meditation and her celebration made anyone else look pale, and sometimes she wouldn't come at all. She was depressed for a few weeks, but then one night she went out dancing with Milarepa and Rafia and made a date for the following week.

On December 9th, I was in the laundry room when Anando came and told me that Nirvano had died from an accidental overdose of sleeping pills.

CHAPTER TWENTY

Sex and Death

I t is strange to me that Osho has been called "The Sex Guru" by people who have obviously never read or heard what Osho has to say about sex. He has never condemned sex, the way religious leaders always have, and that seems to be the only reason that He is criticized. From magazines and newspapers that I see, it seems to me that the world is obsessed with sex, and I presume that to use the word sex in a newspaper headline guarantees readership.

There is a fine line between licentiousness and allowing natural energies to move with totality. Osho has the courage and wisdom to lead people, along this fine line.

Osho's work to help us towards enlightenment is to allow sex, because it is natural, but His emphasis has always been on transcendence. Transcendence cannot come from a repressed mind, so expression has to be the first step. It is so simple.

"...With meditation you will be opening up higher doors of your consciousness, your superconscious. And the energy always needs movement, it cannot remain static. And these new areas will be far more enchanting.

"The sexual area you have experienced. It was good as far as biology goes, but it was an ordinary experience available to all the animals, to all men, to all birds. It was nothing special, nothing unique. But if meditation makes a way towards superconsciousness, and energy is available, that energy will automatically start moving through the new channel that has opened up.

"That is what I mean by transformation." (*The Transmission of the Lamp*)

With my Western conditioning, I have been given the idea that when sex goes, then everything is finished. Osho has been speaking to us and trying to explain that in the East it is a totally different concept. "In the East when sex is disappearing it is a time for rejoicing, whereas in the West if sex is disappearing, it is a calamity."

It has to be that one day the sexual urge, or urgency, disappears and what is left is a playfulness and lightness about sex. No longer pulled in a blind fever towards somebody, it is a wonderful thought that one day it will be possible to be free in one's choice whether to play or not. And I would hope that this can happen before the body is worn out and sexual energy becomes cerebral. I think it can.

"Beloved Master,

I have had a strong feeling of sex and death over the last few weeks. Is it necessary that I understand why?"

Osho's answer:

"It is always necessary to understand how your mind is functioning, how your heart is doing, what is happening to your interior world. Trying to understand it will give you a certain distance from those things, and an awareness that they may be there but you are not identified with them. That is the great alchemy of understanding. Try to understand everything within yourself. In the very fact that you are trying to understand, you become separate from it; it becomes an object. And you can never become an object, you are always the subject; it is not possible to change your subjectivity into an object. So that gives a good distance between you and your feelings, whatever they are. That is one thing.

"The second thing: this distance will give you a possibility of understanding what is happening to you.

Nothing happens without any cause. And sometimes there are things which are very fundamental. For example, the question is one of the most fundamental questions — the connection between sex and death. And if you can see it clearly, slowly the distance between death and sex will disappear and they will become almost one energy.

"Perhaps sex is death in installments. And death is sex wholesale.

"But there is certainly one energy functioning at both corners. Sex is the beginning of life, and death is the end of the same life; so they are the two ends of one energy, two poles of one energy. They cannot be unconnected.

"Death and sex remind me of one spider found in Africa, where death and sex come very close to each other. In man there is a distance of seventy years, eighty years; but in that particular species of spider there is no distance. The male spider makes love only once in his life. While he is making love, the moment he comes to an orgasmic state, the female starts eating him. But he is in such euphoria, he does not care that he is being eaten. By the time his orgasm is finished, he is also finished.

"Death and sex are so close...but whether they are close or distant, they are not different energies. So one can feel them arising together. It is good to see them together, it is a great understanding — because people don't see it. People are almost blind, they never connect death with sex. Perhaps it is an unconscious fear that prevents them connecting the two, because if they start connecting death with sex they may become afraid of sex itself — and that is dangerous for its biological purpose. It is better for biology that they don't connect them.

"It has been noted that whenever people are beheaded — there are still a few countries where this happens — the strangest thing observed is: the moment the man is beheaded, he ejaculates — without exception. It is strange, because while his neck is being broken, is this the time to ejaculate? But it is not within his capacity to control. When death is happening to him, when life is leaving him, it is natural that his sexual energy also leaves. It was part of the whole phenomenon. There is no point in it remaining in his body.

"The question is significant. It does not mean that you are going to die. It simply means your sexual energy is coming to its highest peak; hence you are feeling death also. It would not be felt if the sexual energy was being released.

"Whoever has asked the question must not be making love. Energy is accumulating, coming to such intensity that it is automatic to remember death. Death, if you die consciously, brings you the greatest orgasm you have ever had in your life.

"By the way, woman lives longer than man lives, is healthier than man, is more resistant to disease, does not go mad as easily as man, does not commit suicide so easily. The reason may be that her sexual energy is negative. The positive energy is the active force; the negative energy is the absorbing force.

"Perhaps because of this negative, absorbing energy, she has a healthier body, is more resistant to disease, and lives longer. And if biology could manage to get her free from her monthly periods, she could live even longer and healthier. She could really become the stronger sex.

"So the idea of sex and death arising together, simply shows that the sexual energy is accumulating — positive or negative. And negative energy can be accumulated longer.

"In fact, I have been watching Jaina monks and nuns, who are perhaps the most sincere people in what they are doing. It may be stupid, but their sincerity is beyond doubt. The nuns seem to take it quite easily, remaining celibate. But the monks get into tremendous difficulty — the same difficulty as Christian monks or any other monks.

"Negative energy simply means it is more silent, waiting for the active energy so that it can absorb it. But it has no active force of its own. These are the reasons why I am against things like lesbianism. It is simply stupid — two negative energies trying to reach to some orgasmic peak. It is simply that either they are pretending, or what they are calling their orgasm is only clitoral, it is not vaginal. And clitoral orgasm is nothing compared to the vaginal orgasm. Clitoral orgasm is just a kind of foreplay. It can help to bring the vaginal orgasm, but it cannot replace it.

"It is really very amazing that such an intimate thing as lovemaking has remained in darkness. I am making the statement — and this is for the first time in the whole of history that anyone has made this statement — that clitoral orgasm can be of immense help as foreplay; otherwise the psychologists have been at a loss as to what to make of it, because it has no biological function. To avoid the question, many psychologists even have denied that there is any vaginal orgasm, there is only clitoral orgasm.

"Man's orgasm is so quick that he cannot create the vaginal orgasm in that small period of time — a few seconds. But if clitoral orgasm is created just as foreplay, it is creating a situation for the vaginal orgasm to happen. It has already started: the clitoral orgasm has triggered the process in the body.

"But men pay no attention to the clitoral orgasm, because their orgasm can happen easily only with vaginal contact. They are interested only in their own orgasm, and when they are finished they don't think about the woman at all.

"Lesbianism is spreading in the woman's liberation movement because it is giving them clitoral orgasm; but that is another stupidity because it is simply foreplay. It is as if you had the preface of the book but the book is missing. So you go on reading the preface as long as you want, again and again, but you don't go into the book at all. If the woman is waiting and waiting, she also accumulates a negative energy which she absorbs. If it is too much, then the idea of death can come, because having love in this state, and having a really beautiful orgasmic feeling, will give her an insight into what happens at death.

"There is nothing to fear in it; nothing is destroyed. It is the ultimate peak of your life.

"If you have lived your life unconsciously, in misery, in suffering, then before death comes, you are bound to go into a coma. So you don't experience the orgasm, or the awareness that death is not happening to you, to your being, but is happening only to the body, to the vehicle that you have been using up to now.

"If the question is from a man, the same is to be understood. But rarely can a man come to such a peak that he can start thinking of death. His energy is so dynamic, active, that before he comes to such a peak, the energy is released. So my feeling is the question is from a woman.

"And nobody has listened to the woman. Nobody has even taken care about what she feels, how she feels. One thing has been understood by man for centuries — in India we have paintings, statues, depicting the phenomenon — that man has felt in woman a certain kind of death. That is a misunderstanding. It is not in the woman, it is in your sexual energy itself.

"But that's how men always project things; they cannot see that their own sexual energy brings them close to death. And they cannot see very clearly because their sexual energy never comes to such a peak that it reminds them of death. But women, if listened to, have many things of wisdom to say about the phenomenon.

"The wise woman has been destroyed by Christianity. They were burned in their thousands in the Middle Ages. The word 'witch' simply means a wise woman, but because it was so condemned, even the word has become condemnatory; otherwise it is a compliment. It is equal to the man of wisdom. All over the world there were wise women, and there were matters into which only a wise woman could give an insight.

"The statues in India, and the paintings, are very strange if you don't understand the phenomenon. For example, Shiva is lying down, and his wife, Shivani, is dancing on his chest with a naked sword in one hand, and with a recently cut head in the other hand; she has a garland of heads, blood is oozing out of all the heads and she is in a mad dance. It seems she will kill Shiva. That dance is so mad, and the woman is in such a mad state, there is no hope for Shiva.

"What I have been saying is related to such experiences. In the East, the woman has been listened to. There has never been anything like what happened in the West — killing and burning women. Women of wisdom have always been listened to, and their wisdom has been absorbed — because they are half of man. Man's wisdom is half; unless the woman's wisdom is also absorbed, the wisdom cannot become a whole. She has to be asked what the experience is from her side.

"The woman, in many orgasmic experiences, particularly in the East, has felt death very close, almost hovering around. I say particularly in the East, because in the East in the ancient days, before repressive ideologies started making people split and schizophrenic, love was not to be made until the urge came to its peak.

"It was not that you have to make love every day. Both the partners should wait for each other to come to a state where it is no longer possible to hold on. Naturally, those people were far more wise. They might have been making love once a week or once a month, but their love yielded tremendous experiences which everyday love cannot yield.

"You don't have enough energy for that great experience to happen. It needs to be at the peak of your control, throbbing with energy, and then it is really a dance, a merger and meeting of two energies. And at the highest peak, then man may also feel death surrounding him. The feeling of death is there because it is all one energy, but as the sexual energy is released, the feeling of death disperses.

"Only lately has medical science accepted one fact, that the people who go on making love do not die of heart attacks. But they should ask: do they die of anything else? They live longer, and remain younger. But you can make love at the lowest point...that's where people are making it. It is not satisfying, not gratifying; it does not give you any contentment, it simply leaves you in despair.

"Love should be made at the highest peak, and that needs a certain discipline. People have used discipline to not make love. I teach discipline to make love rightly, so that your love is not just a biological thing, never reaching your psychological world. And it has the potential to reach even your spiritual world. At the highest peak it will reach your spiritual world.

"Why — at that point — is one certainly reminded of death? Because you forget your body, you forget your mind; you remain just a pure consciousness, merged with your partner. It is very, very similar to death.

"As you die — if you are dying consciously — you will forget the body, you will forget the mind, just consciousness...and then suddenly the consciousness merges into the whole. That merging with the whole is a thousand fold more beautiful than is possible through any orgasm. But both these things are certainly deeply related. They are one. And anyone who wants to understand death, has to understand sex — or vice versa.

"But strange — people like Sigmund Freud or Carl Gustav Jung, who are trying to understand sex, are so much afraid of death. Their understanding of sex cannot go very far. And as far as death is concerned, nobody thinks about it, nobody even wants to talk about it.

"If you start on the subject of death people think you don't know your manners. It is something that has not to be talked about; death has to be simply ignored. But by ignoring death you cannot understand life. They are all connected: sex is the beginning, death is the end. Life is just in between, the energy that flows from sex to death. All three have to be understood together.

"The effort has not been made. The experiments have not been made, particularly in the contemporary world. In the East, way back, before Buddha and Mahavira, they must have looked into the phenomenon very closely. Otherwise, what is the need to make Shiva's wife dance on his chest with a garland of skulls. And in her hands? — one hand is holding a recently cut head, blood is flowing, and in the other hand is a naked sword. She looks absolutely mad.

"This is just a pictorial illustration of the deepest state of orgasm; this is how the woman can be depicted. And the man is just lying under her as she dances. She can cut off his head or he may die just from the dance on his chest. But one thing is certain, that death is there. Whether death happens or not, that is another thing.

"Perhaps this is one of the reasons — unconsciously — because in the West they have always been afraid. They chose only one posture to make love in — that is, with the man on top, so that he is in control and the woman cannot go absolutely berserk, the way Shivani goes on Shiva's chest.

"And the woman has been taught for centuries that she must not even move, because that is not lady-like — only prostitutes move. She has to lie down almost as if she is dead, unmoving. She will never attain any orgasm, clitoral or vaginal. But she is a lady, and there is the question of reputation, respectability. She is not allowed to enjoy, she has to be serious in the whole affair. It is only the man who can make movements, not the woman.

"My insight is that this is because of the fear. In the East the common position for love is with the woman on top, not the man. The man being on top is absolutely ugly. He is heavier, he is taller, and he is just crushing a delicate woman unnecessarily. And it will be scientifically right that he is not on the top so that he cannot move much, and the woman has more freedom to move — to scream with joy, to beat the man, to bite the man, to scratch his face, or whatsoever comes to her.

"She has to be a Shivani. She does not have a sword, but she has nails, long nails; she can do much with those nails. And if she is on top she is faster, the man is slower, and that can bring them together to the orgasmic peak. With the man on top and woman under him it is impossible to come together to the orgasmic peak. But the man has not cared; he has simply used the woman.

"The ancient Eastern wisdom had a totally different attitude. In the time of the *Upanishads*, the woman was respected the same as the man. There was no question of inequality. She read all the religious scriptures, she was allowed even to go to great discussions.

"It was the worst day when man decided that woman was second grade and had simply to follow man and his dictates. She is not even allowed to read scriptures, she is not allowed to discuss the great problems of life. And there is no question that she should be asked what the situation is from her side. Her side is half, and this rejection has kept man split, schizophrenic. It is time that we should bring man and woman wholeheartedly together. Their experiences, their understandings, their meditations, should make one whole — and that will be the beginning of a real humanity."
(*Light on The Path*)

I have heard Osho say that the meditator experiences death, not of the body but of the mind, and is therefore born again. *Dwija* (twice born) is the expression used in Sanskrit. It is one thing to sit with Osho as He is talking and be seduced into meditation by the soft rhythmic sound of His voice, falling into the gaps of silence, feeling suspended in timelessness; it is something else to be aware during the day in all the things I do. For instance, when walking I remember to just walk without working something out in my mind; eating, just chew, without the background of a dialogue. I find this fun, almost like a game, and it spreads more and more into my day. But to sit silently in my room is something else. To sit down and do nothing feels like death. I feel as though I am letting go of everything I know, and what else can death be, but letting go of everything? I have heard Osho say that that is why people usually die unconsciously; it is nature's greatest surgery, to separate the "soul" from the body and mind with which it has been identified for your whole life, and so the kindest way is to die unconsciously. That is why people cannot remember their last death, or life.

When I sit silently the first thoughts that come into my mind are: "DO something. There is so much to DO." Somehow even being aware of my movements during the day is a type of DOING — at least there is something to watch. My mind is in fear when I sit silently; it says, "So what if you sit one hour, what do you get afterwards? You will end up more vulnerable and unable to cope with your life." THAT'S the big one. My life is perfectly good, I am enjoying myself, what if I should lose hold on what I have? Ah! I remember the story of the diamond mine, and Osho's promise that there is much much more.

I have read both in scientific papers and newspapers, stories told by people who almost died. People who, on the operating table for instance, experienced death because their heart stopped, or people who had been in coma after a severe accident, and then "come back" to life. When I read the descriptions of the experiences, I was surprised to see that they are exactly the same experiences I have known in meditation.

The "Herald Tribune" last year ran an article where people described their near-death experiences, when in tremendous shock they must have left their bodies. Every one of them talked of a "light" at the end of a tunnel, going through it and feeling tremendous love and blissfulness. Some of these people, being Christians, would interpret the "light" as Jesus, and on recovering from their illness would become religious. I have experienced this in meditation, although I always passed out before the "light" totally engulfed me.

A *sannyasin* asked Osho about this experience in a discourse in *The Hidden Splendor*. He had experienced it as "a big black spot. Inside this black spot there is a white one. This white spot comes nearer and nearer, whirling in a circle. But just before the black spot disappears totally, I open my eyes."

Osho: "What happened to you was tremendously significant, rare and unique. It is one of the contributions of the East to the world: the understanding that between these two eyes there is a third eye inside which normally remains dormant. One has to work hard, bring his whole sexual energy upwards, against gravitation, and when the energy reaches the third eye, it opens."

Osho explained to him to try and resist opening his eyes when it happens.

"...And once you have known the black spot disappearing...that black spot is you and the white spot is your consciousness. The black spot is your ego, and the white spot is your being. Allow the being to spread and let the ego disappear.

"Just a little courage — it may look like death because you have been identified with the black spot and it is disappearing. And you have never been identified with the white spot, so something unfamiliar, unknown, is taking possession of you. "

My understanding is that nothing harmful can happen through meditation, because the watcher, or witness remains. When I told Osho that I sometimes had the desire to faint while meditating, He said: "You have to go beyond the state where you start feeling faint, or passing out. Don't be afraid — pass out, faint, go into it, let it overwhelm you. For a moment all will be lost, but only for a moment. And then suddenly — the dawn; the night is over." (*The Rebel*)

Osho has spoken a lot on death, the greatest mystery and the greatest taboo. In His book *The Rajneesh Upanishad*, He says:

"We have given up our lives at the very moment when we were born, because the birth is nothing but a beginning of death. Each moment you will be dying more and more.

"It is not that on a certain day, at seventy years old, death comes; it is not an event, it is a process that begins with the birth. It takes seventy years; it is mighty lazy, but it is a process, not an event. And I am emphasizing this fact so that I can make it clear to you that life and death are not two things. They become two if death is an event which ends life. Then they become two; then they become antagonistic, enemies.

"When I say that death is a process beginning with birth, I am saying that life is also a process beginning with the same birth — and these are not two processes. It is one process: it begins with birth, it ends with death.

"But life and death are like two wings of a bird, or two hands, or two legs.

"Life is a dialectic — and if you understand this, a tremendous acceptance of death naturally comes to you. It is not against you, it is part of you; without it you cannot be alive.

"And I say to you: death is fiction. There is no death because nothing dies, only things change. And if you are aware, you can make them change for the better.

"That's how evolution happens."

Nirvano's death was sudden, unexpected and shocking. I had the feeling that a part of myself had gone, and I had a feeling of urgency that I had to live more fully from now on. Her death gave me the gift of urgency. If Osho could have got anyone enlightened, if He could have done it for someone, then He would have done it for her. But we have to walk The Path alone, He can only point the way. So many things that Osho said I received as poetry, I did not realize He was giving us the Truth.

Nirvano and I had sat at Osho's feet about ten years ago. We sat in meditation together in His room. He sat in His chair and we both sat on the floor for about an hour. Within the first couple of minutes, I experienced an explosion, and I was lost for a while in colors and light. After a few moments, Osho said, "Okay, come back now." He had a smile on His face and He said that it had been far more than He had expected, and that now we (Nirvano and I) were "twins — energy twins."

Nirvano and I had been living together very intensely for twelve years; at times loving each other and at times "arch enemies" as Osho put it once, "who couldn't be in the same room together." It was a strong relationship. I felt closest to her when we were in Bombay at the end of the World Tour. Osho's laundry room was also her bedroom, and the weather temperature was above 120 degrees. We were right on top of each other, and although the situation was extremely difficult because of space, there was a love between us that I cherished. In her British way she was always a little cool with people, but being in the same room all day together, it dropped. I liked to do her hair for her, to pile it up on top of her head with pins, although it always fell down, it was too silky and heavy.

The last time I saw her alive she was leaving Buddha Hall and I was sitting by the doorway. We looked at each other and smiled. That was my small farewell.

When she died I didn't feel there was anything left over that I had wanted to say to her. In fact, every one of her friends felt a completion with her. She lived totally, and

I had learnt already that I have to be aware with everyone I know that nothing is to be left unsaid. I don't want to behave with a friend unconsciously, because it is a fact that they may never be seen again and what is left unsaid leaves a hole, a wound that cannot heal.

In life Nirvano was the greatest mystery to me, the way she lived, the way she was. One moment she was a child, innocent, and in the next moment a mother Kali brandishing a sword. And her death was as mysterious as her life. I don't know why she died. I know she was desperately unhappy and had talked of wanting to die since I knew her. But I always thought a "click" would happen, a change would happen and one day she would suddenly be enlightened. I think she was close to enlightenment, very close. She was a wise woman, and she was in tune with Osho like nobody else. Many times when He was sick she would intuitively know what the problem was and He said many times how lovingly she cared for Him. She had a clarity and sharpness, and great perception and understanding of people, especially their negative points. Yet, she would swing into a depression so overwhelming that she would be completely helpless and would make it impossible for anyone to help her also. She closed the doors and suffered alone.

As a child her parents took her to Switzerland to hospitals, because she refused to eat. In the last few years that I knew her she had a hormonal or chemical imbalance and was treated with medicine for this. Nothing worked though. Earlier in 1989 she visited a psychiatric hospital in England for treatment, but did not stay for more than two days. She said that the doctors were more insane than her and it made her realize that she could overcome her depression on her own.

The last few months I didn't see her because whenever I went to visit her she would ask me to come back later — and then she would not answer the door. So, I got the message that she didn't want to see me.

It was better for me to stay away from her, because I used to pick up her unhappiness very easily. On the last few occasions that I did visit her she would tell me about the anxiety and incredible pain she felt in her "hara" or lower stomach. For years she would wake each morning with a feeling of nausea in the pit of her stomach. After talking to her about it, the very next morning I would wake up with the same pain in my stomach. I would open my eyes and the first thing to flood me would be, "Oh no! Not another day!" I was accepting her wounds as my own.

The last time I went to visit her we were just gossiping for fun. I was ragging on my boyfriend, because he was with another woman and I was saying a few mean things about him; making him look a bit silly in front of the girls. Afterwards I thought to myself that it wasn't really fair that I talk about someone like that. After all I don't really know his situation, and basically I felt bad about it. I saw Nirvano in the morning and I said to her, please forget what was said, I don't have any right to bad mouth someone when I don't really know what's happening for him.

She said to me, "Oh, for goodness sake. Just a little gossip with the girls. There's no harm in that. Otherwise you'll be walking around half-enlightened. And you can't be half-enlightened around here. You're either totally enlightened, or totally unenlightened."

I think its bloody brilliant to say something like that. For me, she was a wise woman.

When I close my eyes to remember her I can only see her laughing. When she was happy, she was the most ecstatic, alive person I have ever met.

In Buddha Hall, the last time I sat next to her for the meditation with Osho, in the silent period, I could hear a sound coming from inside her. I recognized that sound as one that I make when I am feeling very content, very centered and warm inside. I heard that coming from her. So I had some understanding of the space she was in. That's why, when just one week later she died, I was very shocked, because for me, knowing that space, I don't think I could reach such depths of depression. Although she knew that same meditative feeling, her depression must have been so strong, so overpowering, that nothing could help her.

I know that Osho tried everything possible. He gave her everything she wanted. He wanted to keep her here, but she was also free to go anywhere in the world she liked. Many times she went to England; she would stay for one or two days and then return. She went to Australia earlier that year to start a new life, but after a couple of days she returned. Spain, Switzerland, Thailand, many places she visited but after a few days she returned. I think that if she could have stayed until Osho left His body, that would have been the "click," the turning point for her. He said that her death was untimely.

Nirvano's body was taken that night to the burning *ghats* by the river and, at Osho's request, only a few of her friends attended. I had only seen the open-spaced burning *ghats* overflowing with *sannyasins* before, and now there were only about forty of us standing solemnly awaiting the ambulance to arrive with her body.

I *namasted* her as she was carried to the funeral pyre. My friend, Amiyo, on seeing the body said "That body is not Nirvano — she has gone."

The body was laid on the funeral pyre in the center of the *ghats* and covered with wooden logs. I moved around the fire as it blazed up and found myself standing at Nirvano's right side. "Strange," I thought, "that Nirvano's is the first body I see burning. She is my closest encounter with death."

The logs had been stacked, or had slipped, in such a way that a 'window' was created through which I could see her face, like a pure white mask floating and dissolving in the pale smoke. Her lips were swollen and dark red and in the dance of the flames appeared to be whispering.

Nirvano. I looked up at the waxing moon.

Slowly I backed away from the fire, and fainted. When I opened my eyes I didn't know where I was and thought that maybe I had died too.

Later that night I thought, "She would have been proud of me — fainting at her funeral." It's the kind of dramatic thing that she would do, and she had always said of me that I was wishy-washy.

I could never really know, but I have an idea, just how much He loved her. There was a magic between them that was never disturbed from His side by her moods and temperament. Whenever she returned from a trip that was supposedly for good, she was welcomed back without question. On her return from Australia, after three days, where she had gone "to start a new life," she said to me, "Let's see what my crazy mind can think up next."

Although I have had no experience of past lives I always had the impression that their relationship was ancient. He said in a discourse in 1978 that she had been His girlfriend in her past life (just forty years ago) and she had died at the age of seventeen of typhoid and had promised to come back and take care of Him.

I have heard Osho say never judge a person by his deeds, his actions, by what he does. With Nirvano this was so clear to see how on the one hand she was a beautiful "soul," or energy, and on the other hand a very difficult person. Osho said that she never meditated and she had always disturbed His work. He said that she had always made it difficult for whoever was doing secretarial work for Him. Maybe she lacked an understanding of what Osho's work is? He has thousands of disciples and is working on everyone. This is a fact that can be proved by observing the people who have been open to the changes that come through Osho's meditation techniques.

It is not easy to understand what unconditional love is. A love that asks nothing in return is so rare in a world where we know only love that includes possession and domination. Osho's love and compassion were unchanging and always there for Nirvano. He *is* love and His love is there waiting to be received. Sometimes she wasn't able to receive, but that is true of all of us.

There is so much that will always remain unfathomable, a mystery. It seems that the very nature of things is to not be understood. The more I try to understand what has happened in the last few years, the more I am brought back to the present moment — breath touching my nose, moving through my body; I see the trunk of a tree from my window — solid, there; sunlight, and wind blows through the leaves, moving them like long fingers; the gurgle of water running, birds singing, and I stare into silence.

What is there, really? Maybe it will always be impossible to understand.

"Life is a mystery to be lived, not a problem to be solved." ...Osho

CHAPTER TWENTY-ONE

Osho! Osho! Osho!

When I started to write a chapter on Osho's death, I realized it wasn't possible, because Osho has not died. If He had died then I would feel a sense of loss, but since He left I have not felt any loss. I don't mean that I see His spirit floating around like a ghost, or that I hear His voice coming out of the clouds. No, it is simply that I feel Him as much today as I did when He was in His body.

The energy I felt around Him when He was 'alive' must have been the pure energy, or soul, that which is deathless. Because it feels the same now that He has no body. The more I see Him on videos and read His words the more my understanding grows that He really was not there as a person, even when He was in the body.

"I am as absent as I will be when I will be dead, with only one difference...that right now my absence has a body, and then, my absence will not have a body." Osho, in Uruguay.

He said in so many ways that He was nobody and that He was just an absence, but I could not understand. Once in Uruguay I experienced seeing His chair empty when He was speaking.

I saw the chair empty and through the wall behind Him I could see sky and sea. I saw a tremendous energy rushing through Him, so powerful and moving so fast, that it frightened me because He looked so totally vulnerable. "I'm not going to let existence do that to me," said a voice in my head. I wrote to Him about this and told Him that I was spooked. He answered:

"You have to look deeply into the phenomenon of the enlightened person. He is and he is not — both together. He is because his body is there; he is not because his ego is no longer there.

"...There is no one who can say 'I am,' and yet the whole structure is there, and inside is pure space. And that pure space is your divineness, is your godliness; that pure space is what, on the outside, is pure sky. The sky only appears to be...it does not exist. If you go in search of sky, you will not find it anywhere; it is only an appearance.

"The enlightened man has an appearance like the sky, but if you get in tune with him sometimes you will find he is not. That can make you feel spooky, afraid; and that's what must have happened.

"You got in tune with me. In spite of yourself, once in a while you will get in tune with me. You may forget yourself once in a while and will get in tune with me — because only if you forget your ego can there be a meeting. And in that meeting you will find that the chair is empty. It may be just a glimpse for a moment, but really you had seen something far more real than anything else that you have ever seen. You have looked inside the hollow bamboo and the miracle of the music coming out of it."

After this discourse Osho changed my name from Chetana to Prem Shunyo — love of emptiness.

"My presence is becoming more and more a kind of absence.

"I am, and I am not.

"The more I disappear the more I can be of some help to you." (*The Rajneesh Upanishad*, Bombay 1986)

When I looked at Osho I could see emptiness in His eyes, but I could not accept that He was totally without personality and ego, because I had no way of understanding what that meant. I can see it now that I look back at the way He has been teaching us and gently urging us along the path to discover our deepest mysteries; a path that soars above miseries and torment, and yet a path that takes us to the very heart of being human; a path that goes against every organized religion and yet is true religiousness. I can see that although He spent thirty-five years continuously trying to help people He had nothing invested in it. He would share his wisdom and it was entirely up to us whether or not we listened to Him or understood Him. He was never angry at our inability to grasp what He was trying to show us; never impatient that we kept repeating the same habit patterns over and over.

He said that one day we would get enlightened, because one day it was bound to happen. He said that it didn't matter when.

"I am giving you the taste of my being, and preparing you to do the same, on your part, to others. It all depends on you, whether my words will remain living or will die. As far as I am concerned, I do not care.

"While I am here, I am pouring myself into you. And I am grateful that you are allowing it to happen. Who bothers about the future? There is nobody in me who can care about the future. If existence can find me as a vehicle, I can remain assured that it can find thousands of people to be its vehicle." (*From the False to the Truth*)

He knew He was hundreds of years ahead of his time and said that any genius will never meet his contemporaries. The day Krishnamurti died Osho said: "Now I am alone in the world."

When asked how He would like to be remembered He said:

"I would simply like to be forgiven and forgotten. There is no need to remember me. The need is to remember yourself. People have remembered Gautam Buddha and

Jesus Christ and Confucius and Krishna. That does not help. So what I would like: forget me completely, and forgive me too — because it will be difficult to forget me. That's why I am asking you to forgive me for giving you the trouble. Remember yourself." (*The Transmission of the Lamp*)

He left this earth without even a name. Osho is not a name, it is a term of respect used in Japan for a spiritual guide. Osho arranged that all His books (seven hundred in all) have the name changed from Bhagwan Shree Rajneesh to Osho. The next generation may not even know that someone called Rajneesh ever lived.

"You are a nameless reality.

And it is good, because every name

Creates a boundary around you,

Makes you small." (*The Great Pilgrimage from Here to Here*)

And yet He has left behind a legacy that is incomparable to all the diamonds in the universe. He has left behind His work, in His people. He has brought thousands of people a giant step forward in the evolution of mankind. We may not be fully realized, but we have understood that death does not exist. The biggest taboo, the deepest mystery and the greatest fear is death, and our master has pulled us through it and out the other side. Death happens only to the body and that has been my experience with Osho. The secret of death, heaven, life after death, reincarnation — the secrets are all open now.

The last time I had eye contact with Osho, without fear in my being — I had fear because I could see He was disappearing — the last time I really met Him was the night that Nirvano died.

Nirvano died just before we all went to our meditation in Buddha Hall at 7.00 p.m. That night I was waiting for Osho's car to arrive at Buddha Hall and I opened the door for Him. As He stepped out of the car He gave me a penetrating look, knowing that I knew. I can only presume that He was looking to see how I was with it. I remember looking back at Him and inside saying, "Yes, Osho," and I think I had a small understanding of the pain He must have felt, and I could never really know — but I have an idea — just how much He loved her. I wanted to say to Him that I will be strong.

Osho had stopped dancing with us as He entered Buddha Hall, two months previously. He would walk around the podium very slowly and greet everybody in the Hall. So slowly, right foot sideways, then the left would slide to meet the other, hands folded in front of Him, in *namaste*. He would sometimes look at someone in the first few rows and then His eyes would scan the horizon as though looking at a distant star.

From where I sat, it looked as though less and less He focused on any single person in Buddha Hall. His people were His anchor in this world, but He seemed to be looking more into the distance. With Avirbhava, so innocent, He would play, and again He would be in His body. He would be like a child playing. It was one of the greatest joys to see Him come back to this world to play with Avirbhava. He chuckled and His shoulders would go up and down with the laughter, and He would open His eyes wide and beckon for her to get up on the podium with Him. As part of the game she would scream and fall to the floor.

He sat with us while the musicians played Indian music, interspersed with gaps of silence.

And then, He would be gone again. At times I wanted to shout to Him, "Come back, Come back."

In mid-December Osho sent a message to us that He had heard someone chanting a *mantra*, and it had disturbed the silence. No one else had heard it, but this did not surprise me because I know how much more sensitive Osho's hearing is than other people's.

Despite announcements asking whoever it was to cease,

it continued. The chant began to cause pain in Osho's stomach. He said it was being done deliberately and that while sitting with us in Buddha Hall He was totally open and vulnerable so that we could experience the full depth of His silence. The attack was being made on Him by the same people who destroyed the commune in the U.S.A. He later said that it was the C.I.A. and they were using black magic.

We tried to find the person or persons with the help of a psychic, and also by simple elimination. People were moved from their usual sitting areas in Buddha Hall. The sound came mostly from Osho's right side. He would open His eyes during the meditation and point in the direction of the sound.

One night I sat on Osho's right, half way back in the Hall. I watched everyone around me and one by one, different people were taken outside to see if their absence would eliminate the chant. Osho turned His head many times and stared long and hard in the direction where my "suspect" sat. But it proved to be futile. We were unable to find the person and in the process had disturbed the meditation for a lot of people, by creeping around and asking people to go outside.

We had no idea how to locate the person doing the *mantra*. From our side, it was muddled and we were moving in confusion and darkness, and yet from Osho's side, He was very clear and knew exactly what was happening and where it was coming from. But we could not understand what He was telling us.

We checked all electrical appliances and searched for a machine of new invention that could maybe send out a death ray, or sound that was above the usual human hearing level.

The last thing Osho said to me, while leaving Buddha Hall on 16th January, was, "The man is in the fourth row." That night we videotaped the fourth row of people and watched the film afterwards looking for a suspect. But Osho said there was more than one person, and seeing how helpless and stressed we were becoming, He said to drop the search.

He sent a message saying that He could return the energy to the person, and return it double, but that His reverence for life was total and He could not use any power destructively.

Osho was becoming increasingly weak and the pain in His stomach was worse. He had X-rays taken of His stomach but nothing could be detected on them. The pain was moving towards His *hara*, and he said that if it reaches the *hara*, His life will be in danger. He looked as though He was becoming less of this world.

Sometimes He would come out to see us and, feeling angry in my helplessness, I wanted to stand up in Buddha Hall and scream at Him, "Don't go," but He was going. Whenever I looked at Him, I could hear Him saying to me, "You are alone, you are alone."

I had a desire at this time to move away from Him, to dance at the back of the Hall, because at least there I could feel Him very strongly, and not be disturbed by the look of nothingness in His eyes. One night I danced so madly, I was delirious and almost fell through the mosquito netting that surrounded the Hall. I was blubbering and talking gibberish, like the old *darshan* days. In the front I was so taken over by the fact that I could see He was disappearing, that I couldn't really celebrate. And yet I couldn't move to the back, except that one time.

On His last visit to Buddha Hall, as He walked in I had absolutely no celebration in me. I was sitting just in front of His chair and He walked towards me and stopped just above me and then turned to His right and slowly moved to the far side of the podium to *namaste* the people on that side. I was misery incarnate.

As He stood at the far side of the podium I said to

myself that this is the last time I am going to see Osho and I had better drop my misery — or keep it for the rest of my life. I started to wave my arms and dance to the music. Osho was now slowly moving back across the podium until, once again, He was standing directly over me, just a few feet away.

Our eyes never met, but as He stood there I waved my arms in dance, and said:

"So be it. You have tried to stay in your body for so many years for us. If it is time for you to leave, so be it." And I waved good-bye to Him, saying, "I'm happy for you if you have to go. Goodbye, Beloved Master."

He moved to the back of the podium and just before He left, He turned and, looking slightly to His right — way out into the sky, beyond Buddha Hall, beyond all the people — I saw in His eyes a smile. It was something between a smile and a chuckle. I can try and say it was the look of a traveler who, having traveled a long time, sees his home in the distance. It was a look of knowing. A smile that I can still see if I close my eyes, but I can't describe it. It was in His eyes and it gently brushed His mouth. As He smiled at existence, so a smile spread across my face. The warmest and only genuine smile I had felt for a long long time. My face was glowing and I felt alone.

As He went, I raised my arms in *namaste* above my head. I *namasted* Him and He was gone.

That night while having dinner with a friend, she said that she thought that she had seen Osho for the last time. This is something I would never have admitted to anyone — it was too outlandish. I felt it, I knew it, and I denied it. I saw Rafia and he said to me, "How's Osho? I'm scared," and I replied, "So am I."

The next day I was very disturbed but I couldn't admit to myself that it was because I thought Osho was going to die. After all, I had always believed that if Osho died then I would also die. I couldn't imagine life without Him.

That night we received the message that Osho was going to stay in the safety of His room and we were to meditate without Him. Now I think of the time He said that when His people had reached a depth of silence without Him, then He would leave His body. But on that night I wasn't thinking of any such thing.

The last two nights I had found it impossible to stay in Buddha Hall for the full meditation. During the video discourse I had to get up and run out of Buddha Hall. I went to my laundry room — my womb.

We sat and meditated in Buddha Hall without Him. Indian music and silence. Osho had a preference for Indian music, he said it was more meditative.

In a rickshaw the following day I felt enveloped in a soft blissful feeling. I said to myself that this is my potential, this is what I am capable of, my possibility. This is how I can live if I choose. The rest of the day, watching how I was freaked out but didn't know why, I was having a good look at my reality, my mindliness. I felt the temptation to fall into darkness, the temptation to be depressed, and at the same time I felt the ability to choose, to not be in the dark, and knew I had a choice. It was in this space that I stayed all day.

I sat in my room, which was directly above Osho's room. I was literally living on His ceiling, a very cold ceiling too! I spent the afternoon writing the last chapter of a fairy tale. Just before 6.00 p.m. I was sitting in Anando's office printing the last chapter and Maneesha came in crying. "I think Osho's dying." We both saw an Indian doctor leave the house — Osho never has outside doctors unless He is seriously ill — so this meant something serious was happening.

I went to my room to get ready to go to the meditation at 7.00. My zen friend and lover, Marco, came to visit me. We used to dance and laugh together before we went to the evening meetings, but tonight we stood like phantoms suspended in the dawn of something terrible. He was dressed in his white robe, shawl draped over his shoulder and he said, "The shock in your eyes frightens me. What is happening?" I said that I didn't know yet, but I thought something was happening to Osho.

Maneesha came to my room and told me Osho had left His body. She started crying and saying, "I'm so angry, they've won" ('they' being the U.S. government) and I said, "No, now we will see! They can't kill Him."

She left me and the first thing that I did was to throw myself on my bed and call to Him, that "Osho, it has just begun. I know this is a beginning." After that moment of clarity I then slipped into shock. I moved very slowly up and down the stairs, eyes staring. I didn't know where I was going or what I was doing. By now everybody knew and I could hear crying throughout the house and the commune.

I met Mukta who had to pick roses from His rose garden and place them on the stretcher for the burning. I looked for something beautiful to carry the roses on. It felt good to do something. I found a silver tray, four feet in diameter, that was used for wedding ceremonies in the Parsee religion. His disciple, Zareen, had given it to Him and He always liked it so much.

Avesh, who had been Osho's driver for many years, was standing in the doorway, waiting to know if he was to drive Osho to Buddha Hall that night. He had a frightened look on his face as he said to me that he didn't know what was going on. No one had told him anything. I pulled him close to me and held him in my arms, but couldn't speak. After a few minutes I said to him that I couldn't say the words. He looked at me and said, "He's gone?" Then he broke down crying, but I couldn't stay with him. It felt as though each one of us was deep in our aloneness that night. Every *sannyasin* has his own unique and intimate relationship with Osho where no one else can tread.

I met Anando in the corridor. She looked radiant. She took me to Osho's room, where He was lying on the bed, and she closed the door behind me. I bowed down on the floor, head on the cold marble, and whispered, "My Master." I felt only gratitude.

I helped carry Osho to Buddha Hall, where we put Him on the podium on the stretcher, covered in roses. He was wearing His favorite robe and hat with the pearls given Him by a Japanese seeress.

Ten thousand Buddhas celebrated.

We carried Him to the burning ghat. It is a long walk through the busy streets of Pune. It was dark and there were thousands of people. I couldn't take my eyes off Osho's face. There was music and singing all the way.

The burning *ghat* is next to the river and it is in a hollow, which left room for thousands of people to watch the burning. Milarepa and the musicians played all night, and everyone was wearing white robes. Strange, how Osho always wore white in the old Pune days, and He said it was a sign of purity. I used to think that we would change to white clothes when we got enlightened, and here we were at His death, every *sannyasin* in white.

There were crows that called as though the dawn was breaking. I closed my eyes, would hear the crows, and wonder, "My god, have my eyes been closed that long?" but on opening them I would see it was still the middle of the night.

I felt physically sick and pain all over my body. I didn't feel any of the great things I had imagined I would when the Master leaves His body. Osho's death, for me, gave me a very very good look at my reality.

The next morning I awoke, and although not really thinking about it, I was expecting the *ashram* to be empty. I went out and the *ashram* was full. Meditation was happening in Buddha Hall, people were sweeping the streets and breakfast was ready for everyone. Even though we had all been up most of the night, there was breakfast, so lovingly made. This broke my heart. This gave me the assurance that Osho's dream would be fulfilled.

Amrito and Jayesh were with Osho when He left His body. In Amrito's words:

"Over that night (18th) He became weaker and weaker. Every movement of the body was obviously agonizing. Yesterday morning I noticed that His pulse was also weak and slightly irregular. I said I thought He was dying. He nodded. I asked Him if we could call in the cardiologists and prepare for cardiac resuscitation. He said, "No, just let me go. Existence decides its timing."

I was helping Him to the bathroom when He said, "And you put wall-to-wall carpet in here, just like this bath mat." Then He insisted on walking over to His chair. He sat down and made arrangements for the few items that He has in His room. "Who should this go to?" He said, pointing to His small stereo. "It is audio? Nirupa would like it?" He asked. Nirupa had cleaned His room for many years.

And then He went carefully around the room and left instructions for every item. "Those you take out," He said, pointing to the dehumidifiers which He had found too noisy recently. "And always make sure one air conditioner is on," He continued.

It was incredible. Very simply, in a very matter-of-fact and precise way, He looked at everything. He was so relaxed, as if He were going for the weekend.

He sat on the bed and I asked what we should do for His Samadhi. "You just put my ashes in Chuang Tzu, under the bed. And then people can come in and meditate there."

"And what about this room?" I asked.

"This would be good for the *Samadhi*?" He asked.

"No," I said, "Chuang Tzu will be beautiful."

I said we would like to keep His present bedroom as it is. "So you make it nice," He said. And then He said He would like it marbled.

"And what about the celebration?" I asked.

"Just take me to Buddha Hall for ten minutes," He said, "and then take me to the burning *ghats* — and put my hat and socks on me before you take my body."

I asked Him what I should say to you all. He said to tell you that since His days in the marshal's cell in Charlotte, North Carolina, in America, His body has been deteriorating. He said that in the Oklahoma Jail they poisoned Him with thallium and exposed Him to radiation, which we only came to know when the medical experts were consulted. He said they had poisoned Him in such a way that would leave no proof. "My crippled body is the work of the Christian fundamentalists in the United States government." He said that He had kept His pain to Himself, but "living in this body has become a hell."

He lay down and rested again. I went and told Jayesh what was happening and that Osho was obviously leaving His body. When Osho called again, I told Him Jayesh was here and He said for Jayesh to come in. We sat on the bed and Osho gave us His final words.

"Never speak of me in the past tense."

He said: "My presence here will be many times greater without the burden of my tortured body. Remind my people that they will feel much more — they will know immediately."

At one point I was holding His hand and I started to cry. He looked at me, almost sternly. "No, no," He said, "that is not the way." I immediately stopped and He just smiled beautifully.

Osho then spoke to Jayesh and talked about how He wanted the expansion of the work to continue. He said that now that He was leaving His body, many more people would come; many more people's interest would show, and His work would expand incredibly beyond our ideas. It was clear to Him that not having the burden of His body would actually help His work to flourish.

Then He said, "I LEAVE YOU MY DREAM."

Then He whispered so quietly that Jayesh had to put his ear very close to Him, and Osho said, "And remember, Anando is my messenger." Then He paused, and said, "No, Anando will be my medium."

At that point Jayesh moved to one side, and Osho said to me, "Medium will be the right word?"

I hadn't heard what had preceded it so I didn't understand. "Meeting?" I said.

"No," He replied, "for Anando, medium — she will be my medium."

He lay back quietly and we sat with Him while I held His pulse. Slowly it faded. When I could hardly feel it, I said, "Osho, I think this is it."

He just nodded gently, and closed His eyes for the last time."

Rajneesh means Lord of the Full Moon. Osho had been living in the darkness of His room for almost a year. He only got out of bed to come and visit us in Buddha Hall. His room was so dark – there were double curtains inside and blinds outside the windows — it seemed poetically fitting that He left His body on the dark side of the moon.

It was also perfectly fitting of the universe that twenty-one days after He left His body was full moon and it was totally eclipsed by the sun. I watched the moon all night as it turned from silver to gold and blues, pinks and purples danced across its face. There were so many shooting stars and the whole sky seemed to be celebrating that the Lord of the Full Moon had come home.

I have heard Osho say many times that He is just an ordinary man. He would say that if an ordinary man like Him can get enlightened, then so can we.

In Uruguay, during the talks called *The Transmission of the Lamp*, He said, while answering a question about the release of energy that emits from a dead body:

"...So in India, only the saints are not burned; that's the exception. Their bodies are kept in *samadhis* — in a certain kind of grave, so that their bodies can go on radiating for years, sometimes for hundreds of years.

But ordinary persons' bodies are immediately burned — as quickly as possible."

Osho requested that He be burnt immediately. He did not want to be worshipped as a saint; He wanted to be burnt just like an ordinary man.

Two years have passed and yet more than two years' worth of understanding has grown.

I had needed a master, and although Osho is still my Master — I do not need Him. He has shown me that the time has come when I no longer need to look to anyone else for guidance. Life is so full, so rich that even the idea of enlightenment is not needed because enlightenment is only an idea until it happens.

I can hear the sound of the Mystic's voice echoing across timeless oceans, "I have given you the diamonds. Now GO IN."

About Osho

Most of us live out our lives in the world of time, in memories of the past and anticipation of the future. Only rarely do we touch the timeless dimension of the present — in moments of sudden beauty, or sudden danger, in meeting with a lover or with the surprise of the unexpected. Very few people step out of the world of time and mind, its ambitions and competitiveness and begin to live in the world of the timeless. And of those who do, only a few have attempted to share their experience. Lao Tzu, Gautam Buddha, Bodhidharma... or more recently, George Gurdjieff, Ramana Maharshi, J. Krishnamurti — they are thought by their contemporaries to be eccentrics or madmen; after their death they are called "philosophers". And in time they become legends — not flesh-and-blood human beings, but perhaps mythological representations of our collective wish to grow beyond the smallness and trivia, the meaninglessness of our everyday lives.

Osho is one who has discovered the door to living his life in the timeless dimension of the present — He has called Himself a "true existentialist" — and He has devoted His life to provoking others to seek this same door, to step out of the world of past and future and discover for themselves the world of eternity.

Osho was born in Kuchwada, Madhya Pradesh, India, on December 11, 1931. From His earliest childhood, His was a rebellious and independent spirit, insisting on experiencing the truth for Himself rather than acquiring knowledge and beliefs given by others.

After His enlightenment at the age of twenty-one, Osho completed his academic studies and spent several years teaching philosophy at the University of Jabalpur. Meanwhile, He traveled throughout India giving talks, challenging orthodox religious leaders in public debate, questioning traditional beliefs, and meeting people from all walks of life. He read extensively; everything He could find to broaden His understanding of the belief systems and psychology of contemporary man. By the late 1960s Osho had begun to develop His unique dynamic meditation techniques. Modern man, He says, is so burdened with the outmoded traditions of the past and the anxieties of modern-day living that he must go through a deep cleansing process before he can hope to discover the thought-less, relaxed state of meditation.

In the early 1970s, the first Westerners began to hear of Osho. By 1974 a commune had been established around Him in Pune, India, and the trickle of visitors from the West was soon to become a flood. In the course of His work, Osho has spoken on virtually every aspect of the development of human consciousness. He has distilled the essence of what is significant to the spiritual quest of contemporary man, based not on intellectual understanding but tested against His own existential experience.

He belongs to no tradition — "I am the beginning of a totally new religious consciousness," He says. "Please don't connect me with the past — it is not even worth remembering."

His talks to disciples and seekers from all over the world have been published in more than six hundred volumes, and translated into over forty languages. And He says, "My message is not a doctrine, not a philosophy. My message is a certain alchemy, a science of transformation, so only those who are willing to die as they are and be born again into something so new that they cannot even imagine it right now…only those few courageous people will be ready to listen, because listening is going to be risky.

"Listening, you have taken the first step towards being reborn. So it is not a philosophy that you can just make an overcoat of and go bragging about. It is not a doctrine where you can find consolation for harassing questions. No, my message is not some verbal communication. It is far more risky. It is nothing less than death and rebirth."

Osho left His body on January 19, 1990, as a result of poisoning by US government agents while held incognito in custody on technical immigration violations in 1985.

His huge Commune in India continues to be the largest spiritual growth center in the world attracting thousands of international visitors who come to participate in its meditation, therapy, bodywork and creative programs, or just to have the experience of being in a buddhafield.

Osho Commune

Osho Commune International in Pune, India, is a place to relax from the outward stresses of life and nourish the soul. Osho describes the Commune as a laboratory, an experiment in creating a "New Man" — a human being who lives in harmony with the inner and the outer, with himself and his environment and who is free from all ideologies and conditionings that now divide humanity.

Set in 31 acres in the tree-lined suburb of Koregaon Park, this meditation resort receives thousands of visitors every year from all countries and from all walks of life. Visitors generally spend from three weeks to three months and stay in nearby hotels and apartments.

The Commune houses the unique Osho Multiversity, which offers hundreds of personal growth and self-discovery programs and professional trainings throughout the year, all of which are designed to help people find the knack of meditation: the passive witnessing of thoughts, emotions and actions, without judgment or identification.

Unlike many traditional Eastern disciplines, meditation at Osho Commune is an inseparable part of daily life, whether working, relating, or just being. The result is that people do not renounce the world but bring to it a spirit of awareness, celebration, and a deep reverence for life.

At the center of the Commune is Gautama the Buddha Auditorium where six different one-hour-long meditations are offered every day. Osho Dynamic Meditation: Osho's technique designed to release tensions and repressed emotions, opening the way to a new vitality and an experience of profound silence. Osho Kundalini Meditation: Shaking free dormant energies, and through spontaneous dance and silent sitting, allowing these energies to be redirected inwards. Osho Nataraj Meditation: The inner alchemy of dancing so totally, that the dancer disappears and only the dance remains. Osho Nadabrahma Meditation: Based on an ancient Tibetan humming technique to harmonize the energy flow. Osho No-dimensions: A powerful method for centering the energy, based on a Gurdjieff technique. Osho Vipassana Meditation: Gautam Buddha's technique of dissolving mental chatter through the awareness of breath.

The highlight of the day at the Commune is the evening meeting of the Osho White Robe Brotherhood. This two-hour celebration of music, dance and silence, followed by a videotape discourse from Osho, is unique — a deep and complete meditation where thousands of seekers, in Osho's words, "...dissolve into a sea of consciousness."

Osho Publications

Osho has spoken on almost all of the world's enlightened mystics and masters: on Buddha and Buddhist masters, Zen and Zen masters, Indian mystics, Jesus, Jewish mystics and Western mystics. He has also spoken extensively on Sufism, Tantra, Tao, Yoga, the Upanishads, and on the practice of meditation.

Books: Virtually all of Osho's discourses, including many from the early days of His travels around India, have been transcribed and collected into more than 650 volumes, not only in original English and Hindi but also translated into 41 languages.

Audio: Most of Osho's discourses are available on audiotape and cover every aspect of the development of human consciousness, from love and creativity to power and politics, from sex and death to science, education and humor.

Video: Approximately 1,750 English discourses are available on videotape. There is also a selection of videotapes documenting significant milestones throughout the years of Osho's work, including a beautiful record of the event of His leaving the body in January 1990 (I Leave You My Dream), and Osho's vision for a new world and a new man (The New Manifesto).

Worldwide Web: Comprehensive information on Osho and His vision, including a tour of Osho Commune International as well as on-line audio, an on-line magazine and on-line shopping facilities for all publications. http://www.osho.org

Cable TV: Osho's discourses are shown on 48 cable TV networks in 400 cities throughout 25 states in the USA. Many discourse programs have been specially produced for distribution by Osho Cable Network. Jain satellite TV is telecasting Osho's discourses in over 50 countries throughout Asia.

Osho Times International: A full-color, glossy quarterly magazine dedicated to Osho's vision. Subscriptions to the international edition are available at the osho.org website and from the Osho Commune.

For Further Reading

The Path of Meditation

If a beginner were to choose one book that would introduce him to Osho and meditation, this is it! *The Path of Meditation* is a compact volume fittingly sub-titled, "A step-by-step guide to meditation."

For the reader already familiar with Osho's vision and His many books. *The Path of Meditation* is a precious new resource, revealing techniques never brought to light before. With its uniquely intimate flavor, one feels as if one is actually present and participating in this early meditation camp at which these discourses were delivered, in Mahabaleshwar, India.

ISBN 81 7261 071 8

The Inner Journey

For the inner traveler, *The Inner Journey* describes what is needed for a seeker to clear the path that returns to the self. It is a precise manual for tuning the instrument — body, mind, heart, *hara* — to an inner balance and harmony that will pave the way for the experience of meditation.

ISBN 81 7261 019 X

Hidden Mysteries

The significance of temples, statutes, places of pilgrimage, *mantras* and astrology has been forgotten or lost over the centuries. *Hidden Mysteries* is a scientific, insightful, and at the same time, esoteric exploration of what are often considered the outer trappings and paraphernalia of religion.

"There are many keys in life which can open the doors of treasures even today, but unfortunately we do not know either about the treasures or the locks."
Osho

IBSN 81 7281 008 4

Further Information

For information about visiting the Commune, your
nearest Osho Meditation Center and general information, contact:

Osho Commune International
17 Koregaon Park, Pune 411 001 (MS) India
Tel: +91 (0) 212 628 562   Fax: +91 (0) 212 624 181
e-mail: osho-commune@osho.org

For publishing and copyright information regarding Osho's
books, contact:

Osho International
570 Lexington Ave, New York, NY 10022, USA
Tel: +1 212 588 9888   Fax: +1 212 588 1977
e-mail: osho-int@osho.org

www.osho.org
A comprehensive web site in different languages
featuring Osho's meditations, books and tapes, an online tour
of Osho Commune International, a list of Osho Information
Centers worldwide, and a selection of Osho's talks.

Other titles published by FULL CIRCLE